C O N T E M P O R A R Y ' S

PRE-GED

WRITING SKILLS

CONTEMPORARY'S

PRE-GED
WRITING SKILLS

CONTEMPORARY BOOKS

a division of NTC/CONTEMPORARY PUBLISHING GROUP
Lincolnwood, Illinois USA

Photo Credits
Computer keyboard and mouse, © David Bishop/Phototake; pencils, © Gary Mirando/New England Stock; pen, © John Feingersh/The Stock Market.

Project Editor
Cathy Niemet

Series Developer
The Wheetley Company, Inc.

ISBN: 0-8092-3494-7

Published by Contemporary Books,
a division of NTC/Contemporary Publishing Group, Inc.,
4255 West Touhy Avenue,
Lincolnwood (Chicago), Illinois 60646-1975 U.S.A.
© 1995 by NTC/Contemporary Publishing Group, Inc.
All rights reserved. No part of this book may be reproduced,
stored in a retrieval system, or transmitted in any form or by any means,
electronic, mechanical, photocopying, recording, or otherwise,
without prior permission of the publisher.
Manufactured in the United States of America.

890 CU 109876

Editorial Director	*Editorial Production Manager*	*Cover Design*
Mark Boone	Norma Underwood	Michael Kelly
Editorial	*Production Editor*	*Interior Design*
Nancy Johnson	Thomas D. Scharf	Lucy Lesiak
Lisa Black		
Eunice Hoshizaki	*Electronic Composition*	*Illustrations*
Sandra Hazel	Victoria A. Randall	The Wheetley Company, Inc.

Contents

To the Student

Congratulations on your decision to use *Pre-GED Writing Skills* to strengthen your grammar, usage, and writing skills. Strong writing skills will contribute to your success in other classes that require you to communicate effectively.

Here is an overview of what you will find in this book, along with some tips on using the book.

Writing Skills Pre-Test   The Pre-Test, found on pages 1–11, will help you decide which skills you need to work on the most. It will direct you to the parts of the book you may want to spend the most time with.

Chapter 1: Sentence Basics   By working through Chapter 1, you will review what a sentence is, the parts of a simple sentence, the types of sentences, and nouns and pronouns.

Chapter 2: Verbs   In this chapter you will learn the types of verbs, the different verb tenses, and subject-verb agreement.

Chapter 3: Modifiers   This chapter teaches you how to distinguish between adjectives and adverbs, how to use them, and how to work with phrases as modifiers.

Chapter 4: Sentence Structure   This chapter shows you how ideas are combined in sentences. You will also study sentence problems, style, and diction.

Chapter 5: Capitalization and Punctuation   This chapter addresses problems with capitalization. You will also learn what form of punctuation to use, how the comma is used, and how to use other forms of punctuation.

Chapter 6: Patterns of Organization   This chapter concerns the ways in which writers organize information. You will learn about time order, cause-and-effect order, comparison-and-contrast order, and how to use simple listing to organize ideas for writing.

Chapter 7: Process of Writing   This chapter introduces you to the four steps involved in the process of writing: prewriting, drafting, editing, and publishing your ideas.

Chapter 8: Spelling   This chapter addresses word parts, spelling patterns, letter combinations, and commonly misspelled words.

Journal Writing   Every chapter allows you an opportunity to write about your personal experiences in a notebook, or journal, as a way of learning more about how to express your ideas in writing.

Pre-GED Practice   At the end of every chapter, and sometimes more frequently throughout the book, you will answer items that are formatted with five-item multiple-choice questions to help you prepare for GED-level study. The Pre-GED Practice at the end of each chapter serves as a review of the skills you have learned in the chapter.

Writing Skills Post-Test   The Post-Test, found on pages 233–244, will help you to see how well you have learned the grammar, usage, and writing skills presented in this book. The Post-Test consists of 55 multiple-choice questions.

Answer Key   This feature gives answers and explanations for all the questions in this book. Use the Answer Key only after you have attempted to answer a set of questions in an exercise.

Glossary   Throughout the book, key terms that are important for you to know are printed in boldface and italic type and are defined in the glossary at the back of the book.

Good luck with your studies! Keep in mind that knowing how to use grammar correctly and how to write well are worth learning for many reasons.

Pre-Test

The Writing Skills Pre-Test that follows is a guide to using this book. You should take the Pre-Test before you begin working on any of the chapters. The test consists of 55 multiple-choice questions that test the grammar and usage skills covered in this book.

Answer each question as carefully as possible. Choose the best of five answer choices by filling in the corresponding circle on the answer grid. If a question is too difficult, go ahead one and come back to that question later. When you have completed the test, check your answers on page 10.

Using the Evaluation Chart on page 11, circle the number of each question that you missed. If you missed many of the questions that correspond to a certain reading skill, you will want to pay special attention to that skill as you work through this book.

1 ① ② ③ ④ ⑤   15 ① ② ③ ④ ⑤   29 ① ② ③ ④ ⑤   43 ① ② ③ ④ ⑤

2 ① ② ③ ④ ⑤   16 ① ② ③ ④ ⑤   30 ① ② ③ ④ ⑤   44 ① ② ③ ④ ⑤

3 ① ② ③ ④ ⑤   17 ① ② ③ ④ ⑤   31 ① ② ③ ④ ⑤   45 ① ② ③ ④ ⑤

4 ① ② ③ ④ ⑤   18 ① ② ③ ④ ⑤   32 ① ② ③ ④ ⑤   46 ① ② ③ ④ ⑤

5 ① ② ③ ④ ⑤   19 ① ② ③ ④ ⑤   33 ① ② ③ ④ ⑤   47 ① ② ③ ④ ⑤

6 ① ② ③ ④ ⑤   20 ① ② ③ ④ ⑤   34 ① ② ③ ④ ⑤   48 ① ② ③ ④ ⑤

7 ① ② ③ ④ ⑤   21 ① ② ③ ④ ⑤   35 ① ② ③ ④ ⑤   49 ① ② ③ ④ ⑤

8 ① ② ③ ④ ⑤   22 ① ② ③ ④ ⑤   36 ① ② ③ ④ ⑤   50 ① ② ③ ④ ⑤

9 ① ② ③ ④ ⑤   23 ① ② ③ ④ ⑤   37 ① ② ③ ④ ⑤   51 ① ② ③ ④ ⑤

10 ① ② ③ ④ ⑤   24 ① ② ③ ④ ⑤   38 ① ② ③ ④ ⑤   52 ① ② ③ ④ ⑤

11 ① ② ③ ④ ⑤   25 ① ② ③ ④ ⑤   39 ① ② ③ ④ ⑤   53 ① ② ③ ④ ⑤

12 ① ② ③ ④ ⑤   26 ① ② ③ ④ ⑤   40 ① ② ③ ④ ⑤   54 ① ② ③ ④ ⑤

13 ① ② ③ ④ ⑤   27 ① ② ③ ④ ⑤   41 ① ② ③ ④ ⑤   55 ① ② ③ ④ ⑤

14 ① ② ③ ④ ⑤   28 ① ② ③ ④ ⑤   42 ① ② ③ ④ ⑤

In each of the following sets of words, there may be a misspelled word. If there is a misspelled word, mark the circle on the answer grid. If there is no misspelled word, choose (5).

1. **(1)** witnesses
   (2) halves
   (3) donkeys
   (4) lifes
   (5) no error

2. **(1)** embarass
   (2) correspond
   (3) immediate
   (4) aggressive
   (5) no error

3. **(1)** agreements
   (2) heroes
   (3) valleys
   (4) pennys
   (5) no error

4. **(1)** controlling
   (2) unforgetable
   (3) preference
   (4) repealed
   (5) no error

5. **(1)** sprayed
   (2) angrily
   (3) luckyer
   (4) destroyer
   (5) no error

6. **(1)** uninteresting
   (2) illegible
   (3) dissappear
   (4) mismatched
   (5) no error

7. **(1)** relief
   (2) percieve
   (3) height
   (4) efficient
   (5) no error

The following sentences contain errors in capitalization and punctuation. Choose what correction should be made to each sentence. If you think the sentence is correct, choose (5).

8. **Every four years, in the summertime, the presidential candidates travel East to west, trying to earn support for their campaigns.**
   (1) change *summertime* to *Summertime*
   (2) change *presidential* to *Presidential*
   (3) change *East* to *east*
   (4) change *west* to *West*
   (5) no correction is necessary

9. **However, Lois's list of foods she should not eat included the following, eggs, salt, and bacon.**
   (1) remove the comma after *however*
   (2) change *Lois's* to *Lois*
   (3) change *following,* to *following:*
   (4) remove the comma after *salt*
   (5) no correction is necessary

10. **Do you know that Governor Marquez, the woman who's wearing the gray suit will not be running for office again?**

   (1) change *Governor* to *governor*
   (2) remove the comma after *Marquez*
   (3) change *who's* to *whose*
   (4) add a comma after *suit*
   (5) no correction is necessary

11. **Shona has'nt resigned, but her boss knows that she is moving out of the state after Memorial Day.**

   (1) change *has'nt* to *hasn't*
   (2) remove the comma after *resigned*
   (3) add a comma after *knows*
   (4) change *Memorial Day* to *Memorial day*
   (5) no correction is necessary

12. **A womens' magazine has a survey this month asking its readers if they would like to change jobs.**

   (1) change *womens'* to *women's*
   (2) change *has* to *have*
   (3) change *its* to *it's*
   (4) change *readers* to *reader's*
   (5) no correction is necessary

13. **Craig, nevertheless, thinks he should take courses in French literature and Math this summer.**

   (1) remove the commas before and after *nevertheless*
   (2) change *French* to *french*
   (3) change *Math* to *math*
   (4) change *summer* to *Summer*
   (5) no correction is necessary

14. **The carpenter called to her apprentice "Tony, will you be able to work late tonight?"**

   (1) change *carpenter* to *Carpenter*
   (2) add a comma after *apprentice*
   (3) remove the comma after *Tony*
   (4) add a period after *tonight?"*
   (5) no correction is necessary

15. **While Lydia read a book named *The Call of the wild*, her aunt listened to music.**

   (1) change *Call* to *call*
   (2) change *wild* to *Wild*
   (3) remove the comma after *wild*
   (4) change *aunt* to *Aunt*
   (5) no correction is necessary

The following sentences contain errors in grammar and usage. Choose what correction should be made to each sentence. If you think the sentence is correct, choose (5).

16. **A recent weather study of thunderstorms and tornadoes show that parts of the Midwest are frequently hit by severe storms.**

    (1) change *recent* to *recently*
    (2) change *show* to *shows*
    (3) change *Midwest* to *midwest*
    (4) change *frequently* to *frequent*
    (5) no correction is necessary

17. **Either John or his sister pick up the children whenever their parents work the second shift.**

    (1) change *his* to *him*
    (2) change *pick* to *picks*
    (3) change *their* to *they're*
    (4) change *parents* to *parents'*
    (5) no correction is necessary

18. **Alfredo looked at his work and thought that, even if he tried much harder, it would never be more better than this.**

    (1) change *looked* to *looks*
    (2) change *thought* to *had thought*
    (3) change *much harder* to *more harder*
    (4) change *more better* to *better*
    (5) no correction is necessary

19. **In terms of experience, we think that Ms. Tucker is a worse choice than him.**

    (1) change *we* to *us*
    (2) change *think* to *will think*
    (3) change *worse* to *worst*
    (4) change *him* to *he*
    (5) no correction is necessary

20. **Ho Kye and his wife were upset when they learned that they forgot their traveler's checks.**

    (1) change *were* to *was*
    (2) change *forgot* to *had forgot*
    (3) change *forgot* to *had forgotten*
    (4) change *their* to *there*
    (5) no correction is necessary

21. **If Melanie was more comfortable talking to large groups of people, she would be an excellent comedian.**

    (1) change *was* to *were*
    (2) change *more comfortable* to *comfortabler*
    (3) change *large* to *larger*
    (4) change *an* to *a*
    (5) no correction is necessary

22. **The best mechanic in the shop does really good at repairing the transmissions of the largest trucks on the road.**

    (1) change *best* to *better*
    (2) change *really* to *real*
    (3) change *good* to *well*
    (4) change *largest* to *larger*
    (5) no correction is necessary

23. **Forgetting the time is not hardly an acceptable excuse for your being late for the appointment with Fleming and me.**

    (1) change *not hardly* to *hardly*
    (2) change *an* to *a*
    (3) change *your* to *you're*
    (4) change *me* to *I*
    (5) no correction is necessary

24. **José asked the people which were in charge of last year's picnic if they would be in charge again.**

    (1) change *which* to *who*
    (2) change *were* to *was*
    (3) change *year's* to *years*
    (4) change *would* to *will*
    (5) no correction is necessary

25. **The managers have divided the work equally between you and she.**

    (1) change *have divided* to *has divided*
    (2) change *equally* to *equal*
    (3) change *between* to *among*
    (4) change *she* to *her*
    (5) no correction is necessary

26. **After Teresa had used the new machine for a few weeks, she was able to drill much faster with fewer mistakes.**

    (1) change *had used* to *used*
    (2) change *was* to *were*
    (3) change *much* to *more*
    (4) change *fewer* to *fewest*
    (5) no correction is necessary

27. **When Louis went to the refrigerator to get the iced tea, he found that his father had drank it all.**

    (1) change *went* to *had went*
    (2) change *found* to *finds*
    (3) change *his* to *him*
    (4) change *had drank* to *had drunk*
    (5) no correction is necessary

28. **Neither Tina or her husband makes much money, but they both enjoy their jobs.**

    (1) change *or* to *nor*
    (2) change *makes* to *make*
    (3) change *much* to *more*
    (4) change *enjoy* to *enjoys*
    (5) no correction is necessary

29. **As soon as everyone finishes their meal, we will begin the program with the most exciting film you've ever seen.**

    (1) change *their* to *his or her*
    (2) change *will begin* to *begins*
    (3) change *most exciting* to *more exciting*
    (4) change *seen* to *saw*
    (5) no correction is necessary

30. **The nurse said those checkups are helpful. It is important that Hang Soon goes to his doctor once a year.**

    (1) change *said* to *say*
    (2) change *those* to *them*
    (3) change *are* to *is*
    (4) change *goes* to *go*
    (5) no correction is necessary

31. **On the top shelf is two special plates that Juanita's parents brought her from their trip to Jamaica.**

    (1) change *is* to *are*
    (2) change *Juanita's* to *Juanitas*
    (3) change *her* to *she*
    (4) change *their* to *there*
    (5) no correction is necessary

32. **When Brian visited Minnesota, he found that their lakes were prettier than he had expected.**

    (1) change *visited* to *had visited*
    (2) change *found* to *finds*
    (3) change *their* to *its*
    (4) change *prettier* to *more pretty*
    (5) no correction is necessary

Choose the best correction for the underlined part of each sentence. If you think the original is best, choose (5).

33. **Boston will have no public transportation <u>tomorrow. Because</u> bus drivers are going on strike.**

    (1) tomorrow, because
    (2) tomorrow; because
    (3) tomorrow because
    (4) tomorrow, and because
    (5) tomorrow. Because

34. **Leroy always uses a dictionary <u>when he couldn't remember</u> the spelling of a word.**

    (1) when he was unable to remember
    (2) when he can't remember
    (3) if he couldn't remember
    (4) when, he couldn't remember
    (5) when he couldn't remember

35. **The car starts only on dry <u>days, therefore we</u> leave it garaged on rainy days.**

    (1) days; therefore we
    (2) days, when we
    (3) days; therefore, we
    (4) days, however we
    (5) days, therefore we

36. **<u>Today at this present point in time</u> workers are retraining for new jobs.**

    (1) At this moment in our present time
    (2) Today
    (3) Today in the present
    (4) As always
    (5) Today at this present point in time

37. **The speaker was interesting, <u>conversational, and gave a lot of information.</u>**

    (1) conversational, but gave a lot of information
    (2) conversational, and informative
    (3) conversation and full of information
    (4) a conversational person, and informative
    (5) conversational, and gave a lot of information

38. Hector thinks he is <u>more hardworking than any person</u> on his assembly line.

    (1) more hardworking than any other person
    (2) more harder working than anyone
    (3) more hardworking than everyone
    (4) harder working than everyone
    (5) more hardworking than any person

39. This application must be completed <u>before beginning to work here</u>.

    (1) before new employees begin to work here
    (2) before work begins here
    (3) before they are allowed to work at this company
    (4) until they begin to work here
    (5) before beginning to work here

40. Mr. Rodriguez gave the delivery boy a letter <u>as he passed by</u>.

    (1) as he walked by
    (2) as they passed by
    (3) before he walked by
    (4) as the boy passed by
    (5) as he passed by

41. Byron went to cooking class so that <u>the meals that are cooked by him would be meals that tasted much better</u>.

    (1) he could cook better-tasting meals
    (2) the meals that he could cook would be better-tasting ones
    (3) he would be able to create artistic and delicious meals
    (4) he could cook
    (5) the meals that are cooked by him would be meals that tasted much better

42. We think that our product is <u>more different than any other</u> household cleaner of its kind.

    (1) different than any other
    (2) different from any other
    (3) differenter from any other
    (4) more different than any
    (5) more different than any other

43. <u>The frozen pizzas are for the boys that are in the freezer</u>.

    (1) The frozen pizzas are for the boys.
    (2) The frozen pizzas are for the boys; that are in the freezer.
    (3) The pizzas, frozen for the boys are in the freezer.
    (4) The frozen pizzas that are in the freezer are for the boys.
    (5) The frozen pizzas are for the boys that are in the freezer.

44. The company cannot deliver your furniture <u>today there will be</u> no delivery tomorrow.

    (1) today, there will be
    (2) today, however; there will be
    (3) today; as a result, there will be
    (4) today; furthermore, there will be
    (5) today there will be

45. Please come to the workshop prepared to listen <u>carefully and with many questions</u>.

    (1) carefully, and with many questions
    (2) carefully and to ask many questions
    (3) carefully, and to ask many questions
    (4) carefully but with many question
    (5) carefully and with many questions

46. Paula's son sang a <u>song in the school show, which was humorous</u>.

   (1) song in the humorous school show
   (2) song in the school show which was humorous
   (3) song in the school show being humorous
   (4) song, in the school show, which was humorous
   (5) song in the school show, which was humorous

47. She would have been <u>happier if she will choose</u> a better school.

   (1) happier, if she will choose
   (2) happier if she had chosen
   (3) happier, if she had chosen
   (4) happier if she had chose
   (5) happier if she will choose

48. The <u>restaurant, however, did offer</u> an exciting variety of foods.

   (1) restaurant; however, did offer
   (2) restaurant. However, did offer
   (3) restaurant, however did offered
   (4) restaurant, however; did offer
   (5) restaurant, however, did offer

Choose the best answer to each question.

49. What kind of organization pattern would you use in writing directions for making a pizza?

   (1) time order
   (2) comparison-and-contrast organization
   (3) cause-and-effect organization
   (4) simple listing
   (5) whole-to-whole order

50. What kind of organization pattern would you use in telling what caused the Civil War?

   (1) time order
   (2) comparison-and-contrast organization
   (3) cause-and-effect organization
   (4) simple listing
   (5) whole-to-whole order

51. What kind of organization pattern would you use if you were giving examples of foods developed in North America?

   (1) time order
   (2) comparison-and-contrast organization
   (3) cause-and-effect organization
   (4) simple listing
   (5) whole-to-whole order

52. **What kind of organization pattern would you use in writing a paragraph explaining why you like baseball better than football?**

    (1) time order
    (2) comparison-and-contrast organization
    (3) cause-and-effect organization
    (4) simple listing
    (5) whole-to-whole order

53. **During which step in the writing process should you pay most attention to grammar and spelling?**

    (1) prewriting
    (2) drafting
    (3) revising
    (4) editing
    (5) publishing

54. **During which step in the writing process should you pay most attention to simply putting your ideas down on paper?**

    (1) prewriting
    (2) drafting
    (3) revising
    (4) editing
    (5) publishing

55. **During which step in the writing process should you pay most attention to organizing ideas?**

    (1) prewriting
    (2) drafting
    (3) revising
    (4) editing
    (5) publishing

ANSWERS ARE ON PAGE 10.

PRE-TEST

Pre-Test Answer Key

1. **(4)** Many nouns ending in *f* or *fe* are made plural by changing *f* to *v* and adding *es*.
2. **(1)** You will need to memorize the spelling of this word.
3. **(4)** If the *y* at the end of a word follows a consonant, form the plural by changing the *y* to *i* and then adding *es*.
4. **(2)** Double the final consonant of the root word when these three conditions exist: the stress is on the final syllable of the root word; the root word ends with a single consonant other than *h*, *w*, or *x* preceded by a single vowel; and the suffix begins with a vowel.
5. **(3)** When adding a suffix to a word ending in *y* that is preceded by a consonant, change the *y* to an *i* unless the suffix begins with an *i*.
6. **(3)** When adding a prefix to a root word, do not change the spelling of either part.
7. **(2)** Remember the rule "*i* before *e* except after *c*."
8. **(3)** Do not capitalize names of directions when they refer to a general direction.
9. **(3)** When a series of items is introduced by a complete sentence, a colon is used before the series.
10. **(4)** The phrase *the woman who's wearing the gray suit* is giving additional information. It should be set off from the rest of the sentence with commas.
11. **(1)** In a contraction, the apostrophe is used to replace missing letters. Here it should replace the *o* in *not*.
12. **(1)** *Women* is a plural noun. To form the possessive, add *'s*.
13. **(3)** Do not capitalize the name of a school subject unless it is the specific name of a course.
14. **(2)** Use a comma to set off a direct quotation.
15. **(2)** The main words in a book title are capitalized.
16. **(2)** The subject of the sentence is the singular noun *study*. Since the verb should agree in number with the subject, *shows* is correct here.
17. **(2)** When a compound subject is joined by *either . . . or*, the verb should agree with the closest part of the subject. Here it should agree with the singular noun *sister*.
18. **(4)** *Better* is the form of the adjective *good* that is used to compare two things. Do not use *more* along with this form.
19. **(4)** Mentally put the understood verb after the pronoun: ". . . a better choice than he is." The subject pronoun is needed here.
20. **(3)** This sentence says that two actions occurred in the past. They forgot their traveler's checks before they became upset. To show that losing the checks occurred first, use the past perfect tense.
21. **(1)** This statement is contrary to fact. The subjunctive *were* is needed.
22. **(3)** *Good* is an adjective, which is used incorrectly in this sentence to modify the verb *does*. The adverb *well* is needed.
23. **(1)** *Not hardly* is a double negative. *Hardly* should be used by itself.
24. **(1)** When referring to a person, always use *who* or *that*, never *which*.
25. **(4)** *You* and *she* are objects of the preposition *between*, so the object pronoun *her* is needed.
26. **(5)**
27. **(4)** *Drunk* is the correct past participle of *drink*.
28. **(1)** Always use *nor* with *neither*. *Or* is used with *either*.
29. **(1)** *Their* is a plural possessive pronoun. It cannot be correctly used to refer to the singular pronoun *everyone*. Since *everyone* may refer to either a man or a woman, use the reference *his or her*.
30. **(4)** Use the subjunctive verb form in a sentence expressing urgency.
31. **(1)** The subject and verb are inverted. The subject is *plates*; the verb should be *are*.
32. **(3)** *Their* is plural. It cannot refer to the singular noun *Minnesota*. *Its* is the singular possessive pronoun.
33. **(3)** *Because bus drivers are going on strike* is not a complete sentence. Choice (3) turns it into a dependent clause.
34. **(2)** The verb *uses* is in the present tense. To make the sequence of verb tenses correct, the present tense *can't* should be used.
35. **(3)** *Therefore* is a conjunctive adverb between two complete thoughts. It must be preceded by a semicolon and followed by a comma.
36. **(2)** The underlined phrase is repetitive. *Today* says the same thing without the repetition.
37. **(2)** Using the adjective *informative* makes the sentence structure parallel.
38. **(1)** Hector is one of the people on the assembly line, so he is more hardworking than any *other* person.
39. **(1)** The underlined phrase is a dangling modifier. It doesn't refer to any noun or pronoun in the sentence. It actually says the forms are beginning to work here. Choice (1) adds the needed subject.
40. **(4)** In the original sentence, you can't tell whether *he* refers to the boy or Mr. Rodriguez. Choice (4) makes the reference clear.
41. **(1)** The underlined phrase is wordy and repetitious. Choice (1) keeps the meaning without the wordiness.
42. **(2)** *More different* and *different than* are incorrect. *Different from* is the correct idiom.
43. **(4)** The phrase *that are in the freezer* should be placed next to the word it modifies, *pizzas*. The original sentence implies the boys are in the freezer.

10

44. (4) The original sentence is a run-on. Choice (4) adds a conjunctive adverb with correct punctuation so the two main clauses are correctly connected.

45. (2) The original sentence does not have parallel structure. The two phrases joined by *and* should be in the same form. Choice (2) makes the structures parallel.

46. (1) The pronoun *which* in the original sentence could refer to either the song or the show. Choice (1) makes it clear that the show, not the song, was humorous.

47. (2) This sentence contains a clause beginning with the conditional word *if*. Since the verb form in the first part of the sentence is *would have been*, the *if* clause must be in the past perfect, *had chosen*. No comma is needed.

48. (5)

49. (1) In order for readers to follow the directions accurately, they need to know what to do first, next, and so on. Time order puts events in this order.

50. (3) Use cause-and-effect organization to tell what happened that caused other things, like the Civil War, to happen.

51. (4) Simple listing is used to give examples or characteristics that illustrate some event or idea.

52. (2) Use comparison-and-contrast organization to tell about two or more things. You tell about one thing and then tell how the next is similar and how it is different.

53. (4) During drafting and revising, you should concentrate on expressing your ideas. During editing, you can go back and correct grammar and spelling errors.

54. (2) During drafting, your job is to get your ideas down on paper. During prewriting, you should have collected and organized your facts.

55. (1) During prewriting, you create a plan for telling about your ideas before you start writing.

Pre-Test Evaluation Chart

On the following chart, circle the number of any item you got wrong. Next to each item, you will see the pages you can review for items that gave you trouble. Pay special attention to skills on which you missed half or more of the questions.

Skill Area	Item Number	Review Page
Nouns	1, 3	24–31
Pronouns	19, 24, 25, 29, 32	32–50
Verbs	20, 21, 27, 30	55–73
Subject/Verb Agreement	16, 17, 28, 31	75–87
Modifiers	18, 22, 23	93–112
Sentence Combining	33, 35, 44	117–127
Sentence Problems	34, 37, 39, 40, 43, 45, 46, 47	129–141
Style and Diction	36, 38, 41, 42	143–151
Capitalization	8, 13, 15	157–164
Punctuation	9, 10, 11, 12, 14	166–179
Writing and Organization	49, 50, 51, 52, 53, 54, 55	185–214
Spelling	2, 4, 5, 6, 7	219–229
No Error	26, 48	

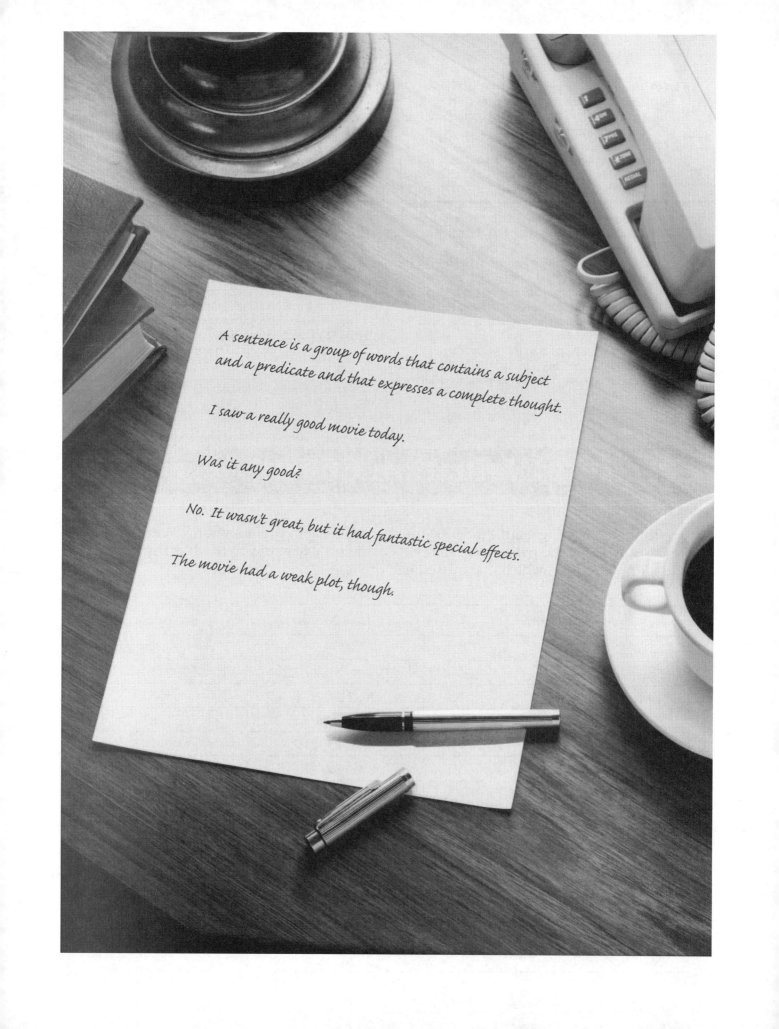

A sentence is a group of words that contains a subject and a predicate and that expresses a complete thought.

I saw a really good movie today.

Was it any good?

No. It wasn't great, but it had fantastic special effects.

The movie had a weak plot, though.

Sentence Basics

SENTENCES

WHAT IS A SENTENCE?

When you're talking with friends, you probably don't worry much about speaking in complete sentences.

"Saw a movie today."

"Any good?"

"Not great. Fantastic special effects. A weak plot, though."

You've probably had conversations like this one. The meaning is clear because you know the situation and understand the subject being discussed. Besides, if you don't immediately know what your friend has said, you can just ask, "What do you mean?"

When you write, though, single words or phrases are not enough to make an idea clear. This is why it's so important for you to write in complete sentences. A sentence makes your ideas clear. Your reader isn't forced to guess what you really mean.

> A **sentence** is a group of words that contains a subject and a predicate and that expresses a complete thought.

The **subject** is whom or what the sentence is about. Whom or what is the following sentence about?

The young woman bought two tickets to Friday's rock concert.

This sentence is about the young woman. Therefore, the subject is *the young woman*.

The **predicate** of a sentence tells what the subject *is* or what it *does*. Everything in the sentence that is not part of the subject is part of the predicate. Find the predicate in the sample sentence above.

You should have identified the predicate as the words *bought two tickets to Friday's rock concert.*

Besides having a subject and a predicate, a sentence must also express a complete thought. When you finish a sentence you should not be asking questions such as *Who did it? What is this about? What happened?*

The sample sentence has a subject and a predicate and expresses a complete thought.

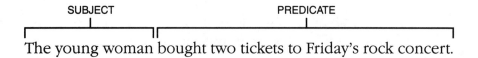

The young woman bought two tickets to Friday's rock concert.

TESTS FOR A SENTENCE

1. It must have a subject that tells whom or what the sentence is about.

2. It must have a predicate that tells what the subject is or does.

3. It must express a complete thought.

EXERCISE 1

Directions: In each of the following sentences, first find the predicate and underline it twice. Then underline the subject once.

Example: <u>Karen Wong</u> <u>drove to Ohio for the weekend</u>.

1. Sarah attacked the chores with enthusiasm.

2. Indira's kitchen table was piled high with fresh baked bread.

3. High winds broke several windows in downtown buildings.

4. Jevon raced to the telephone in the living room.

5. Mr. Zimmer's house will always be our least favorite.

6. The woman answered the police officer carefully.

7. The doctor arrived at the office at 8:30 A.M.

8. Soon Young prepared a huge meal for her parents.

9. The forest fire had destroyed several thousand acres of trees.

10. Marek's grandmother will turn eighty-five this year.

ANSWERS ARE ON PAGE 245.

PARTS OF A SIMPLE SENTENCE
SIMPLE SUBJECTS AND VERBS

The **simple sentence** is the most basic, or simple, form of the complete sentence. It has at least one subject and one predicate.

The subject of a sentence tells whom or what the sentence is about. The **simple subject** is a part of the sentence's subject. It tells what or whom the sentence is about but does not include the descriptive words that are part of the subject.

Look at the following example. Which key word tells what or whom the sentence is about?

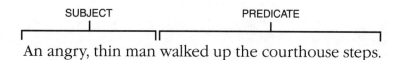

The simple subject is *man*. It tells whom the sentence is about.

Sometimes the subject includes more than one word. A subject that has more than one part connected with words like *and* and *or* is called a **compound subject**. In the following sentence, the compound subject is *my brother and his wife.*

My brother and his wife rented a car for the day.

The predicate is what the subject *is* or *does*. A **verb** is the most important part of the predicate. It is the key word that tells what something is or does. A verb does not include the descriptive words found in the predicate. Often, but not always, the verb shows action, as in the following sentence.

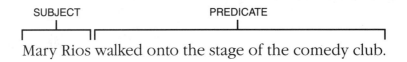

SUBJECT   PREDICATE

Mary Rios walked onto the stage of the comedy club.

In this sentence, the verb is *walked*. It tells what the subject, Mary Rios, does.

Often a verb needs two or more words to express an action or state of being. This is a way of showing whether the action or state of being occurs in the past, present, or future. In the following sentence, the words *had waited* are the verb.

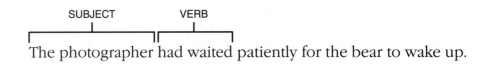

SUBJECT   VERB

The photographer had waited patiently for the bear to wake up.

EXERCISE 2

Directions: In the following sentences, first find the verb and underline it twice. Then underline the simple or compound subject once.

Example: The crisp, autumn <u>leaves and berries</u> <u>had crunched</u> under our feet.

1. The team's manager should win an award.

2. Everyone has ordered something different to eat.

3. Andrej fumbled in his pockets for his car keys.

4. Mr. and Mrs. Hastings complained about the defective lamp.

5. The run-down old bus pulled slowly out of the station.

6. The previous receptionist had been more efficient.

7. Pak Ku runs during his lunch hour every Friday.

8. Christy and Jan became good friends last year.

9. My brother's apartment was burglarized recently.

10. The brilliant writer of this movie has created a suspenseful plot.

ANSWERS ARE ON PAGE 245.

FRAGMENTS

A group of words that does not have a subject and a predicate and does not express a complete thought is called a ***fragment***. A fragment is an incomplete sentence. Look at the following group of words. Is it a sentence or a fragment?

The party last night.

The group of words has a subject, *party*, but there is no predicate. The sentence doesn't express a complete thought. What is it about the party last night? What happened? What was it like? If we add the predicate *was very crowded*, the sentence now expresses a complete thought.

The party last night was very crowded.

Other fragments can result when a group of words begins with a connecting word such as *because, when,* or *if,* and the thought is not completed.

If you leave on the earlier train.

This group of words does not tell what will happen if you leave on the earlier train. An easy way to fix the fragment is to combine it with another sentence.

If you leave on the earlier train, I will drive you to the station.

Now the sentence is complete. The subject is *I* and the predicate is *will drive you to the station.*

TWO WAYS TO CORRECT FRAGMENTS
1. Attach the fragment to the sentence before or after it.
2. Reword or add words to the fragment to give it a subject and a predicate.

EXERCISE 3

Directions: Read each group of words below. Decide whether each group is a sentence or a fragment. Write *S* for sentence or *F* for fragment in the space provided.

Example: __F__ Went to St. Louis for a ball game.

_____ **1.** You need three stamps on that envelope.

_____ **2.** Yesterday, Sam and his nephew fished all morning.

_____ **3.** When that thick magazine fell off the sofa.

_____ **4.** This room is a mess!

_____ **5.** My client in Dallas will send you the brochure.

_____ **6.** Rattled and chugged all the way down the street.

_____ **7.** My former next-door neighbor and good friend.

_____ **8.** The workers walked carefully through the construction area.

_____ **9.** Because you and your co-workers are dependable.

_____ **10.** Florentia received dozens of cards during her illness.

ANSWERS ARE ON PAGE 245.

≡ PRE-GED Practice ≡
PARTS OF A SIMPLE SENTENCE

Choose the best way to write the underlined part of each sentence to make the sentence complete. If you think the sentence is correct, choose (5).

1. **<u>People with homes</u> on the Mississippi's floodplain.**

   (1) People fled their homes
   (2) People in homes
   (3) Living in homes
   (4) Because of record-high levels
   (5) no correction is necessary

2. **<u>Migrated hundreds of miles south</u> from Canada.**

   (1) While migrating south
   (2) Migrating wolves
   (3) Packs of wolves
   (4) Wolves migrated hundreds of miles south
   (5) no correction is necessary

3. **<u>Because the air pollution</u> was so bad.**

   (1) Because, the air pollution
   (2) Laws were enacted because the air pollution
   (3) Air pollution, which
   (4) A source of air pollution that
   (5) no correction is necessary

4. **During the rain, the car's <u>electric window</u>.**

   (1) electric window on the driver's side
   (2) electric window and windshield wipers
   (3) electric window became jammed
   (4) electric window
   (5) no correction is necessary

5. **In high school, <u>my grades in biology were poor</u>.**

   (1) my first two grades in biology
   (2) my grades in biology
   (3) my grades on biology tests
   (4) my grades on biology experiments
   (5) no correction is necessary

6. **Yesterday at the beach, <u>the sun shone brightly</u>.**

   (1) the sun in my eyes
   (2) the sun and sand
   (3) the sun above the clouds
   (4) the sun's harsh rays
   (5) no correction is necessary

ANSWERS ARE ON PAGE 246.

TYPES OF SENTENCES

There are four types of sentences: statements, questions, commands, and exclamations. Each type of sentence is used for a different purpose.

STATEMENT

A ***statement*** gives information or tells something. All of the example sentences used so far have been statements.

The young woman bought two tickets to Friday's rock concert.

QUESTION

A ***question*** asks for or about something.

Where is my math book? Will you go to the concert with me?

In most cases, the subject comes before a predicate in a sentence. In a question, though, this order is reversed. It can make it more difficult to find the subject. You can find the subject more easily if you change the order of the words in a question into a statement.

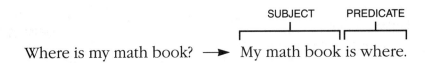

Where is my math book? ➞ My math book is where.

In some questions, the subject falls between parts of the verb. To find the subject, change the order of the words to form a statement.

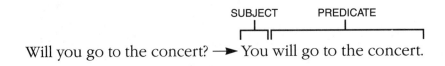

Will you go to the concert? ➞ You will go to the concert.

COMMAND

A ***command*** states an order or a request.

Shut the door.   Move, please.

Get away from there this minute.

Don't go near the edge of the cliff.

These sentences seem to have predicates but no subjects. The subject is actually *you*. *You* is understood without being directly stated.

You + shut the door.   You + move, please.

You + get away from there this minute.

You + don't go near the edge of the cliff.

EXCLAMATION

An ***exclamation*** is an expression of excitement or surprise. As in a command, certain words that are understood may be left out of an exclamation. As in a question, changing the order of the words in an exclamation may help you find the subject.

Fire! ⟶ There is a + fire.

Wonderful! ⟶ This is + wonderful.

Is that a great movie! ⟶ That is a great movie.

◎ FOCUS ON PUNCTUATION

Endmarks

Once you've written a complete sentence, be sure to punctuate it (put in the endmarks) correctly. All sentences begin with a capital letter and end with an endmark. The punctuation you use at the end of a sentence depends on the type of sentence it is.

A statement ends with a period.

> Mount McKinley is North America's highest mountain.
>
> Too much fat in your diet is unhealthy.

A question ends with a question mark.

> Who will be our new senator next year?
>
> Are you running in the Boston Marathon?

A command ends with a period. It has *you* as the understood subject.

> Turn on the air conditioning.
>
> Move that bike out of my way.

An exclamation ends with an exclamation point.

> What a fantastic game!
>
> We won!

EXERCISE 4

Directions: Punctuate each sentence with the correct endmark.

1. Brian slowly got to his feet_____

2. Be careful with that lawn mower_____

3. Smoke is coming from the roof_____

4. Where did you find the book____

5. Stop jumping on the bed____

6. The train stops here every fifteen minutes____

7. Have you seen my radio____

8. Ms. Luna left here at least twenty minutes ago____

9. What a nightmare____

10. Can you see her yet____

ANSWERS ARE ON PAGE 246.

PRE-GED Practice
TYPES OF SENTENCES

Choose what correction should be made to each sentence below. If you think the sentence is correct, choose (5).

1. **Watch out for that falling ladder.**
    (1) add a subject
    (2) change the period to an exclamation point
    (3) change the period to a question mark
    (4) add a verb
    (5) no correction is necessary

2. **Who would like to attend the concert.**
    (1) change the period to an exclamation point
    (2) change the period to a question mark
    (3) add the word *you* to make the subject clear
    (4) restate the sentence as a command
    (5) no correction is necessary

3. **Will you take this book back to the library for me?**
    (1) change the question mark to a period
    (2) change the question mark to an exclamation point
    (3) add a verb to the sentence
    (4) add a subject to the sentence
    (5) no correction is necessary

4. **The grizzly bear is the most dangerous animal!**
    (1) change the exclamation point to a question mark
    (2) change the exclamation point to a period
    (3) add a subject to the sentence
    (4) add a verb to the sentence
    (5) no correction is necessary

5. **Wow.**
    (1) add a subject to the sentence
    (2) add a verb to the sentence
    (3) change the period to a question mark
    (4) change the period to an exclamation point
    (5) no correction is necessary

ANSWERS ARE ON PAGE 246.

NOUNS

WHAT ARE NOUNS?

Read the following paragraph. Pay attention to the words in dark print as you read.

Teresa Rivas pulled her **car** into the small parking **lot**. About fifteen **miles** to the **south** lay the **town** of **Taos, New Mexico**. **Teresa** walked up a **path** to the **top** of a **hill**. A concrete **building** marks the **grave** of **D.H. Lawrence**. It is a **place** of **solitude** and **beauty**. This famous English **novelist** had lived here in the early twentieth **century**. **Lawrence's ranch** now belongs to the **University of New Mexico**.

What do the words in dark print have in common? All of the words in dark print are nouns.

Nouns are words that name people, places, things, or ideas.

PEOPLE:	*Teresa Rivas, Teresa, D.H. Lawrence, novelist, Lawrence's*
PLACES:	*lot, south, town, Taos, New Mexico, top, hill, building, grave, place, ranch, University of New Mexico*
THINGS:	*car, miles, path, century*
IDEAS:	*solitude, beauty*

EXERCISE 5

Directions: Underline the nouns in each sentence.

Example: <u>Bryan's</u> only <u>wish</u> is to have a new <u>car</u>.

1. Hilda says she will return home soon.
2. Construction of the Alaska Highway began in 1942.
3. Superman's first home was Cleveland, Ohio.

4. Two high school students created the superhero.

5. Last year, Louis Padilla moved into an apartment in Washington, D.C.

6. Padilla visits the Smithsonian Institution at least twice a month.

7. The Smithsonian is one of the largest museums in the world.

8. Toni is learning to paint landscapes.

9. William wants to capture the beauty of the outdoors in his photos.

10. Shawna captured the colors of the morning sky in her painting.

ANSWERS ARE ON PAGE 246.

COMMON AND PROPER NOUNS

There are two main types of nouns: proper nouns and common nouns. **Proper nouns** name a specific person, place, thing, or idea. Proper nouns are always capitalized. **Common nouns** name a whole group or general type of person, place, thing, or idea. Common nouns are not capitalized.

	Proper Nouns	**Common Nouns**
PEOPLE:	Billie Smith, Toya Greene, Jay Hawk Wind	artist, mechanic, mayor, writer, police officer
PLACES:	Grand Canyon, Kentucky, Empire State Building	city, mountains, train, valley, restaurant
THINGS:	*Sports Illustrated, Compton's Encyclopedia,* Space Shuttle *Columbia*	newspaper, table, pencil, diploma, computer
IDEAS:	Modernism, Zionism, Roaring Twenties	politics, justice, happiness, religion, patriotism

EXERCISE 6

Directions: Underline each common noun once in the sentences below. Underline the proper nouns twice. The proper nouns have not been capitalized. Cross out the small letter at the beginning of each proper noun and write a capital letter above it.

Example: As they crossed the <u>street</u>, <u><u>~~a~~nna</u></u> grabbed her <u>daughter's</u> <u>hand</u>.

1. The two friends traveled to chicago and visited the sears tower.

2. The salesperson showed melanie two navy blue jackets.

3. While riding on the train, an attorney read the st. louis post-dispatch.

4. The nurse took james's blood pressure and recorded the numbers on the form.

5. My friend yolanda wants to learn more about hinduism.

6. Many people go out of town over memorial day weekend.

7. A chef from france prepared a fabulous meal for the special event.

8. Let's go into the museum when mark and noriko arrive.

9. There are geysers and hot springs in yellowstone national park.

10. Can jeremy stop at the quikstop food store and pick up some milk?

ANSWERS ARE ON PAGE 246.

JOURNAL WRITING

Keeping a journal (notebook) is a good way to get writing practice. In your journal, write at least two paragraphs describing an activity or an event that happened this past weekend. What happened? Who were you with? Describe how you felt at the time. Then go back to see how many common nouns and proper nouns you used in your writing.

PLURAL AND SINGULAR NOUNS

Nouns that name more than one person, place, thing, or idea are called **plural nouns**. Nouns that name only one person, place, thing, or idea are called **singular nouns**. The underlined nouns in the passage below are plural.

Our lives are constantly enriched by the unusual people around us. Marcia, for example, has entertained many people with her taste in clothing. As a child, other children laughed at Marcia's way of dressing. She thought nothing of mixing colors and fabrics in unusual ways. She might mix plaids with stripes or corduroys with silks. Now in her thirties, Marcia still dresses in her own style. Her dresses still do not match her shoes. She delights in wearing shirts with contrasting cuffs and collars. Now, however, both women and men say she is a trendsetter.

Fill in the blanks below with the correct plural form. Several of the plurals are used in the passage above.

1. Most nouns are made plural by adding *s*.

color   ⟶   colors   (line 4)

fabric   ⟶   _____ (line 4)

stripe   ⟶   _____ (line 5)

2. Nouns ending in *s, ch, sh,* or *x* are made plural by adding *es*.

dress   ⟶   _____ (line 6)

match   ⟶   matches

dish   ⟶   dishes

box   ⟶   boxes

3. Nouns ending in *y* are made plural in two ways. If the final *y* follows a vowel (*a, e, i, o,* or *u*), the noun is made plural by adding an *s*. If the *y* follows a consonant (any letter but *a, e, i, o,* or *u*), the plural is formed by changing the *y* to *i* and adding *es*.

Following a Vowel **Following a Consonant**

way ⟶ _____ (line 4) thirty ⟶ _____ (line 5)

corduroy ⟶ _____ (line 5) penny ⟶ pennies

4. Many nouns ending in *f* or *fe* are made plural by changing the *f* to *v* and adding *es*.

Change **No Change**

knife ⟶ knives cuff ⟶ _____ (line 7)

leaf ⟶ leaves roof ⟶ roofs

5. A few nouns do not change form when they are made plural.

clothing ⟶ _____ (line 3) fish ⟶ fish

6. Some nouns take special forms when they are made plural.

woman ⟶ _____ (line 8) foot ⟶ feet

EXERCISE 7

Directions: Look at the plural nouns after each number below. If one plural noun is incorrect, underline it. If all the plural nouns in a group are correct, choose (5).

Example: **(1)** chiefs **(2)** beef **(3)** loafs **(4)** shelves **(5)** correct

1. **(1)** batches **(2)** taxes **(3)** scratchs **(4)** addresses **(5)** correct
2. **(1)** dictionaries **(2)** turkeys **(3)** alloys **(4)** supplies **(5)** correct
3. **(1)** deer **(2)** scissors **(3)** sheeps **(4)** trousers **(5)** correct
4. **(1)** leaves **(2)** knives **(3)** beliefs **(4)** lifes **(5)** correct
5. **(1)** babies **(2)** spys **(3)** butterflies **(4)** alleys **(5)** correct
6. **(1)** congresswomen **(2)** officers **(3)** gentlemen **(4)** salespersons **(5)** correct

7. **(1)** feet **(2)** trouts **(3)** pants **(4)** teeth **(5)** correct

8. **(1)** cities **(2)** countries **(3)** monkeys **(4)** skys **(5)** correct

9. **(1)** boxes **(2)** nieces **(3)** dishs **(4)** messes **(5)** correct

10. **(1)** handkerchieves **(2)** grooves **(3)** halves **(4)** wives **(5)** correct

ANSWERS ARE ON PAGE 247.

POSSESSIVE NOUNS

The way to show ownership or possession is by using a possessive noun. ***Possessive nouns*** are formed by adding an apostrophe and an *s* to a noun.

The dog's name is Griffin.   Carla's shirt is red.

◯ FOCUS ON PUNCTUATION

Apostrophes in Possessive Nouns

1. For singular nouns, add an apostrophe and an *s*.

the lawyer's opinion   Dino's truck

2. For plural nouns ending in *s*, add only an apostrophe.

the Bergs' home   my parents' gifts

3. For plural nouns not ending in *s*, add an apostrophe and an *s*.

people's traditions   the children's shoes

It is easy to confuse plural and possessive nouns. You need to read a sentence carefully to decide if the noun is singular or plural and if it shows possession. If it does not show possession, it should not have an apostrophe. Which sentence is correct?

That <u>singer's</u> shirt is white.

That <u>singers</u> shirt is white.

The word *that* shows there is only one singer. That singer owns the shirt. So the noun is both singular and possessive. *Singer's* is the correct form to use.

Which of the following two sentences is correct?

Those <u>singers</u> shirts are white.

Those <u>singers'</u> shirts are white.

The word *those* shows there is more than one singer. Those singers own the shirts. So the noun is both plural and possessive. *Singers'* is the correct form to use.

Which of the following sentences is correct?

All the <u>singers'</u> have white shirts.

All the <u>singers</u> have white shirts.

The word *all* indicates there are several singers. However, the verb *have* already shows possession. So there is no need to add an apostrophe to the plural noun *singers*.

EXERCISE 8

Directions: Read each of the following sentences. If the underlined noun is correct, write *C* on the line. If the noun is incorrect, write the correct form of the word on the line.

Example: _artists'_ The five <u>artists</u> paintings were already framed.

_____ **1.** Some people believe that our <u>countrys</u> greatest problem is the economy.

_____ **2.** For increased sales, the prices of <u>womens'</u> clothing must be reduced.

_____ **3.** <u>Benjamin's</u> favorite food is spaghetti and meatballs.

_____ **4.** The <u>Millers'</u> have four red chairs in their kitchen.

_____ **5.** Mrs. Chan has trouble sleeping because of her <u>husband's</u> snoring.

_____ **6.** In spite of all my studying, these Spanish <u>books'</u> are still too difficult.

_____ 7. The <u>owners</u> of this restaurant serve great salads.

_____ 8. High stacks of paper always cover my <u>bosses</u> desk.

_____ 9. Rebuilding downtown will require several <u>years</u> planning.

_____ 10. Thomas Jefferson wrote about <u>citizens</u> rights.

ANSWERS ARE ON PAGE 247.

PRE-GED Practice
NOUNS

Read each sentence. Then choose the best correction for each sentence.

1. **The Panthers' coach watched his teams' star forward sink two three-point baskets to win the game.**

   (1) change *Panthers'* to *Panther's*
   (2) change *teams'* to *teames*
   (3) change *baskets* to *baskets'*
   (4) change *teams'* to *team's*
   (5) no correction is necessary

2. **Four churchs' were located along Olive Street on the town's south side.**

   (1) change *churchs'* to *churches*
   (2) change *Olive Street* to *olive street*
   (3) change *town's* to *towns*
   (4) change *town's* to *townes*
   (5) no correction is necessary

3. **Can you guess what dark mysteries' lie hidden in Lake Superior's depths?**

   (1) change *mysteries'* to *mystery's*
   (2) change *mysteries'* to *mysteries*
   (3) change *Lake Superior's* to *lake superior's*
   (4) change *depths* to *depthes*
   (5) no correction is necessary

4. **Two boxs in the corner of Bess's room contained the last of her worldly possessions.**

   (1) change *boxs* to *boxes*
   (2) change *Bess's* to *Bess*
   (3) change *Bess's* to *Besses*
   (4) change *possessions* to *possessions'*
   (5) no correction is necessary

5. **Piri's face grew sad as she watched the suns last rays gleam on the Golden Gate Bridge.**

   (1) change *Piri's* to *Piris'*
   (2) change *suns* to *sun's*
   (3) change *rays* to *rayes*
   (4) change *Golden Gate Bridge* to *golden gate bridge*
   (5) no correction is necessary

ANSWERS ARE ON PAGE 247.

PRONOUNS

Nouns make writing precise. They tell the reader specifically who or what is being discussed. Occasionally, however, too many nouns can make writing dull.

> Jevon is an excellent mechanic. Jevon has worked at Boyer's Garage for six years, and the other mechanics there often come to Jevon with problems that the other mechanics cannot solve. Jevon's wife is very proud of Jevon and Jevon's work. Jevon's wife supports and encourages Jevon, even when Jevon works late.

In this paragraph, two nouns, *Jevon* and *mechanics,* are overused. The writing is repetitive and dull. The writing can be improved by replacing some of the nouns with pronouns. Look how pronouns can improve the paragraph.

> Jevon is an excellent mechanic. **He** has worked at Boyer's Garage for six years, and the other mechanics there often come to **him** with problems that **they** cannot solve. Jevon's wife is very proud of **him** and **his** work. **She** supports and encourages **him**, even when **he** works late.

> A **pronoun** is a word that replaces and refers to a noun. It is used in exactly the same way as the noun it replaces.

There are four kinds of pronouns: subject pronouns, possessive pronouns, object pronouns, and reflexive pronouns.

SUBJECT PRONOUNS

A **subject pronoun** replaces a noun that is used as a subject.

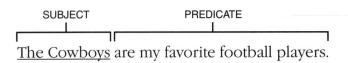

The Cowboys are my favorite football players.

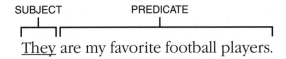

They are my favorite football players.

Pronouns have singular and plural forms. These are the forms for subject pronouns.

SUBJECT PRONOUNS	
Singular	**Plural**
I	we
you	you
he, she, it	they

Nouns and pronouns are often joined with *and* or *or*. Sometimes it may be difficult to know what kind of pronoun to use with the noun. (Remember, subject pronouns are only used to replace a subject or part of a subject.)

Hint: If you're not sure which type of pronoun is correct when a pronoun appears with a noun, try thinking of the pronoun by itself in the sentence.

Lee and Frank are absent today.

***(He, Him)* and Frank are absent today.**

***He* is absent today.**

***He* and Frank are absent today.**

Subject pronouns are also used to rename the subject following a verb of being (*am, are, is, was, were,* and verbs with *be* and *been*). Remember that these verbs act as equal signs. So if the pronoun that follows the verb of being is the same as the noun before the verb, use the subject pronoun.

The chairperson has been *Marie Tso.*

The chairperson has been *she.*

Subject pronouns also replace nouns that give more information about the subject of the sentence.

The two people we hired, *Barry and Sharon,* are former teachers.

The two people we hired, *Barry and she,* are former teachers.

EXERCISE 9

Directions: In each of the following sentences, underline the correct choice in parentheses.

Example: (*Him and Gloria,* <u>*He and Gloria*</u>) both enjoy going to movies.

1. The only guests who arrived on time were *(they, them)*.

2. *(Him and I, He and I)* eat supper together every Friday.

3. My two friends, *(Julian and she, Julian and her)*, planned a surprise party for me last week.

4. Did *(they, them)* sell more tickets to the benefit than the rest of us?

5. Since we had such a terrific time together, *(you and he, you and him)* should plan to visit us again soon.

6. In the beginning, *(we, us)* learned the most from the class.

7. It is *(I, me)*.

8. Although it seems as if we moved in only yesterday, *(the Porters and we, the Porters and us)* have lived in this area for several years now.

9. Our most humorous co-worker is *(he, him)*.

10. Although you and *(I, me)* both love baseball, I go to more games.

11. *(We, Us)* invited the Greens to the play on Friday night.

12. Tina and *(I, me)* are in the same classes together.

13. *(He, Him)* often asks his friend Todd for advice.

14. William and *(her, she)* both have similar interests.

15. *(You and he, You and him)* both did very well on the test.

ANSWERS ARE ON PAGE 247.

POSSESSIVE PRONOUNS

> A **possessive pronoun** replaces a noun that shows ownership.

There are two kinds of possessive pronouns. One type is used along with a noun. The other type is used by itself.

My favorite pastime is fishing. (The pronoun *my* goes with the noun *pastime*.)

Mine is bowling. (The pronoun *mine* stands alone.)

POSSESSIVE PRONOUNS

	Singular	**Plural**
Used with a noun	my	our
	your	your
	his, her, its	their
Standing alone	mine	ours
	yours	yours
	his, hers, its	theirs

Note that possessive pronouns never take an apostrophe.

Incorrect: The old blue car is her's.
Correct: The old blue car is hers.

Possessive pronouns are sometimes confused with contractions. *It's,* for example, is a contraction meaning "it is." *Its* is a possessive pronoun.

> **Hint:** If you are unsure whether or not to use an apostrophe, substitute *it is* or *it has* for *its* and see if the change makes sense.
>
> **(*It's, Its*) hinges are rusty.**
>
> Incorrect: **It *is* hinges are rusty.**
> Correct: **Its hinges are rusty.**

EXERCISE 10

Directions: Choose the correct word to fill each blank.

Example: _yours_ Is this suitcase *(your, yours, your's)?*

1. _____ They were dazzled by *(her, her's, hers)* knowledge.

2. _____ Is this cap *(you'res, yours, your's)?*

3. _____ Sheila said the umbrella by the door was *(her, her's, hers).*

4. _____ You seem very certain of *(your, yours, you're)* opinion.

5. _____ When I opened the book, I noticed that *(its, it's, its')* binding needed to be repaired.

6. _____ Your family's kitchen table is much larger than *(ours, our, our's).*

7. _____ The workers wanted *(they, their, theirs)* break time extended.

8. _____ I'm not sure whether this coat is Carol's or *(mines, my, mine).*

ANSWERS ARE ON PAGE 248.

OBJECT PRONOUNS

An **object pronoun** is used when the pronoun is not the subject of a verb.

OBJECT PRONOUNS	
Singular	**Plural**
me	us
you	you
him, her, it	them

Generally, object pronouns follow a preposition or receive the action of a verb. In the following example, the pronoun *him* replaces the proper noun *Shen*. It is the object of the preposition *to*.

Please give this magazine to *Shen*.

Please give this magazine to *him*.

In the following example, the pronoun *him* replaces the noun *Robert*. In this case, *Robert* receives the action of the verb *hired*. The object pronoun is correct.

Mr. Schwartz hired *Robert* for the job.

Mr. Schwartz hired *him* for the job.

Hint: If a pronoun is joined to a noun in a sentence, it may not always be clear which pronoun is correct. Think of the pronoun by itself.

This book would be helpful to Rosa and *(she, her)*.

This book would be helpful to *her*.

This book would be helpful to Rosa and *her*.

When two or more pronouns are joined and one is *me*, *me* goes last.

Incorrect: The astronomy lecture was interesting to *me and her*.
Correct: The astronomy lecture was interesting to *her and me*.

Using the wrong pronoun after the word *between* is a common error. Because it is a preposition, *between* always takes an object pronoun.

Incorrect: We can split this newspaper between *you and I*.
Correct: We can split this newspaper between *you and me*.

EXERCISE 11

Directions: Choose the correct word to fill each blank.

Example: Please send the tickets to Mr. Arocha or ___*me*___ *(me, I)*.

1. The manager wants to begin regular meetings between himself and

   _____ *(us, we)*.

2. The stray dog followed Arnold and _____ *(she, her)* all the way home.

3. The receptionist was apologetic when she spoke to

   _____ *(me and him, him and me)*.

4. The clerk asked two customers, Donald and _____ *(her, she)*, if they ever used

   credit cards.

5. There is certainly enough food here for you and _____ *(they, them)*.

6. Between _____ *(you and me, you and I)*, I think our best course of action is

   no action at all.

ANSWERS ARE ON PAGE 248.

REFLEXIVE PRONOUNS

> ***Reflexive pronouns*** show action done by the subject to himself
> or herself.

We can finish the work by ourselves.

Bill left himself a note.

Reflexive pronouns are also used to emphasize the subject. They stress that the subject alone performed the action of the verb.

They wanted to do the work themselves.

REFLEXIVE PRONOUNS	
Singular	**Plural**
myself	ourselves
yourself	yourselves
himself, herself, itself	themselves

Reflexive pronouns are sometimes used incorrectly in place of object or subject pronouns.

Incorrect: *Jan and myself* are painting the house.
Correct: *Jan and I* are painting the house.

Incorrect: The lawyer spoke to *Aaron and myself.*
Correct: The lawyer spoke to *Aaron and me.*

Certain forms of reflexive pronouns are also incorrect: *hisself, ourself, theirself, theirselves,* and *themself.*

EXERCISE 12

Directions: In the following sentences, underline the correct pronouns in parentheses.

Example: Stanley filled out the application *(himself, hisself).*

1. We planned last year's vacation *(ourself, ourselves).*

2. Lonnie and *(her, herself, she)* freeze their own vegetables every year.

3. *(I, Myself, Me)* am responsible for meeting the deadline.

4. The second shift workers built those benches *(theirselves, themselfs, themselves).*

5. The bus driver gave Alicia and *(me, I, myself)* transfers that had already expired.

6. The Morrisons repaired the broken furnace *(themself, theirselves, themselves).*

7. Yulian made all the arrangements for the party *(her, herself, she).*

8. Gary and *(I, myself, me)* met at the mall for lunch.

ANSWERS ARE ON PAGE 248.

JOURNAL WRITING

Write a passage of at least two paragraphs describing an activity involving you and one or more friends. You might, for example, tell about going to a ball game, a picnic, or a movie with friends. Use at least three subject pronouns, three object pronouns, and three reflexive pronouns.

SPECIAL PRONOUN PROBLEMS

Some of the most common problems in the use of pronouns have to do with a few specific pronouns. The following guidelines will help you avoid these errors.

Who or *whom* and *whoever* or *whomever*

These pronouns frequently cause confusion. Which words would you use in the following sentences?

(Who, Whom) is that child?

(Who, Whom) are you calling?

The correct choice is easier if you remember which are subject pronouns and which are object pronouns.

Subject pronouns	who, whoever (he)
Object pronouns	whom, whomever (him)

If you have trouble remembering when to use the subject or object pronouns, try substituting *he* and *him*. If the subject pronoun *he* works in the sentence, then use *who* or *whoever*. If the object pronoun *him* fits in the sentence, use *whom* or *whomever*.

(Who, Whom) is that child?

Incorrect: *Him* is that child.
Correct: *He* is that child.
So: *Who* is that child?

Rearranging the subject and verb in a question will sometimes help you make the right choice.

(Who, Whom) are you calling?

You are calling *(who, whom)*?

Incorrect: You are calling *he*?
Correct: You are calling *him*?
So: *Whom* are you calling?

If the sentence is more complicated, look just at the group of words beginning with the pronoun. (You may have to rearrange the words in normal subject-verb order.)

I know that *(whoever, whomever)* the coach picks will help our team.

Rearrange: the coach picks *(whoever, whomever)*

Incorrect: the coach picks *he*
Correct: the coach picks *him*
So: I'm sure that *whomever* the coach picks will help our team.

Pronouns After *than* or *as*

Than and *as* are used to compare two people or two things.

Tomás walks faster *than* Marcia.

Marcia is as tall *as* Tomás.

These sentences have parts that are understood but not stated.

Tomás walks faster than Marcia *(walks)*.

Marcia is as tall as Tomás *(is tall)*.

Because part of the sentence is not stated, choosing the correct pronoun is more difficult.

Tomás walks faster than *(she, her)*.

Marcia is as tall as *(he, him)*.

To chose the right pronoun, mentally complete the sentence.

Tomás walks faster than *she (walks).*

Marcia is as tall as *he (is tall).*

We or *us* Followed by a Noun

The pronouns *we* and *us* sometimes cause problems when they are followed by a noun.

Car dealers are offering better deals to *(we, us)* Americans.

To choose the correct pronoun, mentally drop the noun. Then decide which pronoun is correct. (Remember: *we* is a subject pronoun; *us* is an object pronoun.)

Incorrect: Car dealers are offering better deals to *we.*
Correct: Car dealers are offering better deals to *us.*
So: Car dealers are offering better deals to *us* Americans.

EXERCISE 13

Directions: Three pronouns have been underlined in each sentence. If one of them is incorrect, circle the error. Then write the correct pronoun in the blank. If there is no error, write *Correct.*

Example: __*Ted and me*__ Nancy and <u>he</u> watched <u>me and Ted</u> do our imitation of <u>their</u> dancing.

1. _____ Amy is just as qualified for the job as <u>him</u>, but <u>they</u> did not promote <u>her</u> as quickly.

2. _____ <u>We</u> voters wanted both <u>he</u> and <u>her</u> to run on the ticket.

3. _____ I thought our plans were just between <u>you</u> and <u>myself</u>.

4. _____ Michael and Sarah gave <u>we</u> parents a chance to get away from <u>them</u> and <u>their</u> noise this weekend.

5. _____ <u>You</u> should pay <u>me</u> more than you pay Janet; I work harder than <u>her</u>.

6. _____ The administrators of <u>mine</u> company did not notify <u>us</u> workers of <u>their</u> decision.

7. _____ Would you please tell <u>whoever</u> Marla brings home that <u>we</u> will be home to greet Marla and <u>her</u>?

8. _____ <u>Whomever</u> would like to see <u>our</u> production should buy tickets from either Jean or <u>her</u>.

9. _____ After <u>we</u> left, <u>I and Ted</u> continued laughing at that joke of <u>theirs</u>.

10. _____ <u>We</u> bowlers didn't know that <u>Franco and he</u> had not reserved <u>our</u> lanes.

11. _____ Jodie and <u>me</u> are as excited about <u>our</u> trip to Florida as <u>our</u> husbands are.

12. _____ Manny said that <u>he</u> would go to the store for <u>his</u> mother since <u>herself</u> was too busy to go.

ANSWERS ARE ON PAGE 248.

NOUN-PRONOUN AGREEMENT

Pronouns must always agree with their ***antecedents***. These are the nouns or pronouns they refer to.

Yolanda and *Gary* both went to work, but *she* drove a car and *he* rode a bicycle.

In this example, *she* refers to *Yolanda*. *Gary* is the antecedent of *he*. Each pronoun has the same characteristics as its antecedent. There are four pronoun agreement characteristics: *use, number, gender,* and *person*.

PRONOUN CHARACTERISTICS	
Use	Does the pronoun function as a subject, object, possessive, or reflexive pronoun?
Number	Is the antecedent singular or plural?
Gender	Is the antecedent masculine, feminine, or neither?
Person	Is the pronoun referring to the person speaking, the person spoken to, or the person spoken about?

Use

For more about how pronouns are used in their subject, object, possessive, and reflexive forms, review pages 32–43.

Number

If the pronoun refers to a singular noun (one thing or person), use a singular pronoun. If the pronoun refers to a plural noun (more than one thing or person), use a plural pronoun. Making pronouns agree with their antecedents is usually simple. However, be alert for the following situations.

1. When the pronoun replaces two or more nouns that are joined by *and*, use the plural form of the pronoun.

    Patty and Laura ate *their* meals together.

2. When the pronoun replaces two or more nouns joined by *or, nor, either . . . or, neither . . . nor,* or *not only . . . but also,* the pronoun should agree with the last noun in the series.

    Neither Dale nor *Gordon* likes *his* sandwich.

    Neither Nancy nor her *sisters* liked *their* sandwiches.

3. Some words always require a singular pronoun. These include all words ending in *one, body, other,* and *thing.* Some of these words look like they are plural, but they are actually all singular.

anyone	everyone	no one	someone
anybody	everybody	nobody	somebody
anything	everything	nothing	something
one	another	each	either
much	person	every	neither

Incorrect: *Everyone* should be careful of *their* health.
Correct: *Everyone* should be careful of *his or her* health.

4. Some nouns name a group of people or things. These are called **collective nouns**. Examples include the following:

audience	class	family	group
committee	jury	crowd	staff
faculty	team	band	army

Sometimes a collective noun is replaced by a singular pronoun. Sometimes it is replaced by a plural pronoun.

The jury returned *its* verdict.

The jury took *their* seats.

To decide whether a pronoun that refers to a collective noun should be plural or singular, look at the meaning of the whole sentence. Ask yourself, Is the collective noun acting as a group or individually? In the examples above, there was only one verdict, but more than one person sat down.

5. Some nouns look plural but are singular. Always use a singular pronoun to replace them. The following nouns are singular.

athletics   economics   measles   politics   news
diabetes   mathematics   mumps   physics   United States

Mathematics has *its* own set of symbols.

6. A few nouns have only a plural form even though they name only one thing. Always use a plural pronoun with these nouns.

scissors   eyeglasses   pants   trousers

I need to sharpen my *scissors* because *they* are dull.

Hint: When *pair of* is used with one of these types of plural nouns, use a singular pronoun. In this case, *pair* is the subject.

That *pair of* pants has *its* zipper broken.

Gender

If a noun has a definite gender, use the pronoun that agrees with that noun according to gender.

Masculine pronouns	Feminine pronouns
he, him, his, himself	she, her, hers, herself

Incorrect: The actress seems quite unhappy with *its* role.
Correct: The actress seems quite unhappy with *her* role.

Certain pronouns can be used only in certain ways.

Pronoun	Usage
which	animals and things
who, whom	people only
that	people, animals, and things

Incorrect: The waiter *which* works at Zippos is very clumsy.
Correct: The waiter *who* works at Zippos is very clumsy.
Correct: The waiter *that* works at Zippos is very clumsy.

Hint: If a pronoun refers to a person who may be either male or female, the pronoun should refer to both.

Incorrect: Every baseball fan brought *their* glove.
Incorrect: Every baseball fan brought *his* glove.
Correct: Every baseball fan brought *his or her* glove.

Person

Pronouns change forms in order to agree with the noun.

First person: agrees with the person or persons *speaking*
Second person: agrees with the person or persons *spoken to*
Third person: agrees with the person or persons *spoken about*

FIRST   SECOND   THIRD
PERSON   PERSON   PERSON
↓   ↓   ↓

I asked *you* to see *him*.

There are singular and plural forms for each person.

SINGULAR AND PLURAL PRONOUNS		
	Singular	**Plural**
First person	I, me, my, mine	we, us, our, ours
Second person	you, your, yours	you, your, yours
Third person	he, she, it, him, her, it, his, her, hers, its	they, them, their, theirs

Hint: When checking pronoun agreement in a sentence, make sure the person used is consistent.

Incorrect: When *you* runners train, *they* should get enough rest.
Correct: When *you* runners train, *you* should get enough rest.

EXERCISE 14

Directions: In each of the following sentences, underline the correct pronoun choice given in parentheses. Then underline its noun or pronoun antecedent twice.

Example: <u>People</u> who fall asleep easily should not waste *(his, <u>their</u>)* time on boring movies.

1. Someone who forgets to pay *(his or her, their)* electric bill may end up without lights.

2. The woman *(which, who)* plays the guitar used to play the drums.

3. When Sergeant York tells you to do something, he expects *(him, you)* to do it.

4. The players must have *(his, their)* luggage on the bus by noon.

5. Although I've had *(it, them)* for years, this pair of scissors is still sharp.

6. If people want to succeed in life, *(you, they)* must make plans now.

7. The group was sure *(its, their)* performance would win first prize.

8. The couple giving this party have plenty of food for *(his, their)* guests.

9. Frank put his sunglasses back in *(its, their)* case.

10. Everything must be put in *(its, their)* place before the guests arrive.

11. Everyone should sign *(his or her, their)* name to register for the workshop.

12. Politics has *(its, their)* own set of rules.

13. The pair of pants is missing *(its, their)* belt.

14. The tailor *(which, who)* altered the suit did an excellent job.

15. Neither Velma nor I can work any harder no matter how hard *(I, we)* try.

ANSWERS ARE ON PAGE 249.

PRONOUN REVIEW

Directions: Three pronouns have been underlined in each sentence. If one of them is incorrect, underline the error. Then write the correct pronoun in the blank. If there is no error, write *Correct*.

Example: __*themselves*__ Peter and he taught <u>theirselves</u> to play basketball, and both of <u>them</u> became good players.

1. _____ <u>They</u> have a cat <u>who</u> is always following <u>them</u>.

2. _____ <u>Us</u> lazy people cannot understand why <u>he</u> works whenever the boss asks <u>him</u>.

3. _____ <u>She</u> and <u>I</u> told <u>him</u> that everyone should be well organized.

4. _____ <u>He</u> told <u>us</u> that having three jobs made <u>his</u> life hectic.

5. _____ Just between <u>you</u> and <u>me</u>, Sam, <u>whoever</u> gets this job deserves it.

6. _____ If <u>you</u> were <u>him</u>, would <u>you</u> want this job?

7. _____ When the United States elects <u>its</u> president, <u>your</u> vote will count as much as <u>his</u>.

8. _____ <u>I</u> left <u>me</u> a note so <u>I</u> would remember to write a letter.

9. _____ <u>He</u> will give a ticket to <u>whomever</u> wants to attend <u>his</u> comedy act.

10. _____ On <u>their</u> vacation, <u>they</u> sent greetings to <u>we</u> slaves still on the job.

11. _____ That baby boy showed <u>his</u> parents that <u>it</u> was ready to walk by pulling <u>himself</u> up to a standing position.

12. _____ <u>She</u> proved <u>herself</u> the person <u>which</u> is most qualified.

13. _____ <u>They</u> claimed the money <u>that</u> was on the table was <u>theirs</u>.

14. _____ Do <u>you</u> remember when <u>you</u> and <u>me</u> visited Washington, D.C.?

ANSWERS ARE ON PAGE 249.

≡ PRE-GED Practice ≡
PRONOUNS

Read each sentence. Then choose the best correction for each sentence.

1. **They're not going to like what I have to tell them about my pet monster and it's enormous appetite.**

   (1) change *They're* to *Their*
   (2) change *them* to *they*
   (3) change *my* to *mine*
   (4) change *it's* to *its*
   (5) no correction is necessary

2. **Our friends, Alicia and her, met them at the train station and brought them to his house.**

   (1) change *Our* to *Ours*
   (2) change *her* to *she*
   (3) change *met them* to *met they*
   (4) change *his* to *him*
   (5) no correction is necessary

3. **Just between you and I, whoever takes that job will have problems working with him.**

   (1) change *you* to *your*
   (2) change *I* to *me*
   (3) change *whoever* to *whomever*
   (4) change *him* to *he*
   (5) no correction is necessary

4. **Harry wants me and you to go to the festival with him and her.**

   (1) change *me and you* to *you and me*
   (2) change *me and you* to *you and I*
   (3) change *him and her* to *he and she*
   (4) change *him and her* to *him and she*
   (5) no correction is necessary

5. **Maria and myself are building a doghouse ourselves. Then our two dogs will have a home for themselves and can stay out of ours.**

   (1) change *myself* to *me*
   (2) change *myself* to *I*
   (3) change *ourselves* to *ourselfs*
   (4) change *themselves* to *theirselves*
   (5) no correction is necessary

   ANSWERS ARE ON PAGE 249.

JOURNAL WRITING

Use your journal to practice using pronouns correctly. Write two or three paragraphs about an issue in the news that you don't like. Tell who's involved and what's wrong. Tell what should be done. Use at least one pronoun in every sentence. Use at least one subject, object, possessive, and reflexive pronoun. When you're done, check your writing. Are all your pronouns used correctly?

≡ PRE-GED Practice ≡
SENTENCE BASICS

Choose the best way to write the underlined part of each sentence.

1. **While thousands of ducks** rose from the lake.

   (1) Because the ducks were nervous and
   (2) Feeding on seeds
   (3) Thousands of ducks
   (4) After a brief rest
   (5) no correction is necessary

2. **Gave himself** a pepperoni pizza as a reward for his hard work.

   (1) Jevon gave hisself
   (2) Jevon gave himself
   (3) After finishing the job
   (4) Feeling great, ate
   (5) no correction is necessary

3. **Because his cold** was so bad.

   (1) Because, his cold
   (2) John stayed home from work because his cold
   (3) Feverish and weak, which
   (4) A cough that
   (5) no correction is necessary

4. During that cold **night around the fire.**

   (1) night sitting around the fire
   (2) night, the fire kept them warm
   (3) night as the snow fell
   (4) night without any food
   (5) no correction is necessary

Read each sentence. Then choose the best correction for each sentence.

5. Eric and his brother both have their own businesses. Eric replaces old roofs. His brother builds tables, chairs, and bookshelfs.

   (1) change *their* to *his*
   (2) change *roofs* to *rooves*
   (3) change *chairs* to *chaires*
   (4) change *bookshelfs* to *bookshelves*
   (5) no correction is necessary

6. The zookeeper told me to be careful when returning to my car. The ferocious lions had freed themselves. Had jumped over a wall.

   (1) change *me* to *I*
   (2) change *my* to *mine*
   (3) change *themselves* to *theirselves*
   (4) add the subject *They* to the last sentence
   (5) no correction is necessary

7. As soon as he drove the car off their lot, it began coughing. People pointed at him and his car. Smoke rose from under it's hood.

   (1) change *their* to *their's*
   (2) change *it* to *his*
   (3) change *him* to *he*
   (4) change *it's* to *its*
   (5) no correction is necessary

8. **Will she go to their party with he?**

   (1) change *she* to *her*
   (2) change *their* to *theirs*
   (3) change *their* to *they*
   (4) change *he* to *him*
   (5) no correction is necessary

9. **Carla and three of her friends went bowling. When her friend dropped a bowling ball, she yelled, "Watch out!"**

   (1) change *her friends* to *hers friends*
   (2) change *yelled* to *yelle'd*
   (3) add a subject before "Watch out!"
   (4) change the exclamation point to a period
   (5) no correction is necessary

10. **Mercedes and she were both hungry. They split a pizza between themselves. Whom do you think ate the most?**

    (1) change *she* to *her*
    (2) change *themselves* to *theirselves*
    (3) change *Whom* to *Who*
    (4) change the question mark to an exclamation point
    (5) no correction is necessary

11. **Fire.**

    (1) add a subject to the sentence
    (2) add a verb to the sentence
    (3) change the period to a question mark
    (4) change the period to an exclamation point
    (5) no correction is necessary

12. **Karen wants her son to be a basketball player. She teaches him herself. Already he shoots better than her.**

    (1) change *her* to *hers*
    (2) change *She* to *Herself*
    (3) change *him* to *he*
    (4) change the second *her* to *she*
    (5) no correction is necessary

13. **Us Americans like our cars. We know public transportation is great, but whoever can afford a car has one, sometimes two.**

    (1) change *Us* to *We*
    (2) change *our* to *ours*
    (3) change *We* to *Us*
    (4) change *whoever* to *whomever*
    (5) no correction is necessary

14. **Somebody lost their keys at the drugstore. The manager will give the keys to whoever claims them.**

    (1) change *their* to *his*
    (2) change *their* to *his or her*
    (3) change *whoever* to *whomever*
    (4) change *them* to *it*
    (5) no correction is needed

15. **Most of my friends love to travel. I know many people who don't, but if people want to travel, I think you should.**

    (1) change *my* to *mine*
    (2) change *who* to *whom*
    (3) change *you* to *he or she*
    (4) change *you* to *they*
    (5) no correction is necessary

ANSWERS ARE ON PAGE 250.

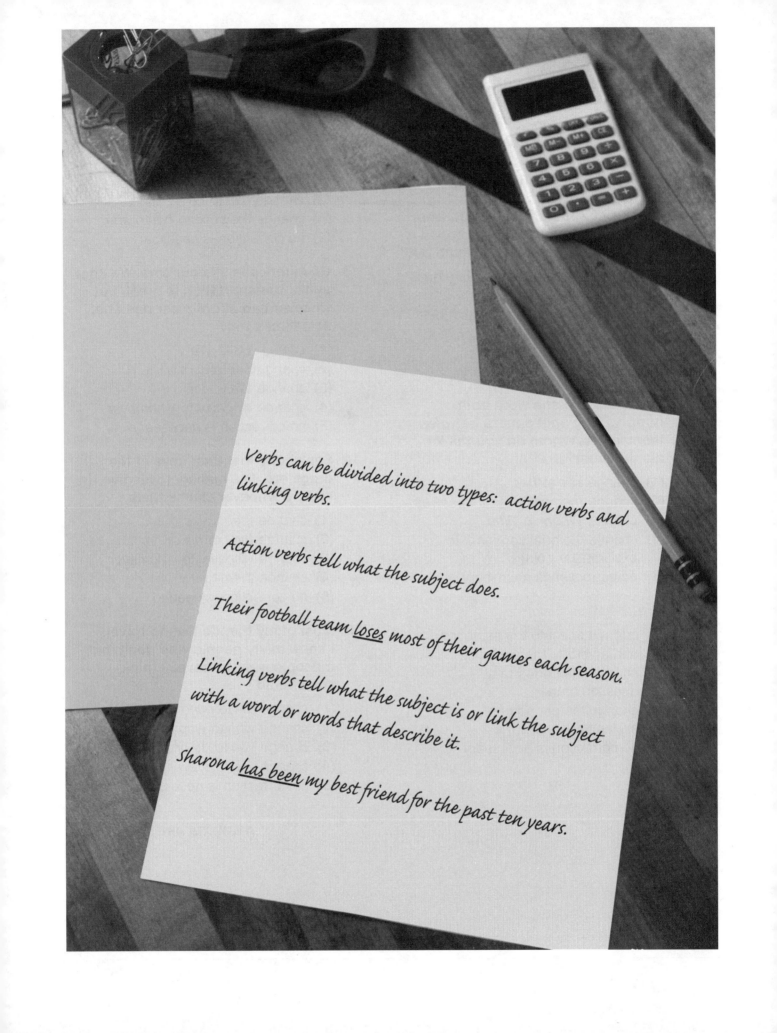

Verbs can be divided into two types: action verbs and linking verbs.

Action verbs tell what the subject does.

Their football team <u>loses</u> most of their games each season.

Linking verbs tell what the subject is or link the subject with a word or words that describe it.

Sharona <u>has been</u> my best friend for the past ten years.

2 Verbs

TYPES OF VERBS

In Chapter 1, you learned that every sentence is made up of a subject and a predicate. The key word in the predicate is the verb. It tells what the subject is or does. Verbs are divided into two types: action verbs and linking verbs.

ACTION VERBS

Action verbs are verbs that tell what the subject does.

Paul *hunts* for his car in the huge parking lot.

Hunts is an action verb that tells what Paul does. Here, the action is physical. Other action verbs tell what mental action the subject does. These can be more difficult to identify. *Know, wish, realize,* and *hope* are common verbs that tell about mental action.

Helena *knows* where her car is parked.

LINKING VERBS

Linking verbs tell what the subject is or link the subject with a word or words that describe it.

When Toshi *became* a father, he *felt* proud.

Note that some sentences, as in the example above, contain more than one verb. Verbs may also be made up of more than one word. *Has been* and *did run* are examples.

Sometimes the words in a verb may be separated by other words. These other words are not part of the verb. In the example below, the verb is *has watched. Always* is not part of the verb.

Harrison *has* always *watched* boxing on television.

> **Hint:** Words in a question are often in a different order than they are in a statement. Usually, the parts of verbs are separated.
>
> *Does* Julie *play* the guitar better than Juan?

EXERCISE 1

Directions: Underline all the verbs in the following sentences.

Example: Julian <u>was</u> sick, so he <u>stayed</u> home from work.

1. Sidney will come to the table when you call him.
2. Did you know that my aunt is still living in Canada?
3. When Veronica saw the picture, she was very surprised.
4. I will be coming to work early tomorrow.
5. When can you come and see my new baby?
6. During our vacation, we camped, cooked, and hiked.
7. By the time we finish this job, our boss will have found two new ones for us.
8. Can you describe the man who just left the store?
9. Although her manager rarely talked to her, Akiko liked her job.
10. Cindy has never missed an Elvis Presley movie that has been shown on television.

11. I will always be grateful that I got a good education.

12. Since she came back from her trip, Raisa has felt much more relaxed.

13. After cleaning, shopping, and fixing lunch, Ida took a nap.

14. What will it be like when we arrive in Florida, I wonder?

ANSWERS ARE ON PAGE 250.

VERB TENSE

In addition to telling what something *is* or *does*, verbs also tell the time of the action.

> The time shown by a verb is called its **tense**.

SIMPLE TENSES

There are three basic or simple tenses.

Present tense: Traci plays soccer on Wednesday.
Past tense: Traci played soccer on Wednesday.
Future tense: Traci will play soccer on Wednesday.

Infinitive and Base Form

Read the following sentence. Pay special attention to the underlined words.

Jim wants <u>to borrow</u> our barbecue grill.

The underlined words, *to borrow,* make up a verb form called an **infinitive**. The infinitive almost always begins with the word *to.* The verb form following *to* is called the base form. The **base form** is what you begin with when you form all verb tenses.

Simple Present Tense

Verbs in the ***simple present tense*** are used in three situations. First, present tense verbs tell what is happening or is true at the present time.

Andrea *gets* herself a second cup of coffee.

Second, present tense verbs show actions that are performed regularly.

We *walk* for an hour every day.

Third, present tense verbs tell about an action that is always true.

The Sonoran Desert *is* hot and dry.

The simple present tense is formed in three ways.

Base Form or Base Form plus *s*

Almost all verbs form their simple present tense from the base form of the verb or from the base form plus *s*. Study the following chart showing the simple present tense of the verb *walk*.

SIMPLE PRESENT TENSE	
Singular	**Plural**
I walk	we walk
you walk	you walk
he, she, it walks	they walk

The only time a regular verb changes its form in the present tense is when the subject is *he, she, it,* or a singular noun. When the subject is one of these, we add *s* (or *es* if the verb ends in *s, x, ch,* or *sh*).

Pedro *plays* basketball every evening.
Kathy *pushes* the pedal to the floor.

Am, *is*, or *are* Plus *ing*

PRESENT TENSE WITH *ING*		
I	am	
He, She, It	is	walking.
We, You, They	are	

When the present tense of verbs are formed in this way, they are used to tell about actions that are true now.

I *am working* too hard.
Evelyn and John *are planning* the company picnic.

Do or *does* with Base Form

The present tense can also be formed by combining *do* or *does* with the base form of the verb. *Do* or *does* gives added emphasis to the verb.

My dog *does eat* at the table with everyone else.

Do you *know* what time it is?

Simple Past Tense

The **simple past tense** shows actions that occurred at a specific time in the past.

Ms. Chavez *asked* me for a ride home from work.
I *hoped* for a promotion.

The simple past is formed by adding *ed* or *d* to the base form.

SIMPLE PAST TENSE	
Singular	**Plural**
I walked	we walked
you walked	you walked
he, she, it walked	they walked

Simple Future Tense

The **simple future tense** shows an action that will occur in the future.

I *will call* you tomorrow.

The simple future tense is formed by using *will* with the base form of the verb.

SIMPLE FUTURE TENSE	
Singular	**Plural**
I will walk	we will walk
you will walk	you will walk
he, she, it will walk	they will walk

EXERCISE 2

Directions: Write the correct form of the base form in each space. Then underline any words that gave you a clue to the correct verb tense.

Example: (open) I ___*will open*___ my birthday gifts <u>tomorrow</u>.

1. (*call*)   We _____ your daughter yesterday.

2. (*wait*)   Stan _____ for his children every afternoon after school.

3. (*move*)   The Rosellos _____ to Columbus two years ago.

4. (*enjoy*)   I always _____ a good mystery book.

5. (*work*)   Mrs. Haynes _____ on your furnace next week.

6. (*happen*)   What _____ to you last night?

7. (*demand*)   Today consumers _____ higher quality products than in the past.

8. (*end*) You _____ your study of the Constitution next Tuesday.

9. (*own*) Simon now _____ a car and a pickup truck.

10. (*talk*) We _____ about you for hours yesterday.

11. (*discuss*) They _____ the issue tomorrow.

12. (*park*) Marissa _____ her car at the airport last Sunday.

13. (*answer*) Martin _____ the phone after the third ring last night.

14. (*smile*) You _____ when you open your gift next Tuesday.

ANSWERS ARE ON PAGE 250.

PRINCIPAL PARTS OF VERBS

As you have learned, there are three simple verb tenses: the past, present, and future tenses. In addition to these simple tenses, there are perfect verb tenses. To understand the perfect tenses, you must understand the principal parts of verbs. These parts are used to form the perfect tenses.

The three **principal parts of verbs** are the base, past, and past participle.

The following chart shows the three principal parts, or forms, of the verb *help*.

PRINCIPAL PARTS OF VERBS		
Base	**Past**	**Past Participle**
help	helped	helped

The base form is used to form the simple present and simple future tenses. The past form is used to form the simple past tense. The past participle form is used to form the perfect tenses, which you will learn about on pages 66–67.

REGULAR VERBS

Regular verbs are verbs that form their past and past participle forms in a regular, or predictable, way. The majority of verbs are regular verbs.

Most regular verbs form the past and past participle by adding *ed* to the base. If the verb ends with an *e* only a *d* is added. In some cases, the final consonant is doubled. If the regular verb ends in a consonant plus *y*, the *y* is changed to *i* before adding *ed.* Here are examples.

EXAMPLES OF REGULAR VERBS		
Base	**Past**	**Past Participle**
walk	walked	walked
praise	praised	praised
stop	stopped	stopped
reply	replied	replied

IRREGULAR VERBS

Verbs that do not form their past and past participle forms by simply adding *ed* are called ***irregular verbs***. There are no simple rules for forming the irregular forms of verbs. You will, however, notice patterns. You have to memorize the spellings of the principle parts of these verbs.

Hint: When you look up an irregular verb in the dictionary, look up the base form. The past and past participle forms will be given for irregular verbs.

Three irregular verbs are so common and so important they need special attention.

HAVE, DO, AND BE			
Base	**Present**	**Past**	**Past Participle**
have	has, have	had	had
do	do, does	did	done
be	am, is, are	was, were	been

The following list gives the principal parts of common irregular verbs. Some verbs have more than one correct form for some parts.

COMMON IRREGULAR VERBS

Base	Past	Past Participle
awake	awoke, awaked	awaked, awoken
become	became	become
bend	bent	bent
bet	bet	bet
bid	bid	bid
bind	bound	bound
bite	bit	bitten
blow	blew	blown
build	built	built
burst	burst	burst
buy	bought	bought
cast	cast	cast
catch	caught	caught
cling	clung	clung
cost	cost	cost
creep	crept	crept
cut	cut	cut
deal	dealt	dealt
dig	dug	dug
draw	drew	drawn
dream	dreamed, dreamt	dreamed, dreamt
drive	drove	driven
fall	fell	fallen
feed	fed	fed
feel	felt	felt
fight	fought	fought
find	found	found
flee	fled	fled
fly	flew	flown
forget	forgot	forgotten
get	got	gotten
give	gave	given
hear	heard	heard
hide	hid	hidden
hold	held	held
hurt	hurt	hurt

COMMON IRREGULAR VERBS

Base	Past	Past Participle
keep	kept	kept
lay	laid	laid
lead	led	led
leave	left	left
lend	lent	lent
lie	lay	lain
lose	lost	lost
make	made	made
mean	meant	meant
meet	met	met
pay	paid	paid
prove	proved	proved, proven
put	put	put
read	read	read
rid	rid	rid
ride	rode	ridden
rise	rose	risen
say	said	said
seek	sought	sought
sell	sold	sold
send	sent	sent
set	set	set
shake	shook	shaken
shine	shone, shined	shone, shined
shoot	shot	shot
sit	sat	sat
sleep	slept	slept
spend	spent	spent
spin	spun	spun
stand	stood	stood
strike	struck	struck
swear	swore	sworn
teach	taught	taught
tell	told	told
think	thought	thought
throw	threw	thrown
understand	understood	understood

EXERCISE 3

Directions: Write the correct form of the verb in the blank. The base form is given in parentheses.

Example: Our house __*shook*__ violently during last week's earthquake. (*shake*)

1. Brian _____ out the runner trying to steal second. (*throw*)

2. The rain _____ as soon as it hits the pavement. (*freeze*)

3. Please _____ this package to the delivery person. (*give*)

4. I didn't know what she _____ when she said she was skating home. (*mean*)

5. Jill's babies _____ tightly to her when she left home. (*cling*)

6. Dilip is the most helpful real estate agent I have ever _____ with. (*deal*)

7. Anna _____ another tale of horror for her young listeners as they squirmed in their seats. (*spin*)

8. If you value your life, don't _____ that can on the table. (*set*)

9. Ms. Tso _____ to the judge that she was telling the truth. (*swear*)

10. Javier leaped excitedly as he _____ the huge fish ashore. (*pull*)

11. The bread dough had _____ after a few hours. (*rose*)

12. I _____ I won the lottery. (*dream*)

13. He _____ the balloon with a pin. (*burst*)

14. Mr. Hanley was _____ by a dog. (*bite*)

ANSWERS ARE ON PAGE 251.

THE PERFECT TENSES

The simple tenses divide time into the three natural periods, the past, present, and future. Verbs also have three perfect tenses: the present perfect, past perfect, and future perfect. Two of the perfect tenses are actually special forms of the past tense. The other perfect tense is a special form of the future tense.

The **perfect tenses** tell that an action has been completed before a certain time or will be continuing to a certain time.

Although you may think of the past as one time, there are actually three levels of past tenses. You already know about the simple past tense. The other two types of past tense are the present perfect and the past perfect.

Present Perfect Tense

The **present perfect tense** tells that an action was started in the past and is continuing in the present or has just been completed.

Pat *has waited* for the bus since three o'clock.

I *have walked* the entire way home.

The present perfect tense of regular verbs is formed by adding either *has* or *have* to the past participle of the main verb.

PRESENT PERFECT TENSE	
he, she, it	has waited
I, you, we, they	have waited

Past Perfect Tense

The ***past perfect tense*** tells that an action was completed in the past before another event or before a certain time in the past.

Pat *had waited* for the bus for ten minutes before we arrived.

The past perfect tense of regular verbs is formed by adding *had* to the past participle of the main verb.

PAST PERFECT TENSE	
I, you, he, she, it, we, they	had waited

Future Perfect Tense

There are two levels or types of verbs in the future tense. You already know about the simple future. It tells what will happen in the future. The other future tense is the future perfect tense.

The ***future perfect tense*** shows an action that will be completed by a specific time in the future.

Pat *will have waited* ten minutes by the time we get there.

The future perfect tense of regular verbs is formed by adding the verbs *will have* to the past participle of the main verb.

FUTURE PERFECT TENSE	
I, you, he, she, it, we, they	will have waited

EXERCISE 4

Directions: In each of the blanks below, write the correct form of the verb in parentheses. These sentences review all six of the verb tenses: present, past, future, present perfect, past perfect, and future perfect.

Example: Ms. Luna ___*will explain*___ the new procedure next week. *(explain)*

1. In two more weeks, I _____ my class. *(begin)*

2. A cup of tea with lunch always _____ good to me. *(taste)*

3. Frank _____ a lot of pictures before he discovered that his camera battery was dead. *(take)*

4. Kathy _____ all over town yesterday. *(rush)*

5. Jose and Molly _____ more than twenty miles by the time they finish the race. *(swim)*

6. Charles _____ several questions before he noticed the information on the sign. *(ask)*

7. The cooks _____ several kinds of desserts tomorrow. *(prepare)*

8. As I _____ before, I'm not going to be talked into taking the first offer I get. *(say)*

9. Since last Tuesday, Sachi _____ the lines to the first act of the play. *(memorize)*

10. Curtis didn't reach the landlady until he _____ six times. *(try)*

11. By next October, Sonya _____ enough money for a new car. *(earn)*

12. Bill Killian _____ the train to work every day since last March. *(ride)*

13. Alexander Graham Bell _____ the telephone. *(invent)*

14. By the end of next week, Maya _____ planning the reunion. *(finish)*

15. While Jay was daydreaming, the runner _____ second base. *(steal)*

ANSWERS ARE ON PAGE 251.

JOURNAL WRITING

Imagine that you're sitting around with friends. They want to know what you've been doing during the past few weeks. Choose one story you'd tell. In your journal, write a short passage of two or three paragraphs. Write it as though you are telling the story to friends. Use as many verb tenses as possible. When you're finished, circle all the verbs. Check that you've used each verb correctly.

SUBJUNCTIVE MOOD

The **subjunctive mood** is a verb form used in three situations: in commands, to express urgency, and to express wishes or a condition that is contrary to fact.

When used for commands or to express urgency, the subjunctive is formed in two ways.

1. Use the base form of the verb. Do not add an *s* to the end of the verb.

Be careful. (command)

It is important that Lee *complete* this questionnaire. (urgency)

2. Use the verb *be* plus the past participle of the main verb.

Mr. Chino insists that this project *be finished* today. (urgency)

To express wishes or something that is contrary to fact, the subjunctive is formed using *were*. *Were* may be used by itself or with the infinitive, past participle, or the *ing* form of the main verb.

If I *were* taller, I could dunk the ball.

If we *were* to leave, we would never know what happened.

If you *were elected* president, would you name me to the Supreme Court?

If he *were lying*, do you think he could keep a straight face?

EXERCISE 5

Directions: Underline the correct verb in parentheses in the following sentences.

Example: If I (*was, were*) a fast runner, I would enter that 10K race.

1. It is necessary that the runner (*complete, completes*) the entire form.

2. If I (*was, were*) stronger, I would run a marathon.

3. It is important that lots of water (*is drunk, be drunk*).

4. If Naoshi (*was, were*) to see me in this race, he would be surprised.

5. The rules require that every runner (*pay, pays*) a small fee.

ANSWERS ARE ON PAGE 252.

ACTIVE AND PASSIVE VOICE

When a sentence is written in the ***active voice***, the subject does the action. When a sentence is written in the ***passive voice***, the subject is acted upon.

Active: LeRoi poured the pancake batter onto the grill.
Passive: Steaming hot pancakes were served to the customer.

The first sentence is in the active voice. The subject, *LeRoi,* performs the action of pouring. The second sentence is in the passive voice. The subject, *pancakes,* is acted upon by being served.

Sentences in the passive voice can be written in any tense. Regular verbs are written in the passive voice by using a form of the verb *be* and the past participle.

PASSIVE VOICE			
Present	I am he, she, it is we, you, they are		
Past	I, he, she, it was we, you, they were	shocked	
Future	I, you, he, she, it, we, they will be		

EXERCISE 6

Directions: Rewrite each of the following passive voice sentences in the active voice.

Example: That wedding dress was worn by my grandmother sixty years ago.

My grandmother wore that wedding dress sixty years ago.

1. The old house was deserted by my grandparents.

My grandparents deserted the old house.

2. The doorway is hidden by large shrubs.

Large shrubs hid the doorway.

3. The cellar door was jammed shut by that fallen tree.

The fallen tree jammed shut the cellar door.

4. The old house will be torn down by the wrecking crew.

The wrecking crew will tear down the old house.

ANSWERS ARE ON PAGE 252.

SEQUENCE OF VERB TENSES

Remember that verb tenses are used to show when an action takes place. As you write, use the correct tenses so your reader is not confused. Do not change tenses within a sentence or between sentences unless it is necessary to show a change in the time of the actions.

Incorrect: Amy *picked* up the keys and *walks* to the door.
Correct: Amy *picks* up the keys and *walks* to the door.
Correct: Amy *picked* up the keys and *walked* to the door.

Sometimes a change in tense is necessary to show that two actions occur at different times.

Abraham Lincoln *had been* (past perfect) a senator before he *became* (simple past) president.

> **Hint:** When trying to decide if two actions occur at the same or different times, look for clues. In the sentence above, for example, the word *before* signals that one event came before the other. Other clues to time include words like *now, yesterday, after, while, next, then,* and *when.*

EXERCISE 7

Directions: In each blank, write the correct form of the verb in parentheses.

Example: Before Yolanda *(come)* ___came___ to see me, she *(go)* ___had gone___ to the bakery.

1. Last year Lauren always *(ride)* ___rode___ the bus to work, but now she always *(ride)* ___rides___ her bike.

2. When we *(measure)* ___measured___ it last, the corn *(grow)* ___grew___ to a height of only five feet.

3. After we *(buy)* _____bought_____ a gas stove, we *(discover)* _____discovered_____ we did not have a gas hookup.

4. Please *(do)* _____do_____ the laundry before we *(be)* _____are_____ ready to eat dinner.

5. Our company *(begin)* _____began_____ a new hiring policy last month while I *(be)* _____was_____ on vacation.

6. Jason *(finish)* _____finish_____ the book by the time class *(begin)* _____begins_____ next week.

7. Audrey *(sweat)* _____sweat_____ when she *(return)* _____returned_____ from carrying the box of books up two flights of stairs.

8. Rosa *(open)* _____opened_____ a box of letters that *(hide)* _____hid_____ in the attic for twenty years.

9. I *(hope)* _____hoped_____ that when you testified you *(give)* _____would have given_____ the correct information.

10. The earthquake *(shake)* _____shook_____ the entire region, and people *(talk)* _____talked_____ about it for months afterward.

11. Last season Doug *(plant)* _____planted_____ daisies; this year he hopes he *(see)* _____sees_____ them spring up.

12. Last night Luiz *(realize)* _____realized_____ his library book was overdue, so later today he *(take)* _____will take_____ the book back.

13. On Saturday Dalia *(drop)* _____dropped_____ her clothes off at the cleaners; they *(ready)* _____are ready_____ to be picked up today.

ANSWERS ARE ON PAGE 252.

═ PRE-GED Practice ═
VERBS AND VERB TENSES

Read each sentence. Then choose the best correction for each sentence.

1. **Javier crossed the finish line after John arrives at the track.**

    (1) change *crossed* to *will have crossed*
    (2) change *crossed* to *had crossed*
    (3) change *arrives* to *had arrived*
    (4) change *arrives* to *has arrived*
    (5) no correction is necessary

2. **Scientists will study Jupiter when the satellite reachs the planet.**

    (1) change *will study* to *study*
    (2) change *will study* to *studied*
    (3) change *reachs* to *reaches*
    (4) change *reachs* to *will reach*
    (5) no correction is necessary

3. **Before the lawyer asked any questions, the witness had swore she would tell the truth.**

    (1) change *asked* to *asks*
    (2) change *had swore* to *had sworn*
    (3) change *had swore* to *swears*
    (4) change *would tell* to *tells*
    (5) no correction is necessary

4. **Yolanda had written the address on a slip of paper while she stood at the station.**

    (1) change *had written* to *had wrote*
    (2) change *had written* to *writes*
    (3) change *had written* to *wrote*
    (4) change *stood* to *stands*
    (5) no correction is necessary

5. **It is important that Sid connects the wires properly or the battery will go dead.**

    (1) change *connects* to *connect*
    (2) change *will go* to *went*
    (3) change *will go* to *goes*
    (4) change *will go* to *will have gone*
    (5) no correction is necessary

6. **Maya exchange the purple skirt for a white one so that she could wear more blouses with it.**

    (1) change *exchange* to *exchanged*
    (2) change *exchange* to *will exchange*
    (3) change *could wear* to *has worn*
    (4) change *could wear* to *wore*
    (5) no correction is necessary

7. **After Ted gets his tax return, he bought a computer.**

    (1) change *gets* to *will get*
    (2) change *gets* to *get*
    (3) change *bought* to *will buy*
    (4) change *bought* to *buy*
    (5) no correction is necessary

8. **When Thelma was given a promotion, she will thank her boss.**

    (1) change *was given* to *gave*
    (2) change *was given* to *give*
    (3) change *will thank* to *thanks*
    (4) change *will thank* to *thanked*
    (5) no correction is necessary

ANSWERS ARE ON PAGE 252.

SUBJECT-VERB AGREEMENT

Besides knowing how to make verb tenses agree, you also need to know how to make verbs and subjects agree.

SIMPLE SUBJECTS

The key to making subjects and verbs agree is to look at the simple subject. (Remember that the simple subject is the noun or pronoun that the sentence is about.) Then look at the verb. If the simple subject is singular, the verb must also be singular. A plural verb must be matched with a plural subject. How would you correct these sentences?

Juan leap up the stairs.
The birds flies to the feeder.

In the first sentence, the simple subject is *Juan,* a singular noun. *Leap* is the plural form of the verb, so use the singular verb *leaps.*

Juan *leaps* up the stairs.

In the second sentence, the simple subject is *birds,* a plural noun. To correct this sentence, you must change the singular verb *flies* to the plural verb *fly.* Another way to correct this sentence would be to change the plural noun *birds* to the singular noun *bird.*

The birds *fly* to the feeder.
The *bird* flies to the feeder.

To check whether you have correctly matched subjects and verbs in a sentence replace the subject noun in a sentence with a pronoun. The pronoun helps you see what is correct. Look at the pattern below.

I
You ⎤
We ⎦ *swim* in the pool.
They

He
She ⎤
It ⎦ *swims* in the pool.

Adding an *s* or an *es* to a present tense verb makes it agree with the singular pronouns *he, she,* and *it,* as well as with all singular nouns that they replace.

Special Problems with Linking Verbs

Linking verbs can cause confusion in subject-verb agreement. For example, which of the following is correct?

Our best hope *is* our children.
Our best hope *are* our children.

If you're not sure, find the simple subject of the sentence—*hope.* Since *hope* is singular, it should be used with the singular verb form *is.*

Our best hope *is* our children.

EXERCISE 8

Directions: Find the simple subject in each sentence and underline it once. Then choose the correct verb form in the parentheses and underline it twice.

Example: The women across the street *(is, are)* my aunts.

1. Those fish *(has, have)* been jumping since we got here.
2. Our problem *(is, are)* getting the tent set up.
3. We in the jury *(believe, believes)* he is innocent.
4. My muscles *(ache, aches)* from all the exercise.
5. The security guards at the store *(want, wants)* a raise.
6. I *(come, comes)* to all my son's baseball games.
7. The order *(include, includes)* paper clips, folders, and tape.
8. My favorite movie *(is, are) The African Queen.*
9. Michiko's three huge dogs *(pull, pulls)* her helplessly along.
10. The price of those strawberries *(seem, seems)* awfully high.

ANSWERS ARE ON PAGE 252.

COMPOUND SUBJECTS

Sentences can have two or more nouns or pronouns as their subject. These are called **compound subjects**, and they can cause confusion in subject-verb agreement. Are the following sentences correct?

Alicia and Patrick buy tickets to every concert.
Alicia or Patrick buy<u>s</u> tickets to every concert.

Both sentences are correct. To decide which verb form to use, look at how the parts of the compound subject are connected. In the sample sentences, they are connected by *and* and *or.*

Compound Subjects Joined by *and, or, either . . . or, neither . . . nor,* or *not only . . . but also*

When a compound subject is connected by *and,* the subject is plural. Use the present tense verb that does not end in *s.*

Incorrect: Juanita and George plays tennis every week.

Correct: Juanita and George play tennis every week.

Words such as *or* and *neither . . . nor* split the parts of a compound subject. Each noun or pronoun in the compound subject is considered separately. The verb agrees with the part closer to it.

Neither Helen nor Maria *wants* to go to the game.

Either David or the twins *take* the dog for a walk.

Not only Tomás but also his three brothers *work* at the factory.

EXERCISE 9

Directions: Underline the correct verb in each sentence.

Example: Either Sarah or her two children *(does, <u>do</u>)* the dishes.

1. Mr. Fletcher and Ms. Ortega *(<u>were</u>, was)* a good sales team.

2. Not only three books but also a new CD *(appear, <u>appears</u>)* on my son's Christmas list.

3. My favorite lunch *(are, <u>is</u>)* fruit and cheese.

4. Neither the twins nor Jeffrey *(plan, <u>plans</u>)* to go to the reunion.

5. Either Veronica or they *(has, <u>have</u>)* the keys to my apartment.

6. My roommate and best friend, Mitch, often *(<u>give</u>, gives)* parties.

7. My car and Stan's pickup *(is, <u>are</u>)* in the repair shop.

8. Zelda, Pearl, and Tonya *(<u>complain</u>, complains)* constantly.

9. Either the mechanics or the manager *(<u>figure</u>, figures)* the bill.

10. Not only the director but also the actors *(<u>want</u>, wants)* another rehearsal.

ANSWERS ARE ON PAGE 252.

JOURNAL WRITING

Think about the last time you did something with several of your friends. What did you do? Who got you together? Where did you go? In your journal, write three paragraphs describing the get-together. When you're finished writing, check your subject-verb agreement.

INTERRUPTERS

Many sentences look more complicated than they really are because they have interrupting phrases. An interrupting phrase is a group of words that comes between the simple subject and the verb. Because of these interrupters, it's easy to make an error in subject-verb agreement. Many interrupters are prepositional phrases.

The building *with the white shutters* needs painting.

> A **prepositional phrase** is a word group that starts with a preposition and ends with a noun or pronoun. The prepositional phrase can be removed, and the sentence will still be complete.

A **preposition** is a word that connects a noun with another part of the sentence. There are many of them in English. Here are a few.

SOME COMMON PREPOSITIONS

above	by	into	through
at	for	near	to
before	from	of	under
between	in	on	with

When you write a sentence with a prepositional phrase, use these three steps to make sure the subject and verb agree.

1. Draw a line through any prepositional phrases.

My mother's biscuits and barbecued chicken ~~off my father's grill~~ *(is, are)* my favorite foods.

2. Find the simple subject.

My mother's *biscuits and* barbecued *chicken* ~~off my father's grill~~ *(is, are)* my favorite foods.

3. Choose the verb that agrees with the subject.

My mother's *biscuits and* barbecued *chicken* ~~off my father's grill~~ *are* my favorite foods.

A special group of words can make interrupting prepositional phrases especially troublesome. These are words that seem to make the subject plural. Actually, they introduce an interrupting phrase.

as well as	besides	including	together with
along with	in addition to	like	

These words usually introduce phrases that are set off by commas. Treat the phrase as an interrupter, not as part of the subject.

My *sister,* along with my brother, *likes* horror movies.

INVERTED SENTENCES

In most sentences, the subject comes first and is followed by the verb. Sometimes, however, the subject and verb are reversed, or inverted. ***Inverted sentences*** can cause confusion in subject-verb agreement. Which of the following is correct?

In her hand *is* two red roses.
In her hand *are* two red roses.

Notice that this sentence begins with a prepositional phrase, *In her hand.* The phrase is followed by the verb and the subject comes last. Often, it is easier to figure out correct subject-verb agreement in an inverted sentence by rephrasing it in normal order.

Two red roses *is* in her hand.
Two red roses *are* in her hand.

Now it is easy to see that the subject is *roses* and the correct verb is *are*.

Sentences Beginning with *Here* and *There*

Sentences beginning with *here* and *there* can also be confusing. Which of the following sentences is correct?

Here *is* my new car.   **Here *are* my new car.**

Neither *here* nor *there* are nouns or pronouns so they cannot be the subject of a sentence. You know, then, that this is an inverted sentence. Rearrange the sentence in normal subject-verb order. Then choose the verb.

My car *is* here.   **My car *are* here.**

Car is a singular subject so it takes the singular verb *is*.

EXERCISE 10

Directions: Underline the correct verb in parentheses.

Example: On top of the suitcase *(is, are)* my tennis shoes.

1. At the end of the dusty road *(stand, stands)* two old water pumps.
2. There *(is, are)* no clues to tell who the robber is.
3. Antonio, along with his two sons, *(waits, wait)* beneath the tree.
4. Across the front windows *(stretch, stretches)* a yellow ribbon.
5. Three lost dogs, including my collie, *(walk, walks)* into the yard.
6. Here *(is, are)* my old hiking boots.
7. Later in the day, the clouds in the west *(grow, grows)* thick and dark.
8. Why *(do, does)* those two dead plants still sit on your desk?

ANSWERS ARE ON PAGE 253.

CLAUSES

Another group of words that often causes problems in subject-verb agreement is a clause. A **clause** is a group of words that contains a subject and a verb. Sentences often contain more than one clause.

An article *that explains the scandals* appears in today's newspaper.

When a sentence has more than one clause, you must be careful to identify which verb goes with which subject. When you're not sure, draw a line under the interrupting clause. Then check the subject-verb agreement in the main sentence and also in the clause.

In the sample sentence, *article* is the main subject of the sentence and should agree with the verb *appears*. *That explains the scandals* is a clause. *That* is a pronoun and goes with the verb *explains*.

Errors in subject-verb agreement are often caused by the pronouns that introduce interrupting clauses. Many pronouns, you recall, can be either singular or plural, depending on the nouns they replace. *That, who,* and *which* are examples. To be sure subject-verb agreement is correct, you need to know if the pronoun refers to a plural or a singular noun.

Kyoko is one of those people *who love to read mystery novels.*

In the sample sentence, the clause is *who love to read mystery novels.* The verb of the main sentence is *is,* which agrees with the simple subject, *Kyoko.* The verb in the clause is *love* and its subject is *who.* In this sentence, *who* replaces *people,* a plural noun. *Love* is a plural verb so the subject and verb do agree.

EXERCISE 11

Directions: In each of the sentences below, underline the correct verb form in parentheses.

Example: Do you know the woman who *(is, are)* selling those plants?

1. Molly is one of those people who *(argue, argues)* about everything.

2. Pak is taking all the orders that *(is, are)* placed this morning.

3. He has two lamps that *(need, needs)* new shades.

4. The solution, which *(seems, seem)* quite simple, is to hire more help.

5. Larry reads books that *(require, requires)* a lot of concentration.

6. The speakers have suggested a plan that *(appear, appears)* to be logical.

7. My niece is one of those children who *(love, loves)* being outdoors.

8. June's office has several computers that *(are, is)* no longer needed.

9. This childproof cap is one of many useful inventions that *(drive, drives)* me crazy.

10. The two brothers who *(like, likes)* to go fishing, usually go to Beck Lake.

11. The answer, which *(appear, appears)* to be correct, is, in fact, incorrect.

12. Mr. Lee, who has several tables and chairs to refinish for his customers, *(plan, plans)* to finish them by Tuesday.

13. His nephews, who *(arrive, arrives)* next week, plan to meet Don at Metro Airport at noon.

ANSWERS ARE ON PAGE 253.

SPECIAL AGREEMENT PROBLEMS
Singular Subjects that seem Plural

One of the most common mistakes in subject-verb agreement is caused by a certain group of pronouns. They look plural but are really singular. Which sentence is correct?

Everybody on the team win.   Everybody on the team wins.

Everybody seems to refer to all people. So it's plural, right? No. What it really says is *every body,* and *body* is singular. The correct sentence is the second one, which has the singular verb *wins.* All of the following pronouns are singular.

SINGULAR PRONOUNS		
another	either	no one
anybody	everybody	nothing
anyone	everyone	one
anything	everything	somebody
each	neither	someone
each one	nobody	

Here's a way you can easily remember most of these words. Look at the second part of the words. The words *one, thing,* and *body* are all singular. The words they are part of are also singular.

> **Hint:** Many of these pronouns are often followed by a prepositional phrase. Remember to ignore the interrupting phrase when deciding on the correct verb.

Neither of the whales *is* happy living in the tank.

Each of those sharks *weighs* more than 500 pounds.

Subjects that are Always Plural

Just as some pronouns are always singular, some are always plural.

PLURAL PRONOUNS	
both	few
many	several

I liked these books. *Both* are science fiction.

Lots of people like Lovecraft's books. *Many* have all his books.

Some nouns are always plural even though they seem to be one thing. They always take a plural verb.

NOUNS THAT ARE ALWAYS PLURAL	
clothes	scissors
eyeglasses	trousers
pants	

Your *clothes are* all over the house!

Those *scissors look* very sharp.

Subjects that can be Singular or Plural

Certain subjects can be either singular or plural, depending on their meaning in a sentence.

WORDS THAT ARE EITHER SINGULAR OR PLURAL		
all	most	half (and other fractions)
any	none	some
more	part	

When these words refer to a singular noun, they take a singular verb. In the following examples, *some* refers to *cake,* which is singular. *Half* refers to *game,* which is singular.

Some of the cake *is* gone.

Half of the game *remains.*

When these words refer to a plural noun, they take a plural verb. In the following examples, *some* refers to the plural noun *people. Half* refers to the plural noun *children.*

Some of the *people* have left.

Half of the *children* arrive late.

Collective Nouns

A **collective noun** names a whole group of people or things. It may be either singular or plural. The following chart shows examples of common collective nouns.

COLLECTIVE NOUNS		
audience	committee	group
band	corporation	jury
class	crowd	number
club	faculty	staff
collection	family	team

A collective noun is singular when it refers to the group as a single unit. Then it takes a singular verb. The collective noun is plural when it refers to individual members of the group. Then it takes a plural verb.

The *band plays* its first concert tonight.

The *band tune* their instruments.

In the first example, the band, as a unit, plays the concert. The verb is singular. In the second sentence, each member of the band tunes his or her own instrument. The verb is plural.

EXERCISE 12

Directions: Underline the correct verb in parentheses in each sentence.

Example: One of the most popular diets *(stress, stresses)* the importance of exercise.

1. The news of the election *(make, makes)* me want to run for Congress.

2. Everyone in these offices *(ride, rides)* the bus to work.

3. Most of the meat *(are, is)* grilled.

4. This new pair of eyeglasses *(give, gives)* me great vision.

5. Everything in those shops *(look, looks)* expensive.

6. Unfortunately, this crowd *(laugh, laughs)* at all the comedian's jokes.

7. None of the voters *(are, is)* happy with any of the candidates.

8. Of all the restaurants, few *(serve, serves)* good Mexican food.

9. Each bill and coin *(was, were)* counted carefully.

10. Of all the people in the building, half *(is, are)* sick with the flu.

11. Neither of these paintings *(appeals, appeal)* to me.

12. The scissors *(belongs, belong)* in the desk drawer.

ANSWERS ARE ON PAGE 254.

≡ PRE-GED Practice ≡
SUBJECT-VERB AGREEMENT

Read each sentence. Then choose the best correction for each sentence.

1. **Shen and Mike plan to visit the Air and Space Museum, which is part of the Smithsonian Institution. Neither of them want to miss the historic airplanes. The collection includes many famous planes.**

   (1) change *plan* to *plans*
   (2) change *is* to *are*
   (3) change *want* to *wants*
   (4) change *includes* to *include*
   (5) no correction is necessary

2. **Rosa, along with her sister, jump out of the stalled car and walks the rest of the way home. The sisters, who get there at the same time, rush through the front door.**

   (1) change *jump* to *jumps*
   (2) change *walks* to *walk*
   (3) change *get* to *gets*
   (4) change *rush* to *rushes*
   (5) no correction is necessary

3. **Everybody says mass transit is a good idea. Many use the buses and trains we have. Neither Sachi nor Andrew have ever been on a bus, however.**

   (1) change *says* to *say*
   (2) change *is* to *are*
   (3) change *use* to *uses*
   (4) change *have ever been* to *has ever been*
   (5) no correction is necessary

4. **John and Sarah Kelly have all the food. This barbecue, which they planned, starts the moment they arrive. Here is the Kelly family now.**

   (1) change *have* to *has*
   (2) change *starts* to *start*
   (3) change *arrive* to *arrives*
   (4) change *is* to *are*
   (5) no correction is necessary

5. **Here is your tickets. When the band plays tonight, it will be before a full house. José and Kathy, as well as the Tucker family, seem eager to hear it. Everyone wants to hear this hot band.**

   (1) change *is* to *are*
   (2) change *plays* to *play*
   (3) change *seem* to *seems*
   (4) change *wants* to *want*
   (5) no correction is necessary

6. **The choir, which perform its first concert tonight, is quite excited. Everybody says they will sing well.**

   (1) change *perform* to *performs*
   (2) change *is* to *are*
   (3) change *says* to *say*
   (4) change *will sing* to *sang*
   (5) no correction is necessary

7. **Jed, along with his brother Thomas, run ten miles a day. They plan to compete in the marathon and win.**

   (1) change *run* to *runs*
   (2) change *plan* to *plans*
   (3) change *compete* to *competed*
   (4) change *win* to *will win*
   (5) no correction is necessary

8. **The committee, which meets every Friday, decide the company's policies and how to carry them out.**

   (1) change *meets* to *meet*
   (2) change *meets* to *would have met*
   (3) change *decide* to *decides*
   (4) change *carry* to *carries*
   (5) no correction is necessary

9. **Some of the residents oppose the building ordinance that requires overnight guests to obtain a permit to park overnight.**

   (1) change *oppose* to *opposes*
   (2) change *requires* to *require*
   (3) change *obtain* to *obtains*
   (4) change *park* to *parks*
   (5) no correction is necessary

10. **The car, which is speeding down the dirt road, raise a cloud of dust. The car behind it has a hard time seeing what is ahead.**

   (1) change *is speeding* to *will speed*
   (2) change *is speeding* to *speed*
   (3) change *raise* to *will raise*
   (4) change *raise* to *is raising*
   (5) no correction is necessary

ANSWERS ARE ON PAGE 254.

JOURNAL WRITING

In your journal, write two or three paragraphs telling the plot of a favorite movie. Write it in the present tense as though you are describing actions as you watch them happen. You may, however, use past and future tenses to add background information or to set the stage for what will happen. When you're finished writing, look at your verbs. Check that you have used tenses correctly and that your subjects and verbs agree.

PRE-GED Practice
VERBS

Read each sentence. Then choose the best correction for each sentence.

1. **The security guard who walks the long halls is exhausted at the end of his shift.**

   (1) change *walks* to *walked*
   (2) change *walks* to *had walked*
   (3) change *is exhausted* to *are exhausted*
   (4) change *is exhausted* to *had been exhausted*
   (5) no correction is necessary

2. **The computer class will start next week. Everyone who is interested in computers are welcome. A fee of $25.00 has been set.**

   (1) change *will start* to *will have started*
   (2) change *who is* to *who are*
   (3) change *are welcome* to *is welcome*
   (4) change *has been* to *was*
   (5) no correction is necessary

3. **Lucinda arrived at the store after the sale has ended.**

   (1) change *arrived* to *has arrived*
   (2) change *arrived* to *arrive*
   (3) change *has ended* to *had ended*
   (4) change *has ended* to *ends*
   (5) no correction is necessary

4. **Somebody whom I do not know send me a birthday card every year.**

   (1) change *do not know* to *does not know*
   (2) change *do not know* to *do not knows*
   (3) change *send* to *will send*
   (4) change *send* to *sends*
   (5) no correction is necessary

5. **Ana had given the package to Curtis while they stood at the door talking.**

   (1) change *had given* to *had give*
   (2) change *had given* to *gave*
   (3) change *stood* to *have stood*
   (4) change *stood* to *stand*
   (5) no correction is necessary

6. **Everybody says athletics are a great way to stay healthy. Something that results in bruises and broken bones does not seem healthy to me.**

   (1) change *says* to *say*
   (2) change *are* to *is*
   (3) change *results* to *result*
   (4) change *does not seem* to *do not seem*
   (5) no correction is necessary

7. **It is necessary that the club manager signs this contract or the band will quit.**

   (1) change *is* to *will be*
   (2) change *signs* to *sign*
   (3) change *will quit* to *will have quit*
   (4) change *will quit* to *quits*
   (5) no correction is necessary

8. **Sonia, along with her two little brothers, were given tickets to the game.**

   (1) change *were given* to *were give*
   (2) change *were given* to *was given*
   (3) change *were given* to *are give*
   (4) change *were given* to *were gave*
   (5) no correction is necessary

9. **Shawna has overslept. She hurries to leave so she will not be late for work. Her little daughter has hid her car keys.**

   (1) change *has overslept* to *had overslept*
   (2) change *hurries* to *had hurried*
   (3) change *will not be* to *is not*
   (4) change *has hid* to *has hidden*
   (5) no correction is necessary

10. **Not only Maya but also her two cousins lives in those apartments. Maya moved in last September, after she had taken the job at the bank.**

    (1) change *lives* to *live*
    (2) change *lives* to *has lived*
    (3) change *moved* to *has moved*
    (4) change *had taken* to *had took*
    (5) no correction is necessary

11. **Before the amusement park had opened, neither Martha nor Kim had ever seen such a large roller coaster.**

    (1) change *had opened* to *have opened*
    (2) change *had opened* to *opened*
    (3) change *had ever seen* to *had ever saw*
    (4) change *had ever seen* to *have ever seen*
    (5) no correction is necessary

12. **The jury do not look happy as they enter the courtroom. They stand as the judge takes her place.**

    (1) change *do not look* to *does not look*
    (2) change *enter* to *enters*
    (3) change *stand* to *have stood*
    (4) change *stand* to *will stand*
    (5) no correction is necessary

13. **Simon stoops to pick up the broken pot, and his eyeglasses slips down his nose.**

    (1) change *stoops* to *stoop*
    (2) change *stoops* to *has stooped*
    (3) change *slips* to *slip*
    (4) change *slips* to *had slipped*
    (5) no correction is necessary

14. **If Louis was chosen the winner, I would be amazed. Before he entered the art contest, he had never been taught anything about painting.**

    (1) change *was chosen* to *were chosen*
    (2) change *entered* to *enters*
    (3) change *entered* to *had entered*
    (4) change *had never been taught* to *has never been taught*
    (5) no correction is necessary

15. **Beside the new garage rests three tired carpenters. They will be going home when the work is done.**

    (1) change *rests* to *rest*
    (2) change *will be going* to *went*
    (3) change *is done* to *was done*
    (4) change *is done* to *will be done*
    (5) no correction is necessary

ANSWERS ARE ON PAGE 254.

Adjectives are words that modify, or describe, a noun or a pronoun.

James is a <u>devoted</u> father to his two children.

Adverbs are words that modify, or descibe, a verb, an adjective, or another adverb.

The bluebird flew away <u>suddenly</u>.

3 Modifiers

ADJECTIVES AND ADVERBS

Nouns and verbs give sentences their main structure. They tell you what the sentence is about and what is happening. By themselves, though, nouns and verbs make language pretty dull. Modifiers give language color. Read the following paragraph. The underlined words are modifiers. Notice what they add to the writing.

One of nature's <u>worst</u> storms moved <u>slowly</u> toward the <u>unprotected</u> land. <u>Worried</u> people were preparing for <u>this</u> hurricane. It would hurl <u>powerful</u> winds and <u>mountainous</u> waves at them. <u>Already, gigantic</u> waves were beating <u>savagely</u> against <u>that</u> shore. <u>One</u> town was <u>nearly empty</u>. <u>Wisely</u>, its people had run toward <u>higher</u> land <u>far away</u> from the <u>dangerous sea</u>.

Modifiers are words that describe other words in a sentence. There are two kinds of modifiers: adjectives and adverbs.

ADJECTIVES

> ***Adjectives*** are words that modify, or describe, a noun or pronoun.

An adjective can modify a noun in several ways. It can tell what kind, which one, and how many.

what kind ⟶ *worst* storms   *mountainous* waves
which one ⟶ *this* hurricane   *that* shore
how many ⟶ *one* town

Often a noun is modified by more than one adjective.

safer, higher land

ADVERBS

> ***Adverbs*** are words that modify, or describe, a verb, an adjective, or another adverb.

modifying a verb ⟶ moved *slowly*
modifying an adjective ⟶ *already* gigantic
modifying an adverb ⟶ *far* away

Adverbs can modify words in several ways. They can tell how, when or how often, where, and to what extent.

how ⟶ moved *slowly*
when ⟶ *already* gigantic
where ⟶ land *far away*
to what extent ⟶ *nearly* empty

> **Hint:** To figure out whether a modifier is an adjective or an adverb, look for the word it modifies.

EXERCISE 1

Directions: Look at the underlined modifier in each sentence. On the first blank, write which word is modified, or described. On the second blank, tell whether the underlined modifier is an adjective or an adverb.

Example: __*flower*__ The snow fell on the <u>red</u> flower. __*adjective*__

_____ **1.** The mail arrived <u>late</u> today. _____

_____ **2.** A <u>late</u> dinner was served at the restaurant. _____

_____ **3.** <u>Four</u> children came to my door this afternoon. _____

_____ **4.** Andrew moved too <u>quickly</u> in the darkness and fell. _____

_____ **5.** He made an <u>absolutely</u> amazing discovery as he got up. _____

_____ **6.** <u>This</u> chair goes over there in the corner. _____

_____ **7.** The music played <u>quietly</u> in the distance. _____

_____ **8.** Juan lives <u>here</u> with his two brothers. _____

_____ **9.** What an <u>awful</u> noise was heard in the basement! _____

_____ **10.** My <u>new</u>, red sports car has a dent in it! _____

ANSWERS ARE ON PAGE 255.

FORMING ADJECTIVES AND ADVERBS

Adjectives and adverbs are both modifiers, but they modify different kinds of words. Therefore, you should not use one in place of the other. Usually adjectives and adverbs are formed in different ways. By knowing how they are formed, you can be sure to use them correctly.

Adjectives do not have a special form. Many adverbs, however, are formed by adding *ly* to an adjective.

ADVERBS FORMED WITH *LY*	
Adjectives	**Adverbs**
loud screaming	scream *loudly*
warm clothes	*warmly* dressed
beautiful photograph	paints *beautifully*

Some adverbs are formed from adjectives in other ways.

If the adjective ends in

ll add only a *y*	full → fully
y change the *y* to *i* and add *ly*	happy → happily
le change the *le* to *ly*	horrible → horribly
ic add *al* before adding *ly*	frantic → frantically

Some adjectives and adverbs have the same form. The chart below shows some of these. Note especially that words ending in *ly* are not always adverbs.

ADJECTIVES AND ADVERBS WITH THE SAME FORM			
daily	fast	ill	right
early	hard	low	straight
far	high	near	weekly

Remember that there is not an adverb for every adjective.

EXERCISE 2

Directions: If the adjectives and adverbs in each sentence are correct, write *C* in the blank. If an adjective or adverb is incorrect, write the correct form.

Examples: __*C*__ Paul spoke kindly to the frightened child.

__*slowly*__ The parks committee worked slow.

_____ **1.** The runners moved rapid toward the finish line.

_____ **2.** This new calculator is supposed to work easy.

_____ **3.** Andre willingly agreed to help me move that heavy chair.

_____ **4.** I fully expect you to complete this project by noon.

_____ **5.** The extremely heat and lack of rain is hard on the crops.

_____ **6.** Rico buys the paper daily.

_____ **7.** I read the contract careful before signing it.

_____ **8.** Molly hurt her foot bad.

_____ **9.** She looked straightly into my eyes and said it was broken.

_____ **10.** Susan said she had a practically solution to my problem.

_____ **11.** Hector lovingly gave his girlfriend Rosa a dozen roses on her birthday.

_____ **12.** The old road winds crooked through the hills.

ANSWERS ARE ON PAGE 255.

PROBLEMS WITH ADJECTIVES AND ADVERBS

Adverbs can often be moved around in a sentence without changing the meaning or making the sentence unclear.

Reading my favorite book relaxes me *slowly.*
I am relaxed when I read my favorite book *slowly.*

Sometimes putting an adverb in the wrong position can change the meaning of a sentence. Compare the meaning of these two sentences.

Mia *actually* told me that they eat worms.
Mia told me that they *actually* eat worms.

When an adverb is placed too far from the word it modifies, it can make the meaning of the sentence unclear.

I'll *just* give you two hours to get out of town.

A reader might wonder exactly what is meant in this sentence. Moving the adverb will make it clear.

I'll give you *just* two hours to get out of town.

Modifiers Used with Linking Verbs

Remember that linking verbs are words like *is, are, seems, appears,* and *looks.* They connect a noun with another word that describes it or renames it.

Certain verbs can be used as either linking verbs or action verbs. These include the following:

BOTH LINKING AND ACTION VERBS			
appear	feel	look	smell
become	grow	seem	taste

A modifier that follows these words can be an adjective or an adverb. To know which is correct, decide what word is being modified. If the word describes the noun, it must be an adjective. A common mistake is to use the adverb because it seems to modify the verb that it follows.

Incorrect: That anvil looks *heavily.*
Correct: That anvil looks *heavy.* (A heavy anvil)

Incorrect: Jason grew *quick.*
Correct: Jason grew *quickly.* (How Jason grew)

Hint: Use this trick to help you decide whether a verb is used as a linking verb or an action verb. Mentally replace the verb with the linking verb *is* (or *are*). If the sentence still makes sense, the verb is a linking verb. The modifier should be an adjective. If the sentence doesn't make sense, it is an action verb. Then the modifier should be an adverb.

Sarah grew angry.   ⟶   Sarah *is* angry.
Jeremy grew quickly.   ⟶   Jeremy *is* quickly.

EXERCISE 3

Directions: Read each sentence. If the underlined modifiers are correct, write *C* in the blank. If an underlined modifier is incorrect, write the correct one in the space.

Example: __*delighted*__ Laura seemed <u>delightedly</u> to see us.

1._____ The <u>early</u> morning sky became <u>darkly</u> with thunderclouds.

2._____ Will you be <u>sadly</u> if you don't see him again?

3._____ When the two dogs look <u>fiercely</u> at Gopal, he crosses <u>quick</u> to the other side of the street.

4._____ The doctor felt Ann's swollen arm <u>careful</u>.

5._____ Kyle seems fairly <u>surely</u> that they will take a <u>long</u> vacation <u>next</u> summer.

6._____ I feel <u>happily</u> that you are my friend.

7._____ The sun shone <u>bright</u> after the storm.

8._____ The robber looked <u>evil</u> at the woman as he snatched her purse.

9._____ Mrs. Valdez <u>lightly</u> scented her wrist with perfume.

10._____ The volume on the radio seemed too <u>loudly</u>.

11._____ Weeds <u>slow</u> covered our neighbor's backyard.

12._____ Smoking is <u>harmful</u> to your health.

ANSWERS ARE ON PAGE 255.

ADJECTIVES AND ADVERBS IN COMPARISONS

When writing, you often want to compare different things or actions. Adjectives are used to compare people, places, things, and ideas. Adverbs are used to compare actions.

Claudia is *tall*.
Claudia is *taller* than William.
Claudia is the *tallest* person in her family.

In the first sentence, the basic form of the adjective *tall* is used to describe Claudia. In the second sentence, the adjective *taller* is used to compare two people, Claudia and William. In the third sentence, *tallest* is used to compare three or more people. These are the three degrees or levels of comparison. Both adjectives and adverbs have these degrees. Here are examples of the three degrees of the adverb *quickly*.

Hyung walks *quickly*.
Sachi walks *more quickly* than Hyung.
Kim walks the *most quickly* of the three friends.

Comparing Two Things or Actions

When two things or actions are compared, the correct adjective or adverb is usually formed in two ways. If the modifier is short—one or two syllables—add *er*. If the modifier is longer—three or more syllables—use the word *more* plus the adjective or adverb. Always use *more* with adverbs ending in *ly*. If an adjective ends in a consonant plus *y*, change the *y* to *i* before adding *er*.

Adjectives

Kathy's job is *harder* than his.
This shirt is *more expensive* than that one.

Adverbs

Steve's band plays *louder* than Ken's band.
Of those two stars, that one sparkles *more brightly*.

The opposite of *more* is *less*. You can also make comparisons using *less*.

That house is *less expensive* than ours.
I clean the kitchen *less carefully* than my mother does.

Hint: Never use *more* or *less* along with the *er* ending.

Incorrect: A bicycle is *more cheaper* than a motorcycle.
Correct: A bicycle is *cheaper* than a motorcycle.

Comparing Three or More Things or Actions

There are two ways to form modifiers that compare three or more things or actions. To the short adjectives and adverbs, add *est* to the end of the word. For longer modifiers—and all adverbs ending in *ly*—use *most* plus the regular form of the adjective or adverb. For adjectives ending in a consonant plus *y*, change the *y* to *i* before adding *est*.

Adjectives

Of the three children, John is *sleepiest.*
This book is the *most interesting* one I've read all year.

Adverbs

Our team plays the *hardest* of all.
Maria works the *most carefully* of the four employees.

You can compare three or more things or actions using *least.*

What is the *least* amount of salt I can use in this recipe?
This car runs the *least dependably* of any I've ever owned.

FORMING COMPARISONS		
Types of Modifiers	**Comparing two things or actions**	**Comparing three or more things or actions**
Short modifiers	add *er: taller, harder*	add *est: tallest, hardest*
Adjectives ending in a consonant plus *y*	change *y* to *i* and add *er: happier*	change *y* to *i* and add *est: happiest*
Long modifiers and all adverbs ending in *ly*	Use *more* or *less: more quickly, less intelligent*	Use *most* or *least: most quickly, least intelligent*

Irregular Forms of Comparisons

Like verbs, adjectives and adverbs have both regular and irregular forms. Most adjectives and adverbs are regular and comparisons are formed as already described. Comparisons for some of the most commonly used irregular adjectives and adverbs are given below.

IRREGULAR COMPARISONS		
Describing one thing or action	**Comparing two things or actions**	**Comparing three or more things or actions**
bad	worse	worst
far	farther	farthest
good	better	best
ill	worse	worst
little	less	least
many	more	most
much	more	most
well	better	best

Comparison Problems with Modifiers

When making comparisons, check how many things or actions are being compared. If two items are being compared, always use the *er, more,* or *less* forms. If more than two items are being compared, always use the *est, most,* or *least* forms. Errors often result from not using these forms correctly.

Incorrect: Of the *two* sisters, she is the *shortest.*
Correct: Of the *two* sisters, she is the *shorter.*

Incorrect: *All* the workers do well, but Martha does *better.*
Correct: *All* the workers do well, but Martha does *best.*

Be alert to comparisons between one thing and a group of things. It may seem as though you are comparing many things. In fact, it is two things: one thing and one group.

Incorrect: He speaks *most slowly* than the *other men.*
Correct: He speaks *more slowly* than the *other men.*

EXERCISE 4

Directions: Write the correct form of the modifier in parentheses.

Example: __*hungrier*__ Elena is *(hungry)* than Margo.

1._____ This is the *(little)* enthusiastic group of volunteers we have ever had.

2._____ Rice, beans, and macaroni are the *(cheap)* items I buy at the grocery store.

3._____ Everyone knows that Noriko is the *(fast)* of the two typists.

4._____ I think Soon Young would be the *(good)* house painter among all those people who applied.

5._____ Mark always dresses *(neat)* than Tamiko.

6._____ Tony has *(few)* duties now than he had in his last job.

7._____ Helena is *(serious)* about starting a business than I am.

8._____ Of all the movies you've seen this summer, which was the *(exciting)*?

9._____ I feel *(much)* relaxed after swimming than after biking.

10._____ Susan was never *(happy)* than she is now.

11._____ Andy's has the *(good)* buys on fruits and vegetables in our area.

12._____ Ben traveled *(far)* on his bike yesterday than Tim did.

13._____ Anita's allergies are *(bad)* during the summer than during the winter.

ANSWERS ARE ON PAGE 256.

MORE PROBLEMS WITH ADJECTIVES AND ADVERBS

There are four common mistakes in the use of modifiers.

Well or *Good*; *Badly* or *Bad*

Well and *badly* are adverbs. *Good* and *bad* are adjectives. Be careful to use them correctly.

Adjectives	**Adverbs**
Take a *good* look at this example.	She plays *well*.
Do you think this is a *bad* idea?	The toast is *badly* burnt.

Be especially careful when using linking verbs. Remember they connect a subject to its modifier, which is always an adjective.

This book is *good*. Those rotten apples smell *bad*.

There is an important exception to this rule. When the modifier after a linking verb refers to health, always use *well* instead of *good*.

Are you feeling *well*?

Double Negatives

A negative word is one that means *no* or *not*.

NEGATIVES		
hardly	nobody	nothing
neither	none	nowhere
never	no one	*n't* in contractions
no	not	scarcely

Never use more than one negative in a clause.

Incorrect: I do *not* want *nothing*.
Correct: I do *not* want anything.
Correct: I want *nothing*.

Look for words like *don't, won't, wouldn't, can't,* and *shouldn't*. These words are negatives. The *n't* stands for *not*. Do not use them in a sentence with another negative.

Incorrect: She *can't* go *nowhere.*
Correct: She *can't* go anywhere.
Correct: She can go *nowhere.*

A common mistake is to forget that *hardly* and *scarcely* are negatives.

Incorrect: Teresa *can't hardly* see well enough to drive.
Correct: Teresa can *hardly* see well enough to drive.
Correct: Teresa *can't* see well enough to drive.

This, That, These, Those, and *Them*

This and *that* are adjectives used to point out singular nouns. *This* points to something that is close by. *That* points to something that is not close.

This book goes in *that* bookcase.

These and *those* are adjectives used to point out plural nouns. *These* points to things that are nearby. *Those* points to things that are not nearby.

These books go in *those* bookcases.

Because *this* and *these* mean "here," do not use *this here* or *these here.* For the same reason, do not use *that there* or *those there.*

Incorrect: *These* pencils *here* are mine.
Correct: *These* pencils are mine.

Them cannot be used in place of *those* to point out a noun. *Them* is always an object pronoun.

Incorrect: Did you see *them* cars?
Correct: Did you see *those* cars?

A and *An*

The words *a* and *an* are adjectives. They modify nouns to show they are singular. *An* is used before all words that begin with a vowel sound. (The vowels are *a, e, i, o, u.*)

    an ape   *an* opinion   *an* unusual day

Use *an* before a word that begins with an *h* if the *h* is not pronounced.

    an hour   *an* honor   <u>but</u> *a* hospital

Use *a* before all other words.

    a boring speech   *a* lazy dog   *a* flower

There is one vowel to watch out for. Use *a* before words beginning with a *u* that is pronounced like *you.*

    a unicorn   *a* usual day   *a* union

EXERCISE 5

Directions: In each sentence, underline the correct word or group of words in parentheses.

Example: Hilda visited (*a, an*) university last week.

1. I have already read *(those, them)* books.

2. Sarah *(hadn't scarcely, had scarcely)* begun to clean her house.

3. That coffee tastes *(bitter, bitterly)*.

4. When Jon had a cold and didn't feel *(well, good)*, who *(careful, carefully)* nursed him back to health?

5. There is *(a, an)* easier way that *(wouldn't hardly, would hardly)* cost any more money.

6. Jill is *(a, an)* ideal candidate for mayor.

7. We don't have time to sponsor *(no, any)* special events.

8. Slice *(these, this)* carrots and add *(those, that)* cup of peas to the pot.

9. When I'm sick, there isn't *(nothing, anything)* anybody can do to make me feel *(best, better)*.

10. It's good for your health if you eat *(a, an)* variety of fruits and vegetables each day.

11. We couldn't find the little girl *(anywhere, nowhere)*.

12. Carry *(this, these)* basket over to the dining room table.

13. I *(can hardly, can't hardly)* wait for spring to arrive so that I can see the flowers in bloom.

14. That is *(a, an)* unusual house because it is *(more angular, most angular)* than the house next to it.

ANSWERS ARE ON PAGE 256.

☰ PRE-GED Practice ☰
ADJECTIVES AND ADVERBS

Choose what correction should be made to each sentence below. If you think the sentence is correct, choose (5).

1. **The nervous man drove careful down the busy street. He seemed glad when he turned onto the side road.**

   (1) change *nervous* to *nervously*
   (2) change *careful* to *carefully*
   (3) change *busy* to *busily*
   (4) change *glad* to *gladly*
   (5) no correction is necessary

2. **The regular salesperson has not been feeling good. When she had good health, she rarely missed work. Now she misses more work.**

   (1) change *regular* to *regularly*
   (2) change *feeling good* to *feeling well*
   (3) change *good health* to *well health*
   (4) change *more* to *the most*
   (5) no correction is necessary

3. **I didn't hardly ever do anything fun while I lived in that city. After a few months, I moved back to this city where I know more people.**

   (1) change *didn't hardly ever do* to *hardly ever did*
   (2) change *that* to *those*
   (3) change *this* to *that*
   (4) change *more* to *most*
   (5) no correction is necessary

4. **My manager wants our small department to be the most successful in the company. She tries to hire the better people she can find.**

   (1) change *small* to *smaller*
   (2) change *most successful* to *successfullest*
   (3) change *most successful* to *more successful*
   (4) change *better* to *best*
   (5) no correction is necessary

5. **If I were more wiser, I would quickly learn to save more and instantly forget how to spend it so well.**

   (1) change *more wiser* to *wiser*
   (2) change *quickly* to *quick*
   (3) change *instantly* to *instant*
   (4) change *well* to *good*
   (5) no correction is necessary

6. **The oak tree is highest than the maple tree in our yard. We get more shade early in the morning from the oak tree.**

   (1) change *highest* to *high*
   (2) change *highest* to *higher*
   (3) change *more* to *most*
   (4) change *early* to *earliest*
   (5) no correction is necessary

ANSWERS ARE ON PAGE 256.

PHRASES AS MODIFIERS

Sometimes a whole group of words acts to modify, or describe, another word in a sentence. A ***phrase*** is a group of words that contains either a noun (or pronoun) or a verb, but not both. A phrase also includes some other words that describe the noun or verb or that ties the group of words to the rest of the sentence.

PREPOSITIONAL PHRASES

As you learned in Chapter 2, a ***prepositional phrase*** is a group of words that begins with a preposition and ends with a noun or pronoun. In a sentence, a prepositional phrase works as an adjective or an adverb. When it serves as an adjective, it modifies a noun or a pronoun.

The water *in the pool* is clear.

When a prepositional phrase is used as an adverb, it modifies a verb, an adjective, or an adverb.

Cindy jumped *off the high board.*
She is skillful *at diving.*
Cindy began diving soon *after her older sister.*

Hint: A prepositional phrase can be placed either before or after the word it modifies. However, the sentence will be clearer if the phrase is close to the word it modifies.

Confusing: Cindy teaches children to jump off the low board from the grade school.

Better: Cindy teaches children from the grade school to jump off the low board.

VERB PHRASES

Another group of words that acts as a modifier is the **verb phrase**. A verb phrase begins with a verb form.

Tired after a long day, José took his dog for a walk.
José used a leash *to walk his dog.*
Breaking the leash, the dog was free.

◎ **FOCUS ON PUNCTUATION**

Introductory Phrases

A modifying phrase is often used to begin a sentence. When it is, use a comma to separate it from the rest of the sentence. A comma is not always needed if the phrase occurs somewhere else in the sentence.

Stumbling over the curb, Mindy almost fell.

EXERCISE 6

Directions: Underline the modifying phrase in each sentence. Write the word it modifies.

Example: __Jan__ Walking home, Jan watched dark clouds gather.

1. _____ Louis saw the bus at the corner.

2. _____ Opening the door, Shen looked outside.

3. _____ The smell of barbecued chicken made Shawna hungry.

4. _____ The exhausted runner, seeing the finish line, speeded up.

5. _____ Julie was sorry to lose the watch.

6. _____ Jacobo left his books at the library.

7._____ Already soaked to the skin, Ms. Atole opened her umbrella.

8._____ The basketball game ended soon after sunset.

9._____ The police car left the crime scene in a hurry.

10._____ Hoping to get more customers, the store manager lowered prices.

11._____ Locking the door, Mr. Henshaw left his apartment.

12._____ Mrs. Cosmos crossed over the Canadian border.

13._____ Sitting between her parents, Lenore felt quite happy.

ANSWERS ARE ON PAGE 257.

RENAMING PHRASES AS MODIFIERS

A *renaming phrase*, also called an appositive, is a group of words that gives more information about a noun in a sentence. It is made up of a noun and other words that modify it.

John Tenorio, *a truck driver,* left the warehouse at noon.

As with other phrases, a renaming phrase must be placed carefully in the sentence. Otherwise, it can be confusing or misleading. Usually, a renaming phrase comes directly after the noun it modifies. Occasionally, it may come before the noun.

A retired state senator, Margaret Fisher stayed active in politics.

Usually, renaming phrases are separated from the rest of the sentence by commas. If the renaming phrase occurs in the middle of a sentence, a comma comes before and after it.

EXERCISE 7

Directions: Find the renaming phrase in each sentence and punctuate it correctly.

Example: Neil Armstrong the astronaut was the first person on the moon.

Neil Armstrong, the astronaut, was the first person on the moon.

1. Yuri Gagarin the first human in space was from the Soviet Union.

_____

_____

2. Ham a chimpanzee tested the U.S. spacecraft.

_____

_____

3. Alan Shepard the first American in space wrote a book about the early space program.

_____

_____

4. Shepard went into space in Redstone 3 a tiny spacecraft.

_____

_____

5. Shepard an astronaut and test pilot went to the moon many years later.

_____

_____

ANSWERS ARE ON PAGE 257.

PRE-GED Practice
PHRASES AS MODIFIERS

Choose what correction should be made to each sentence below. If you think the sentence is correct, choose (5).

1. **Jumping up from the ground Isabel, my mother's friend, ran after the children.**

   (1) move the phrase *jumping up from the ground* to the end of the sentence
   (2) add a comma after *ground*
   (3) remove the comma after *Isabel* and after *friend*
   (4) add a comma before *after the children*
   (5) no correction is necessary

2. **Tomás watched the truck in the driveway. His neighbor, a mechanic, was busy, under the hood.**

   (1) add a comma before *in the driveway*
   (2) move *in the driveway* to the beginning of the sentence
   (3) remove the commas on each side of *a mechanic*
   (4) remove the comma after *busy*
   (5) no correction is necessary

3. **Janet, a photographer, was always on the go. Finishing one assignment, she would grab her camera an expensive Japanese model and race to the next.**

   (1) remove commas on each side of *a photographer*
   (2) remove the comma after *assignment*
   (3) add commas before and after *an expensive Japanese model*
   (4) add a comma after *race*
   (5) no correction is necessary

4. **Losing his wallet, Jerome called the security office to report his loss. Leonard Chino, chief of security, told him the wallet had been found.**

   (1) move *losing his wallet* to the end of the sentence
   (2) remove the comma after *wallet*
   (3) add a comma after *office*
   (4) remove the commas before and after *chief of security*
   (5) no correction is necessary

5. **To rescue her cat Ann called the fire chief, an old friend. He sent a young fire fighter up a long ladder to save the cat.**

   (1) add a comma after *To rescue her cat*
   (2) move *To rescue her cat* to the end of the sentence
   (3) add a comma after *called*
   (4) add a comma after *ladder*
   (5) no correction is necessary

6. **After we left the movie theater we stopped for some coffee. My friend Albert, an avid film buff, discussed the movie with me for about an hour.**

   (1) add a comma after *theater*
   (2) remove the comma after *Albert*
   (3) remove the comma after *buff*
   (4) add a comma after *me*
   (5) no correction is necessary

ANSWERS ARE ON PAGE 257.

JOURNAL WRITING

You already use modifiers in your writing. You may not think much about them, however. To see how you do use them, write a short journal entry about someone you know. Choose someone who is an interesting or funny character. Write two or three paragraphs. Then look at your writing. Underline each adverb or adjective once. Underline each phrase twice. Did you use all of them correctly?

≡ PRE-GED Practice ≡
MODIFIERS

Read each sentence. Then choose the best correction for each sentence.

1. **Ann Watson, manager of the grocery store, hired two new employees. The younger one will help Sid the produce manager.**

   (1) change *new* to *newer*
   (2) change *younger* to *youngest*
   (3) change *younger* to *more young*
   (4) add a comma after *Sid*
   (5) no correction is necessary

2. **Noriko can't hardly go to work today. Her car, a beat-up old jalopy, won't start. It has seen better days.**

   (1) change *can't* to *can*
   (2) change *hardly* to *scarcely*
   (3) remove the commas before and after *a beat-up old jalopy*
   (4) change *better* to *best*
   (5) no correction is necessary

3. **After I put them cans in the cooler, I added a big bag of ice. In this hot weather, the ice melted fast.**

   (1) change *them* to *those*
   (2) change *this* to *these*
   (3) remove the comma after *weather*
   (4) change *fast* to *faster*
   (5) no correction is necessary

4. **To buy that new car, Sheri signed a application for a loan.**

   (1) change *that* to *these*
   (2) remove the comma after *car*
   (3) change *a application* to *an application*
   (4) change *a loan* to *an loan*
   (5) no correction is necessary

5. **Taro's car looks much shinier than it did. That there wax really makes it look good.**

   (1) change *much* to *more*
   (2) change *shinier* to *shiniest*
   (3) remove *there*
   (4) change *good* to *well*
   (5) no correction is necessary

6. **The letter carrier looks nervous at the dog. It is the most ferocious of all the dogs on that street.**

   (1) change *nervous* to *nervously*
   (2) change *most ferocious* to *more ferocious*
   (3) change *most ferocious* to *ferocious*
   (4) change *that* to *these*
   (5) no correction is necessary

7. **Those steaks smell bad. They looked fresh when I picked them out.**

    (1) change *Those* to *Them*
    (2) change *bad* to *badly*
    (3) change *bad* to *more bad*
    (4) change *fresh* to *freshly*
    (5) no correction is necessary

8. **The funnier book I have ever read is *Roughing It*. Mark Twain, a nineteenth-century writer, is the author.**

    (1) change *funnier* to *most funny*
    (2) change *funnier* to *more funnier*
    (3) change *funnier* to *funniest*
    (4) remove the commas around *a nineteenth-century writer*
    (5) no correction is necessary

9. **Lee Chung did not feel very good yesterday. He feels even worse today.**

    (1) change *good* to *well*
    (2) change *worse* to *more bad*
    (3) change *worse* to *worst*
    (4) change *worse* to *worser*
    (5) no correction is necessary

10. **If I were more smarter, I would have bought this television last week. That sale was better than the sale this week.**

    (1) change *more smarter* to *most smarter*
    (2) change *more smarter* to *smarter*
    (3) change *better* to *more better*
    (4) change *better* to *best*
    (5) no correction is necessary

11. **That basketball player has scarcely any competition. Watch how he sets up the play so easy.**

    (1) change *That* to *Those*
    (2) change *That* to *That there*
    (3) change *any* to *no*
    (4) change *easy* to *easily*
    (5) no correction is necessary

12. **That computer is less expensive than this one. However, it isn't scarcely the best one that I have ever seen.**

    (1) change *less* to *least*
    (2) change *this* to *these*
    (3) change *isn't* to *is*
    (4) change *best* to *better*
    (5) no correction is necessary

13. **Waving frantically, the hungry, shipwrecked sailor screamed loud at the passing ship.**

    (1) change *frantically* to *frantic*
    (2) remove the comma after *frantically*
    (3) change *hungry* to *hungrily*
    (4) change *loud* to *loudly*
    (5) no correction is necessary

14. **Patty seemed extremely happy when she was given those tickets there.**

    (1) change *extremely* to *extreme*
    (2) change *happy* to *happily*
    (3) change *those* to *them*
    (4) remove *there*
    (5) no correction is necessary

15. **Mark looks closely at that small print. A guarantee should be easier to read.**

    (1) change *closely* to *close*
    (2) change *that* to *those*
    (3) change *small* to *smaller*
    (4) change *easier* to *easily*
    (5) no correction is necessary

    ANSWERS ARE ON PAGE 257.

The most basic form of a sentence is the simple sentence. It contains one subject and one predicate and expresses a complete thought.

Jerome wanted to buy a portable CD player. He didn't have enough money.

Jerome wanted to buy a portable CD player, but he didn't have enough money.

COMBINING IDEAS IN SENTENCES

Read these two paragraphs. Which do you like best?

> The U.S. Army is dumping tanks into the Gulf of Mexico. They are trying to improve fishing. Old tanks are cleaned up. The army no longer wants them. All poisonous chemicals are removed. Then the tanks are taken out to sea on ships. The tanks are dumped overboard. This part of the gulf is flat. It has few natural hiding places for fish. Dumping the tanks creates artificial places. Fish can hide and reproduce.

> The U.S. Army is dumping tanks into the Gulf of Mexico in order to improve fishing. Old tanks that the army no longer wants are cleaned up, and all poisonous chemicals are removed. Then the tanks are taken out to sea on ships and dumped overboard. This part of the gulf is flat; it has few natural hiding places for fish. Dumping the tanks creates artificial places where fish can hide and reproduce.

Both paragraphs are correct, and both give the same information. The first one, however, is made up entirely of simple sentences. When you read it, it sounds choppy. In the second paragraph, the sentences have been combined to create more variety in sentence length and structure. Ideas are also more closely linked so you know how they are related.

FORMING COMPOUND SENTENCES

The most basic form of a sentence is the **simple sentence**. It contains one subject and one predicate and expresses a complete thought.

Yolanda wanted a radio for her birthday. She got two.

Simple sentences like these can often be combined to make a more interesting sentence.

Yolanda wanted a radio for her birthday, and she got two.

This new sentence has two subject-predicate sets. In fact, the two original simple sentences were not changed at all. They were linked by the word *and.* The result is a compound sentence.

> A **compound sentence** contains two or more connected simple sentences.

CONJUNCTIONS

Compound sentences are most often linked by a **conjunction**. These are words like *and, or, but,* and *yet.*

Mr. Ruiz does not have a lawn mower. He doesn't want one.
<u>becomes</u>
Mr. Ruiz does not have a lawn mower, and he doesn't want one.

Please bring the cooler. The soda will become warm.
<u>becomes</u>
Please bring the cooler, or the soda will become warm.

Conjunctions link sentences by showing how ideas are related. Each conjunction shows a certain kind of connection between ideas.

CONJUNCTIONS AND THEIR USES	
Conjunction	**Use**
and	adds extra information
but, yet	shows how ideas are different
or	shows a choice between ideas
nor	shows a rejection of both ideas
for	connects an effect to a cause
so	connects a cause to its effect

Here are some examples of compound sentences. Notice that when two simple sentences are combined using a conjunction the original sentences are not changed. The only exception is *nor.* Then the subject and verb in the second sentence are reversed.

Laura bought a coat, and Sara bought a pair of gloves.
Pan hated painting, yet he finished the whole room.
The Tuckers had a long trip before them, so they left early.
Jim's baby wouldn't be quiet, nor would she keep still.

◉ FOCUS ON PUNCTUATION

Commas used before Conjunctions

A comma is used before the conjunction in compound sentences. Remember, however, that a compound sentence has two subject-verb sets, and each expresses a complete thought. If either part of the compound sentence does not express a complete thought or does not have a subject-verb set, then don't use a comma before the conjunction.

Jerry bought flowers but forgot to give them to Julie.
Jerry bought flowers, but he forgot to give them to Julie.

The second part of the first sentence does not have a subject, so no comma is needed. The second sentence has two complete subject-verb sets, so a comma is needed.

OTHER CONJUNCTIONS

Some conjunctions made up of two parts are used in pairs.

both . . . and   either . . . or
not only . . . but also neither . . . nor

These conjunctions are often used in the pairs listed below. Place them next to the words they are connecting.

Not only do I take sugar in my coffee, but I also take milk.
Either it rains when I go fishing, or it's sunny when I work.

A comma is used when conjunctions connect two subject-verb sets.

JOINING IDEAS WITH A SEMICOLON
Semicolons with Conjunctive Adverbs

Simple sentences can also be joined using a semicolon and a conjunctive adverb. A **conjunctive adverb** is a word or phrase that works like a conjunction. As with conjunctions, it is important to choose the right conjunctive adverb to say what you mean.

CONJUNCTIVE ADVERBS		
To show contrast	however otherwise	nevertheless on the other hand
To explain	for example furthermore besides	in other words in fact moreover
To show a result	consequently as a result	then therefore

These words are used like conjunctions to join sentences. Place a semicolon before the conjunctive adverb. Put a comma after all conjunctive adverbs except *then*.

Food prices keep rising; *in fact,* our weekly grocery bill is
ten dollars higher than last year.
Noriko took tennis lessons; *then* she beat me all the time.

Semicolons Without Conjunctions

Two simple sentences can also be joined without using a conjunction or a conjunctive adverb. A semicolon shows the ideas are linked.

Benito likes to barbecue; ribs are his specialty.

FORMING COMPOUND SENTENCES

You've seen that compound sentences can be formed in three ways:

1. using conjunctions and commas

2. using conjunctive adverbs and semicolons

3. using semicolons

One common error in forming compound sentences is caused by forgetting to use one of these methods. The result is a ***run-on sentence***.

Incorrect: Hieu needed new shoes he bought some at the sale.

Run-ons can be corrected by using one of the methods you've learned for forming compound sentences.

Correct: Hieu needed new shoes, so he bought some at the sale.
Correct: Hieu needed new shoes; consequently, he bought some at the sale.
Correct: Hieu needed new shoes; he bought some at the sale.

A second common error in forming compound sentences is caused by stringing several sentences together with the word *and*.

Incorrect: He went on vacation to New Mexico *and* visited Pueblo Villages *and* saw hot-air balloons *and* rode on a tram up the mountain.

Correct: He went on vacation to New Mexico *and* visited Pueblo Villages; he also saw hot-air balloons *and* rode on a tram up the mountain.

A third common error in forming compound sentences is caused by the comma splice.

Incorrect: I keep sneezing, I think I'm catching a cold.
Correct: I keep sneezing, so I think I'm catching a cold.
Correct: I keep sneezing; I think I'm catching a cold.

EXERCISE 1

Directions: Rewrite each of the following pairs of simple sentences as a compound sentence. Use the conjunction, conjunctive adverb, or semicolon shown in parentheses to connect the sentences. Add correct punctuation.

Example: Bill likes sports. He especially enjoys touch football. *(and)*

Bill likes sports, and he especially enjoys touch football.

1. Ann starts a new job soon. She hasn't told her present boss. *(but)*

_____

_____

2. There are no good movies in town. A great rock band is playing. *(however)*

_____

_____

3. My house is a mess. I never seem to have time to clean it. *(semicolon)*

_____

_____

4. The plane's wings were covered with ice. The departure was delayed. *(as a result)*

_____

_____

5. The waitress took their orders. She brought us coffee. *(then)*

_____

_____

6. I could never keep the washer fixed. I bought a new one. *(so)*

_____

_____

7. Snow is forecast for tonight. We should change our travel plans. *(therefore)*

_____

_____

8. Max is a good dog. I don't want him eating off the table. *(nevertheless)*

_____

_____

9. The storm knocked out electric power. Lights are off all over town. *(semicolon)*

_____

_____

10. Janet has a sore arm. She's going bowling. *(yet)*

_____

_____

11. The game was really exciting. Hugo made the winning touchdown. *(because)*

_____

_____

12. We had a good time at the party. It ended too soon. *(but)*

_____

_____

13. I went swimming at the beach yesterday. The water was just the right temperature. *(semicolon)*

_____

_____

14. Alexandra got the flu yesterday. She will stay home for a few days. *(so)*

_____

_____

ANSWERS ARE ON PAGE 258.

FORMING COMPLEX SENTENCES

Another kind of sentence is the ***complex sentence***. It is made up of two or more clauses. Remember that a clause is a group of words that contains a subject and a predicate. A clause may express a complete thought, or it may not. In a complex sentence only one clause expresses a complete thought and can stand alone as a sentence. Look at the clauses in this sentence.

While Rosa loaded the car, Michael got the kids ready to go.

The first clause in this sentence is not a complete thought. When you read it, you want to know, What happened while Rosa loaded the car? This clause is called a ***dependent clause*** because it needs the second clause to explain it. The second clause is an independent, or main, clause. An ***independent clause*** expresses a complete thought and can stand alone.

A complex sentence is made up of one or more dependent clauses linked to one independent clause.

Simple sentences can be combined to form complex sentences. One simple sentence will be the independent clause. A second sentence will be linked to it by a type of conjunction that makes it dependent.

You are such a good friend. I'll help you out.
<u>becomes</u>
Because you are such a good friend, I'll help you out.

Marty grilled some hamburgers. Denise fixed a salad.
<u>becomes</u>
While Marty grilled some hamburgers, Denise fixed a salad.

Elmer likes to visit Greece. Peter prefers Italy.
<u>becomes</u>
Whereas Elmer likes to visit Greece, Peter prefers Italy.

Here is a list of conjunctions that make dependent clauses.

CONJUNCTIONS	
To show time before after while when whenever until as soon as as long as	*Before* I got out my camera, the bear had Manuel up a tree. Sylvia hurried home *while* it was still light.
To show reason because in order that since so that	Alicia went home early *because* she was sick.
To show conditions if unless whether	*Unless* you want trouble, don't pester that bee.
To show contrast though although even though in spite of the fact that despite the fact that whereas	*Even though* Pak Ku was tired, he helped fix dinner. Jennifer went to the meeting *despite the fact that* she had lost the election.
To show similarity as though as if	The day looked *as if* it would be clear and warm.
To show place where wherever	Jan went *wherever* her sister went.

When you are combining sentences, be careful to choose the conjunction that says what you mean. Which conjunction would you use to combine these two clauses?

Phillip forgot to open the door _____ he saw the ghost following him.

When and *because* make sense here. Try some other conjunctions, like *unless* or *as though.* They do not make sense at all. Make sure your sentence makes sense when you use a conjunction. Here is another example. Think what relationship there is between the clauses.

Lana went to the show _____ she hated gangster movies.

Several conjunctions would work here—*although, even though, in spite of the fact that, despite the fact that.* All of them show contrast between the ideas. Try other conjunctions from the list. Do you see that they do not make sense here?

◎ FOCUS ON PUNCTUATION

Dependent Clauses

When a dependent ***introductory clause*** comes at the beginning of a sentence, use a comma to separate it from the independent clause. If the dependent clause comes at the end of the sentence, no comma is needed.

Because Jerry arrived late, he was criticized.
Jerry was criticized because he arrived late.

Although it was still dark out, Maria was getting ready for work.
Maria was getting ready for work although it was still dark out.

EXERCISE 2

Directions: Complete each complex sentence. In the blank, write one of the conjunctions from the chart of conjunctions on page 125 to link the clauses.

Example: __When__ the hurricane approached, people left the island.

1. _____ backing into the garage, Sarah loaded the truck.

2. Melissa wants to go to the zoo _____ the weather turns cold.

3. _____ the bats still live in Carlsbad Caverns, there are fewer of them today.

4. Gilbert cast his fly _____ he had seen the large trout jump.

5. _____ I tell Santwana I saw a spider, she will want to leave.

6. Few salmon live in the Snake River _____ huge dams were built.

7. _____ that dog has a loud bark, it's really very friendly.

8. _____ you said the dog was friendly, I tried to pet him.

9. _____ you were bitten, I still say the dog is gentle.

10. The doctor says the wound will heal _____ I keep it bandaged.

ANSWERS ARE ON PAGE 258.

JOURNAL WRITING

Practice using compound and complex sentences by writing three paragraphs in your journal. Describe an experience you've had with an animal. It might be a favorite pet, or it might be the ferocious or friendly dog up the street. You might even describe an encounter with a wild animal. Use a mixture of simple, compound, and complex sentences. When you've finished writing, check your use of conjunctions. Have you chosen the words that say what you really mean?

☰ PRE-GED Practice ☰
COMBINING IDEAS IN SENTENCES

Choose what correction should be made to the underlined part of each sentence. If the underlined word is the best choice, choose (5).

1. **<u>Since</u> Mrs. Tenorio saw her unharmed son, tears of relief streamed down her face.**

    (1) As though
    (2) Where
    (3) As soon as
    (4) Until
    (5) no correction is necessary

2. **I usually read a magazine <u>as soon as</u> I eat lunch.**

    (1) when
    (2) since
    (3) although
    (4) even though
    (5) no correction is necessary

3. **You will receive only one more issue <u>so that</u> you renew your subscription.**

    (1) because
    (2) in spite of the fact that
    (3) whether
    (4) unless
    (5) no correction is necessary

4. **Michiko bought healthy plants, <u>but</u> all of them are wilted now.**

    (1) and
    (2) so
    (3) for
    (4) or
    (5) no correction is necessary

5. **Will you please answer the phone <u>despite the fact that</u> I am in the shower?**

    (1) whether
    (2) while
    (3) as soon as
    (4) unless
    (5) no correction is necessary

6. **He won't pay his bills on time <u>whether</u> he didn't get his paycheck.**

    (1) while
    (2) so that
    (3) because
    (4) as though
    (5) no correction is necessary

ANSWERS ARE ON PAGE 258.

SENTENCE PROBLEMS

MISPLACED MODIFIERS

Modifiers—whether they are words, phrases, or clauses—should be placed as close as possible to the words they modify. When they are not, confusing ideas sometimes result. What does this sentence mean?

Julian is following a stray cat *wearing yellow sneakers.*

The writer probably meant that Julian, not the cat, was wearing yellow sneakers. However, that is not what the sentence says. This is an example of a misplaced modifier.

A ***misplaced modifier*** is a word or phrase whose meaning is unclear because it is out of place.

A misplaced modifier can be corrected by moving the modifier closer to the word it modifies.

Wearing yellow sneakers, Julian is following a stray cat.

Here are some other examples.

Incorrect: Carmen bought milk from the grocery store *that was spoiled.*
Correct: Carmen bought milk *that was spoiled* from the grocery store.

Incorrect: Sharon read a story about a woman who won the lottery *in the elevator.*
Correct: *In the elevator,* Sharon read a story about a woman who won the lottery.

DANGLING MODIFIERS

Another sentence problem is the dangling modifier. This error is sometimes more difficult to identify than the misplaced modifier.

A **dangling modifier** is a phrase or clause that does not modify any word in the sentence.

While entering the cave, bats flew out of the darkness.

Who entered the cave? The bats? You probably know what the writer means, but the message isn't quite clear. *While entering the cave* does not modify a word in the sentence.

There are two ways to correct a dangling modifier. One way is to change the dangling modifier into a dependent clause. (Add a subject to the phrase.)

While I was entering the cave, bats flew out of the darkness.

A second way to correct a dangling modifier is to add a word for the phrase to modify. When rewriting the sentence, place the modifier as close as possible to the word it modifies.

While entering the cave, *I heard* bats fly out of the darkness.

Here is another example.

Incorrect: *To get home quickly,* a creepy path by the river was taken. (Who wants to get home quickly?)

Correct: To get home quickly, *they took* a creepy path by the river.
Correct: *Because they wanted to get home quickly,* a creepy path by the river was taken.

EXERCISE 3

Directions: Underline the misplaced or dangling modifier in each sentence. Then rewrite the sentence to correct it. If there is no error, write *C* on the blank.

Example: While reading an exciting book, Gretchen's telephone rang.

While Gretchen was reading an exciting book, her telephone rang.

1. Your bill should be paid before going on vacation.

_____

2. Hanging on the wall, Javier stared at the beautiful painting.

_____

3. After cooking breakfast, the fan had to be turned on to remove the smoke.

_____

4. To remember my childhood stories, I wrote them in a diary.

_____

5. The parade included clowns, elephants, and bands beginning on Bradford Road.

_____

6. When only six years old, my grandfather gave me his big pocket watch.

_____

7. Being very proud, Emily's new ring was shown to everyone.

_____

8. Driving down the highway, the scenery Pam saw was beautiful.

_____

ANSWERS ARE ON PAGE 258.

SENTENCES WITHOUT PARALLEL STRUCTURE

Many sentences have compound parts that are connected by a conjunction such as *and* or *or*. These parts may be adjectives, verbs, adverbs, phrases, or other sentence parts. Compound parts should always have the same form.

> Combining ingredients, stirring the mixture, and kneading the dough are steps in making bread.

The words *combining, stirring,* and *kneading* have the same form. The sentence has **parallel sentence structure**. Using parallel structure makes a sentence easier to read. Now look at this sentence.

> Jerome's goal is to build a boat, to quit his job, and sailing around the world.

This sentence does not have parallel sentence structure. The words *to build, to quit,* and *sailing* do not have the same form. The first two verbs are infinitives and the third ends in *ing.* Here are two ways to correct this sentence.

> Jerome's goal is *to build* a boat, *to quit* his job, and *to sail* around the world.

> Jerome's goal is *building* a boat, *quitting* his job, and *sailing* around the world.

Nonparallel structure can occur with compound verbs, nouns, adjectives, and adverbs.

> Incorrect: This morning I *did* the grocery shopping, *bought* a bus pass, and *had looked* for a job.

> Correct: This morning I *did* the grocery shopping, *bought* a bus pass, and *looked* for a job.

In the incorrect sentence above, *did* and *bought* are in the simple past tense. The other verb, *had looked,* is in the past perfect tense. The corrected sentence changes them all to the simple past.

> Incorrect: The clothes were *wrinkled, smelly,* and *needed washing.*

> Correct: The clothes were *wrinkled, smelly,* and *dirty.*

The incorrect sentence includes two adjectives and a verb phrase. The corrected sentence changes them all to adjectives.

EXERCISE 4

Directions: Rewrite each sentence to create parallel structure.

Example: Veronica told me to sit back, to relax, and enjoying the afternoon.

Veronica told me to sit back, to relax, and to enjoy the afternoon.

1. I spent the weekend working in the yard, painting a door, and to fix a cracked window.

_____

_____

2. Regina said she would fix supper, set the table, and that she would clean up afterwards.

_____

_____

3. That candidate has energy, concern, and she is honest.

_____

4. When Taro got home, he found mud on the carpet, scratch marks on the furniture, and having broken glass on the floor.

_____

_____

5. Jo likes people who are kind, thoughtful, funny, and when they are rich.

_____

_____

6. The fortune teller told Ana that she would get a great job, that she would lose money, and she should move to another city.

_____

_____

7. The workshop explained how to speak clearly, appearing skilled, and how to ask for a raise.

_____

_____

ANSWERS ARE ON PAGE 259.

INCORRECT VERB SEQUENCE
Sequence of Verbs

As you learned in Chapter 2, verbs have tenses to show when actions occur. When a sentence has more than one verb, the verbs must work together to tell when the different actions happened. This is called the **verb sequence**. What's wrong with the verb sequence in the following sentence?

It *rained* for five days before the sun *had come* out.

Rained is the simple past tense. *Had come* is the past perfect tense. The past perfect tells that an event occurred in the past before another event in the past. Here, the verb tenses say that the sun came out before it rained for five days. That doesn't make sense. Here is the correct verb sequence.

It *had rained* for five days before the sun *came* out.

To check verb sequence, first decide if the action of each verb occurs in the past, present, or future. If the actions are in the past, for example, decide if they happened at the same time or if one happened before another. Here are some examples of correct verb sequence.

I *eat* too much when I *worry.*
(Both verbs are in the present tense.)

I *ate* too much yesterday because I *worried* about work.
(Both verbs are in the past because both actions happened in the past, were completed in the past, and happened at the same time in the past.)

I *had eaten* three sandwiches before I *realized* it.
(Both actions happened in the past. One action—eating the sandwiches—took place before the other action—realizing it. The earlier action is correctly shown by the past perfect tense.)

Conditionals

A **conditional** clause is one that begins with the word *if.*

If Marie Valdez is elected, taxes will increase.

Sentences with conditional clauses must have certain verb sequences. In the example above, the conditional clause uses the present tense verb *is.* The main clause uses the future tense verb *will increase.* Here are some examples using the past, subjunctive, and past perfect tenses in the conditional clause.

If you *had* a million dollars, you *could buy* any car.
If Jim *were* rich, he *would give* his money to charity.
If Nancy *had been* more careful, this accident *would have been* avoided.

The following chart summarizes the correct verb sequence to use in sentences containing conditional clauses.

CONDITIONAL VERB TENSES
Form of verb in *if* clause
present *(is elected)* past *(had)* subjunctive *(were)* past perfect *(had been)*
Form of verb in main clause
future *(will increase)*
would, could, or *should* plus the base form of the verb *(could buy, would give)*
would have, could have, or *should have* plus the past participle *(would have been)*

Problems with Helping Verbs

A **helping verb** is a verb such as *is, was, have, has,* and *had.* A helping verb is used to form different tenses of a verb. These helping verbs must be used in the correct combination with verbs in the other part of the sentence. Some cannot be used when the verb in the second part of the sentence is in the past tense.

HELPING VERBS	
Not used in past tense	**Can be used in past tense**
can	could
may	might
must	had to
will	would
shall	should

Incorrect: When I *looked* at my study habits, I *decided* that I really *can work* harder.

Correct: When I *looked* at my study habits, I *decided* that I really *could work* harder.

In the example, *looked* and *decided* are both in the past tense. *Can,* therefore, is an incorrect choice as a helping verb with *work.* The helping verb *could* is correct. Try some other verbs from the chart that can be used in the past tense. All of them could be used correctly in this sentence.

EXERCISE 5

Directions: In each of the following sentences, a verb is underlined. If the verb shows correct verb sequence, write *C*. If the verb shows incorrect verb sequence, write the correct form of the verb.

Example: I am sure that I <u>would be</u> a better soccer player if I go to the

training camp. *will be*

1. Toni was convinced that she <u>will get</u> lost. _____

2. We were so hungry at noon that we ate the meal we <u>had prepared</u>

   for supper. _____

3. Leroy finally realized that he <u>locked</u> himself out of his apartment. _____

4. Maria's neighbor asked her whether he <u>can</u> borrow a hammer. _____

5. We would buy a new refrigerator if we <u>were</u> able to afford one. _____

6. Sonia says that she <u>would</u> wash her hair before the party. _____

7. The police officer said he <u>will</u> give the driver a warning ticket. _____

8. If Bert had known it was you who found his wallet, he <u>had not</u>

   <u>panicked</u>. _____

9. Tamara <u>is pleased</u> that she will receive an award. _____

10. Vince decided that he <u>could</u> interview for the job tomorrow morning. _____

ANSWERS ARE ON PAGE 259.

CONFUSING PRONOUN REFERENCES

Pronouns are words that take the place of nouns or refer to nouns. Errors in using pronouns occur when it is not clear what noun the pronoun refers to. This happens in two situations. It happens when more than one noun comes before the pronoun. It also happens when there is no noun before the pronoun.

Pronouns with More Than One Preceding Noun

Read the following example. Who is entering the room?

Amy glanced at Sara as *she* entered the room.

To which noun does the pronoun *she* refer? You cannot tell whether it is to *Amy* or *Sara.* This sentence is an example of an unclear pronoun reference.

There are different ways to correct sentences with unclear pronoun references. Here are two ways to correct the example.

Amy glanced at Sara as *Amy* entered the room.
As she entered the room, Amy glanced at Sara.

Here is another example of a sentence with an unclear pronoun reference.

Confusing: I'm reading a story in this book, *which* is very good.
Clear: I'm reading a very good story in this book.

Pronouns Without a Preceding Noun

Sometimes pronouns are used without any noun preceding them.

After we put seeds in the bird feeder, *they* never came around.

What is probably meant is that the birds never came around. However, it is better to be specific.

After we put seeds in the bird feeder, the *birds* never came around.

Another common mistake is to use a pronoun to refer to a general idea. For example:

The Changs give a lot of money to charity, which is admirable.

Here, *which* refers generally to giving money to charity. However, pronouns should refer to specific nouns. Then the sentence's meaning cannot be misunderstood.

The Changs give a lot of money to charity; *this generosity* is admirable.

One other common problem occurs with the use of pronouns like *they, you,* and *it.*

They* say that too much salt is not good for *you.

Who are *they?* Who is *you?* Notice how the following sentence makes the meaning more exact.

Health experts* say that too much salt is bad for *people.

EXERCISE 6

Directions: Decide if each of the following sentences has a clear pronoun reference. If it does, write *C* in the space. If the reference is not clear, rewrite the sentence correctly.

Example: Mr. Berg and his son David took his car to the mechanic.

Mr. Berg and his son David took David's car to the mechanic.

1. When I saw Ms. Rivera standing with her son, I thought he looked tall.

_____

_____

2. Cathy told her son to clean his closet and his room since it was a mess.

_____

_____

3. The walls were bright green and the carpeting pale gray, which we thought was really ugly.

_____

_____

4. People are actually living without heat and hot water, and this must be taken care of.

_____

_____

5. They say that crime is increasing in our city.

_____

_____

6. Rosa told her daughter that she would be able to drive in two weeks.

_____

_____

7. Thaddeus helped Steve to move into his new house.

_____

_____

8. Beth talked with them as they walked down the street.

_____

_____

9. He said I have to buy a parking sticker for my windshield or I will have to pay a fine.

_____

_____

10. The person fixing my car said that it should be taken care of immediately.

_____

_____

11. Angel gave Noreen the coat that she had left at her house.

_____

_____

ANSWERS ARE ON PAGE 259.

JOURNAL WRITING

Use your journal to practice the correct use of pronouns and verb sequence. Write two or three paragraphs about a birthday party or holiday celebration that you remember. Use different verb tenses as you write. When you are finished writing, review your use of pronouns and verb sequence. Are your pronoun references clear? Have you correctly used verb tenses to show when actions took place?

PRE-GED Practice
SENTENCE PROBLEMS

Read each sentence. Then choose the best correction for each sentence.

1. It had snowed overnight, but the sun had come out by 7:00 A.M. Looking outside, Juan told his son that it would be great skiing.

  (1) change *had snowed* to *snowed*
  (2) change *had come* to *came*
  (3) change *his son* to *Juan's son*
  (4) change *would be* to *can be*
  (5) no correction is necessary

2. If Marsha had gone to the movie, she will take her little sister with her.

  (1) change *had gone* to *has gone*
  (2) change *she* to *Marsha*
  (3) change *will take* to *would have taken*
  (4) change *with her* to *with Marsha*
  (5) no correction is necessary

3. Isabel told her daughter that she would go on vacation after all.

  (1) change *told* to *tells*
  (2) change *her daughter* to *Isabel's daughter*
  (3) change *she* to *Isabel*
  (4) change *would go* to *goes*
  (5) no correction is necessary

4. Mr. Ho likes to read as he rides to work. Yesterday he read a short story about a haunted house on the train.

  (1) change *rides* to *has ridden*
  (2) change *he read* to *Mr. Ho read*
  (3) change *he read* to *he would have read*
  (4) move *on the train* so it comes right after *Yesterday*
  (5) no correction is necessary

5. If you will go to the store, pick up some milk, and rent a movie, I will cook dinner.

  (1) change *will go* to *had gone*
  (2) change *will go* to *could go*
  (3) change *rent* to *renting*
  (4) change *will cook* to *would cook*
  (5) no correction is necessary

6. Barry told Boris that he is a better athlete because he can run faster.

  (1) change *told* to *tell*
  (2) change *is* to *am*
  (3) change *because* to *although*
  (4) change the second *he* to *Barry*
  (5) no correction is necessary

ANSWERS ARE ON PAGE 259.

STYLE AND DICTION

Sometimes problems with writing are not caused by errors in grammar or sentence structure. In fact, writing can be grammatically and mechanically correct, and yet the meaning may still be unclear. These problems can result from poor style or mistakes in diction.

Style is how you use words and sentences to express your meaning. ***Diction*** refers to your choice and use of words.

ECONOMY AND PRECISION IN WRITING

When you write, your most important goal should be to make your meaning clear. To write clearly, do not confuse your reader with more words than are necessary. Choose words that are as exact as possible. Here is an example of a sentence in which too many words make the meaning unclear.

An article in a book that Sue was reading states that walking in which the walker moves briskly is exercise that is excellent.

Grammatically, there is nothing wrong with this sentence. However, to know what is said, you must read carefully. The problem is too many words. To make this kind of writing easier to understand, simplify it.

An article in a book Sue was reading states that brisk walking is excellent exercise.

Even more simplification makes the meaning clearer.

An article states that walking is excellent exercise.

In making the sentence so brief, some ideas were lost. However, this information is probably not important to the reader. The message in the final revision is what the writer really wants readers to understand.

Here are some suggestions for making writing more economical and precise.

Avoid Repeating Ideas

Writers often unnecessarily repeat ideas. For example:

Lemonade is *equally as refreshing as* orange juice.

Equally refreshing and *as refreshing as* mean the same thing.

Better: Lemonade is as refreshing as orange juice.
            <u>or</u>
            Lemonade and orange juice are equally refreshing.

A common example of repetition occurs when writers want to avoid sounding too sure of themselves. Then phrases like *I think* creep into the writing.

In my opinion, I think you should use a hammer.

In my opinion and *I think* repeat the same idea. Sometimes this is important information. Often it is not, because it is already understood that the writer is expressing a personal opinion.

Better: I think you should use a hammer.
Best: You should use a hammer.

Repetitious: In my opinion, it seems to me that nowadays there's too
            much violence on TV.
Better: In my opinion, nowadays there's too much violence on TV.
Best: There's too much violence on TV.

Use the Active Voice

Most verbs have both an active and a passive form. Remember that the subject of an active verb is the performer of the action. The subject of a passive verb has the action done to it. Sentences using passive forms usually need more words to say the same thing.

Passive: The bread was baked by Maya.
Active: Maya baked the bread.

Besides needing fewer words, active verbs make sentences more direct and forceful.

Passive: The speech had been given by the world-famous civil rights leader, Dr. Martin Luther King, Jr.

Active: The world-famous civil rights leader, Dr. Martin Luther King, Jr., gave the speech.

Passive: Soap operas are loved by people all over the world.
Active: People all over the world love soap operas.

Passive: The lamp was broken by me.
Active: I broke the lamp.

Passive: The movie was enjoyed by the whole audience.
Active: The whole audience enjoyed the movie.

Passive: Royko's column is read by many people each day.
Active: Many people read Royko's column each day.

Passive: A vacation is taken by the Hills family each summer.
Active: The Hills family takes a vacation each summer.

EXERCISE 7

Directions: Rewrite each sentence to state the idea more precisely and economically.

Example: My neighborhood has several new buildings that were recently built near my house last year.

In my neighborhood, several buildings were built last year.

1. Heatwise, the temperature should get to eighty degrees warm.

_____

_____

2. People's names are often forgotten by me all the time.

_____

_____

3. The first step is to make a detailed list of each of the necessary ingredients right away.

_____

_____

4. The reason I don't write letters is because I never have enough time to write them.

_____

_____

5. He said that he thought the new salespersons were ready to go out into the field for further training.

_____

_____

ANSWERS ARE ON PAGE 260.

COMMON PROBLEMS WITH DICTION

Idioms are groups of words that have been used together so often that they have developed a special meaning. For example, *to keep up with, to come between,* and *to make believe* are idioms. You wouldn't know exactly what the phrases mean just by knowing what the separate words mean.

Idioms, like other words, have to be used precisely. Sometimes problems occur because idioms are used incorrectly.

Problems with Prepositions

1. Use *different from,* not *different than.*

Incorrect: Pecans are *different than* walnuts.
Correct: Pecans are *different from* walnuts.

2. Use the preposition *at* or *in* with the verb *to be,* not the preposition *to.*

Incorrect: Juan was *to* the game yesterday.
Correct: Juan was *at* the game yesterday.

3. Use the preposition *as* when a subject-verb combination follows, even if the verb is implied. Use the preposition *like* in all other cases.

Incorrect: My daughter looks *as me.*
Correct: My daughter looks *like me.*

Incorrect: *Like you know,* she is already as tall as me.
Correct: *As you know,* she is already as tall as me.

4. Use *between* when referring to only two things. Use *among* when referring to more than two things.

Incorrect: The argument was *among the two brothers.*
Correct: The argument was *between the two brothers.*

Incorrect: The four couples divided the cost *between themselves.*
Correct: The four couples divided the cost *among themselves.*

5. Use the preposition *from* after the word *borrow*, not the preposition *off* or *off of.*

Incorrect: I will borrow the bicycle *off* Melissa.
Incorrect: I will borrow the bicycle *off of* Melissa.
Correct: I will borrow the bicycle *from* Melissa.

6. Use the preposition *off*, not *off of.*

Incorrect: Warner got *off of* the train from Kansas City.
Correct: Warner got *off* the train from Kansas City.

7. After the verbs *could, should,* and *would*, do not use the preposition *of.* The correct phrase is *could have, would have,* or *should have.*

Incorrect: I *should of* known the answer.
Correct: I *should have* known the answer.

Problems with Verbs

Be alert for incorrect and unidiomatic uses of verbs. The following are a few of the more common errors.

1. Do not use the phrase *try and.* Use *try to* instead.

Incorrect: Ms. Clemente says she will *try and* be here by three.
Correct: Ms. Clemente says she will *try to* be here by three.

2. Use an infinitive after the word *ought. Should* means the same thing but does not need an infinitive.

Incorrect: The team *ought try* to recruit a really tall center.

Correct: The team *ought to try* to recruit a really tall center.
Correct: The team *should try* to recruit a really tall center.

3. Do not use the phrase *can't help but.* Use *can't help* plus the *ing* form of the verb.

Incorrect: I *can't help but think* I should have taken that job.
Correct: I *can't help thinking* I should have taken that job.

Problems with Comparisons

1. Be sure you are comparing similar things.

Dep's bowling score was better than his partner.

Look closely. This sentence is comparing a *bowling score* with a *partner.* Here is what the writer means.

Dep's bowling score was better than his partner's (bowling score).

2. Don't confuse *any* with *any other.*

Katie is a better swimmer than *any* girl in her class.

Katie is a girl, so she cannot be a better swimmer than any girl. The writer means she is better than any *other* girl.

Katie is a better swimmer than *any other* girl in her class.

EXERCISE 8

Directions: Decide if each of the following sentences contains an incorrect usage. If there is an error, rewrite the sentence correctly. If there is no error, write *C.*

Example: Julie's dog is very different than my dog.

Julie's dog is very different from my dog.

1. Lee told us that Greg should of received the package by now.

_____

_____

2. Like I've said before, most people never know how well off they are.

_____

_____

3. Sarah divided the remaining cake between the three of us.

_____

_____

4. Roland will certainly be to the game Saturday to see his brother play.

_____

_____

5. When she got up off of the ground the last time, Yoko gave up skating.

_____

_____

6. Tina's got a sharper memory than any person I know.

_____

_____

7. That movie was so realistic, I couldn't help but scream.

_____

_____

8. Sid said he knew someone who would try and get us some tickets.

_____

_____

9. Do you think you could borrow a snow shovel off the neighbor?

_____

_____

10. New York City has more people than any other city in the United States.

_____

_____

11. Garlan could of gotten home sooner if his train hadn't been late.

_____

_____

ANSWERS ARE ON PAGE 260.

JOURNAL WRITING

Use your journal to think about your writing style and diction. Write three paragraphs about your plans for this weekend. Plan what you want to do, not what you probably will do. Use the active voice throughout. When you're finished, look at each sentence carefully. Have you chosen words that mean exactly what you want to say? Underline any idioms you may have used. Have you used them correctly?

≡ PRE-GED Practice ≡
SENTENCE STRUCTURE

Read each sentence. Then choose the best correction for the underlined part of each sentence. If you think the original is best, choose (5).

1. **Taro is <u>different from Tamara because he would of been</u> nervous speaking before a large group.**

   (1) different than Tamara because he would of been
   (2) different than Tamara because they would have been
   (3) different from Tamara; because he would have been
   (4) different from Tamara because he would have been
   (5) no correction is necessary

2. **Barb <u>was upset when she has discovered that she had forgotten</u> her keys.**

   (1) was upset when she discovers that she had forgotten
   (2) was upset when she discovered that she had forgotten
   (3) was upset; although she had discovered that she had forgotten
   (4) was upset because she has discovered that she had forgotten
   (5) no correction is necessary

3. **Rhode Island <u>not only is the smallest state but also near the ocean</u>.**

   (1) is both the smallest state but also near the ocean
   (2) is not only the smaller state but it is also near the ocean
   (3) not only is the smallest state but also is near the ocean
   (4) not only is the smallest state but near the ocean
   (5) no correction is necessary

4. **<u>The hurricane brought high winds and driving rains the</u> damage was not severe.**

   (1) Although the hurricane brought high winds and driving rains, the
   (2) Although the hurricane brought high winds and driving rains the
   (3) The hurricane brought high winds and driving rains, however, the
   (4) The hurricane brought high winds and driving rains and
   (5) no correction is necessary

5. **The climate in the Caribbean is considered <u>tropical even though it has</u> lots of sun and rainfall.**

   (1) tropical, even though it has
   (2) tropical, however; it has
   (3) tropical since it has
   (4) tropical, since it consists of
   (5) no correction is necessary

6. **John's brother and his mother <u>took his injured dog</u> to the veterinarian.**

   (1) took the dog that had been injured
   (2) took John's injured dog
   (3) took her injured dog
   (4) took his or her injured dog
   (5) no correction is necessary

7. **<u>In the future time before us, world leaders around the globe</u> must make tough decisions.**

   (1) In the future, world leaders
   (2) In the future time, world leaders
   (3) In the time before us, world leaders around the globe
   (4) World leaders of the future that's before us
   (5) no correction is necessary

8. **<u>If you pay that fine you will</u> lose your driver's license.**

   (1) Unless you pay that fine, you will
   (2) Unless you pay that fine you will
   (3) If you pay that fine, you would
   (4) However you pay that fine you will
   (5) no correction is necessary

9. **Cheryl's serve <u>is faster than any other tennis player</u> in the league.**

   (1) is the fastest of any other tennis player
   (2) is faster than the serve of any other tennis player
   (3) is faster than any tennis player
   (4) is more fast than any other tennis player
   (5) no correction is necessary

10. **Murray Mugford bought a used <u>car at an auto dealership that was on sale for $2,000</u>.**

   (1) car, at an auto dealership that was on sale for $2,000
   (2) car at an auto dealership for $2,000
   (3) car, that was at an auto dealership for $2,000
   (4) car that was on sale for $2,000 at an auto dealership
   (5) no correction is necessary

11. **<u>Like Mr. Murray said, about</u> two hundred people applied for this job.**

   (1) Like Mr. Murray said, around
   (2) As Mr. Murray said, about
   (3) As Mr. Murray said about
   (4) Like Mr. Murray said around
   (5) no correction is necessary

12. **The trio is singing <u>tonight in spite of the fact that the</u> lead singer has a bad cold.**

   (1) tonight, in spite of the fact that the
   (2) tonight, because the
   (3) tonight, since the
   (4) tonight, in spite of the fact that, the
   (5) no correction is necessary

13. **If Marie Rosello were <u>mayor, this city would not have been</u> in debt.**

   (1) mayor, this city will not be
   (2) mayor, this city were not
   (3) mayor, this city would not be
   (4) mayor this city would not be
   (5) no correction is necesary

14. **Clean water, <u>clean air, and protecting our other natural resources</u> should be the goal of every elected official.**

   (1) cleaning the air, and protecting our other natural resources
   (2) clean air, and to protect our other natural resources
   (3) to clean the air, and protecting our natural resources
   (4) clean air, and protection for our other natural resources
   (5) no correction is necessary

15. **<u>Juicy and hot, Brian took the sausages off the grill.</u>**

   (1) Brian, juicy and hot, took the sausages off the grill.
   (2) Brian took the juicy and hot sausages off the grill.
   (3) Brian took the sausages off the grill juicy and hot.
   (4) Brian took the sausages off the juicy and hot grill.
   (5) no correction is necessary

16. **After months of work on the construction project, <u>at last it was finally completed by Jim</u>.**

   (1) at last, it was finally completed by Jim
   (2) at last Jim finally completed it
   (3) Jim finally completed it
   (4) Jim finally completed it at last
   (5) no correction is necessary

17. <u>Wanting so badly to own a sheep farm in Australia,</u> Ted and his wife Sonia packed up their things and left the country.

   (1) Because they wanted so badly to own a sheep farm in Australia,
   (2) Although they badly wanted to own a sheep farm in Australia,
   (3) Wanting so badly to own a sheep farm in Australia;
   (4) Their want of a sheep farm in Australia was great, so
   (5) no correction is necessary

18. <u>The bitter disagreement among Dr. Freud and Dr. Jung</u> developed gradually over many years.

   (1) The bitter disagreement, which was among Dr. Freud and Dr. Jung,
   (2) Because the bitter disagreement between Dr. Freud and Dr. Jung
   (3) The bitter disagreement between Dr. Freud and Dr. Jung
   (4) As a result of the bitter disagreement between Dr. Freud and Dr. Jung
   (5) no correction is necessary

19. <u>Calmed by the doctor and because he was under medication,</u> Manuel finally was able to sleep.

   (1) Calmed by the doctor, because he was under medication,
   (2) The doctor having arrived, and because he was on medication,
   (3) Calmed by the doctor and quieted by the medication,
   (4) Having been calmed by the doctor, and because he was on medication,
   (5) no correction is necessary

20. Wendy's speech <u>was both dramatic and it also inspired the audience.</u>

   (1) was not only dramatic but it was also inspiring to the audience
   (2) was both dramatic and inspirational to the audience
   (3) was both dramatic and it inspired the audience
   (4) being both dramatic and inspirational to the audience
   (5) no correction is necessary

   ANSWERS ARE ON PAGE 260.

i really like my english class mrs. peters is a great teacher she knows the subject well her writing assignments are interesting im learning a lot

With capitalization and punctuation, the sentences in this paragraph are much easier to read and understand.

I really like my English class. Mrs. Peters is a great teacher. She knows the subject well. Her writing assignments are interesting. I'm learning a lot.

Capitalization and Punctuation

CAPITALIZATION

Read the passage below. What's wrong with it?

herman melville spent five years on a whaling boat between 1839 and 1844 he sailed the atlantic ocean and on other oceans too drawing upon this experience melville wrote several masterpieces of american literature you have probably heard of moby dick it was melville's most famous novel it is the story of captain ahabs vengeful search for the white whale which had maimed him on one level the book can be read as an exciting adventure story at a deeper level the book is an in depth study of mans struggle against nature and the forces of evil for decades melvilles book went unnoticed but after world war I students of american literature rediscovered melville today his works enjoy a wide audience

You probably noticed that capitalization and punctuation are missing. Although neither punctuation nor capitalization will make poor writing great, both help make all writing clear and understandable.

You know that the first word in every sentence should be capitalized. In addition, nouns that name specific people, places, and things are capitalized. For example, Herman Melville is a specific person. His masterpiece, *Moby Dick,* is a specific book. The Atlantic Ocean is a specific ocean.

Nouns that name general people, places, or things are not capitalized. The word *ocean* is a general name. It could refer to any ocean. *Masterpieces, whaling boat,* and *novel* are also a few of the general nouns.

WHEN TO CAPITALIZE
Geographic Locations

Stick to this rule: Capitalize specific names; do not capitalize general names. The rule applies to names of geographic places.

General: My friend lives in a large *city*.
Specific: My friend lives in *San Francisco*.

Note that the rule also applies to specific names that are used as adjectives.

General: I ordered bread.
Specific: I ordered *French* bread.

Directions, such as north, southeast, easterly, and western, are not capitalized when they refer to a direction. They should be capitalized when they name a specific region of the country or of a city.

General: We drove *south* to the coast and then *northeast* into Georgia.

Specific: We visited Sante Fe, which is in the *Southwest*.

Titles and Names

Capitalize words used as titles that refer to a specific person.

When *Senator* Jones spoke, the audience listened carefully.
I asked *Doctor* Basulto to look at my arm.

Sometimes titles are used by themselves as though they were a name. This occurs when you are speaking directly to someone.

Will it heal, *Doctor*?
Tell me how you will reduce crime, *Mayor*.

If a title is used only to refer to an occupation, do not capitalize it.

The judge gave her decision.

Hint: If you are not sure whether a title that stands by itself should be capitalized, try replacing it with the person's name. If the sentence makes sense, capitalize the title. If it does not make sense, do not capitalize the title.

I wrote a letter to my aunt. → I wrote a letter to my Maria.
Thank you for the letter, Aunt. → Thank you for the letter, Maria.

Capitalize the first word and all important words in titles of books, plays, poems, or other written works.

I read the book *Death Comes for the Archbishop.*
Did you see the play *The Importance of Being Earnest*?
He memorized the poem *Jazz Fantasia.*

Buildings and Other Places

Capitalize the names of buildings and other places when they stand for specific buildings or places.

Empire State Building   White House
Lottie's Laundromat   Grand Avenue

Words like *building, house, laundromat,* and *avenue* are not always capitalized. Capitalize them only if they are part of the specific name. Look at how the words are used in the sentence to decide.

That building is one of the tallest in the city.
Let's visit the Empire State Building.

She washes her clothes every Saturday at the laundromat.
Her favorite place to wash her clothes is at Lottie's Laundromat.

There's a white house on the corner of our block.
The Mendez family toured the White House.

Madison Street is a grand avenue.
Grand Avenue is lined with stately oak trees.

EXERCISE 1

Directions: Three words in each of the following sentences are underlined. One of the words has incorrect capitalization. Write the word, with correct capitalization, on the line.

Example: <u>Mr.</u> Wang is a <u>Congressman</u> from <u>Missouri</u>.

   congressman

1. To get to the <u>supermarket</u>, turn <u>East</u> on <u>Riverdale Road</u>.

   _____

2. A famous <u>monument</u> to <u>president</u> Lincoln is in <u>Springfield</u>, Illinois.

   _____

3. The <u>english</u> <u>highways</u> are crowded with <u>automobiles</u> traveling at unbelievable speed.

   _____

4. My <u>physician</u>, <u>Dr. Ressa</u>, told me I must quit this <u>High-fat</u> diet immediately.

   _____

5. A <u>production</u> of the play *My Fair Lady* will be presented by <u>southeast</u> High School.

   _____

6. A department store in <u>Rochester</u>, <u>New York</u>, has a new <u>Program</u> for training its employees to be more efficient.

   _____

7. <u>langston hughes</u> is one of <u>America's</u> greatest <u>poets</u>.

   _____

8. <u>Margo Johnson</u> is a <u>senator</u> from <u>north Carolina</u>.

   _____

ANSWERS ARE ON PAGE 261.

≡ PRE-GED Practice ≡
WHEN TO CAPITALIZE

Read each sentence. Then choose the best correction for each sentence.

1. **Lonnie and Felicia went to a Los angeles Lakers basketball game.**

   (1) change *Felicia* to *felicia*
   (2) change *Los angeles* to *Los Angeles*
   (3) change *Lakers* to *lakers*
   (4) change *basketball* to *Basketball*
   (5) no correction is necessary

2. **Last year I canoed on three Rivers in the Northeast, including the Kennebec.**

   (1) change *year* to *Year*
   (2) change *Rivers* to *rivers*
   (3) change *Northeast* to *northeast*
   (4) change *Kennebec* to *kennebec*
   (5) no correction is necessary

3. **When you told me you were from New York, you never mentioned the East Side, which is the area where my grandmother grew up.**

   (1) change *New York* to *new york*
   (2) change *East Side* to *east side*
   (3) change *area* to *Area*
   (4) change *grandmother* to *Grandmother*
   (5) no correction is necessary

4. **Whenever Lucha's sister hears "Moon River," she cries because that song reminds her of her first boyfriend.**

   (1) change *sister* to *Sister*
   (2) change *Moon River* to *moon river*
   (3) change *song* to *Song*
   (4) change *boyfriend* to *Boyfriend*
   (5) no correction is necessary

5. **I want you to know, Dad, that I really enjoyed going to the Baseball game at Tiger Stadium.**

   (1) change *Dad* to *dad*
   (2) change *Baseball* game to *baseball* game
   (3) change *Tiger Stadium* to *Tiger stadium*
   (4) change *Tiger Stadium* to *tiger stadium*
   (5) no correction is necessary

ANSWERS ARE ON PAGE 261.

OTHER CAPITALIZATION RULES
Quotations

The first word of every sentence is capitalized. When you are writing a quotation, follow the same rule.

Celeste asked, "*Should* we buy groceries now, or wait till later?"

In the example, the quotation would stand alone as a complete sentence. It should begin with a capital letter. If the quotation is not a complete sentence, don't begin it with a capital letter.

Ken described the color of Cindy's new car as a "*seasick* green."

In the following sentence, the quotation makes up a complete sentence. However, it is divided by words introducing the speaker. Capitalize the first part of the quotation because it begins a complete sentence. Do not capitalize the second part of the quotation because it is a fragment.

"*A* fire broke out this morning," the newscaster reported, "*and* three people were injured."

Abbreviations and Initials

Capitalize the letters that make up abbreviations and initials.

CPA (Certified Public Accountant)
NFL (National Football League)
Kathy Chung, *PhD.* (Doctor of Philosophy)
Samuel Dickens, *Jr.* (junior)

Dates

Capitalize the names of days of the week and months. Do not capitalize seasons.

My vacation begins next *Friday, October* 3.
I love to take my vacations in the *autumn.*

Capitalize the names of holidays.

I always think of *Memorial Day* as the first day of summer.

School Subjects

Capitalize the names of school subjects only when you refer to specific courses. If you are referring to a general kind of class, do not capitalize it.

I am taking a *biology* class and *History* 101.

Note that you always capitalize words that name a specific language, like *English* and *Spanish.*

Organizations

Names of government and social organizations are always capitalized.

Anna's father works for the *Department of Transportation.*
All profits will be donated to the *American Diabetes Association.*

EXERCISE 2

Directions: Three words in each of the following sentences are underlined. One of the words has incorrect capitalization. Write the word using correct capitalization on the line below.

Example: My favorite <u>month</u> is <u>December</u> because I love <u>christmas</u>.

Christmas

1. Last <u>Wednesday</u>, members of the <u>PTA</u> formed a special committee that will meet <u>Weekly</u> until the end of the school year.

   _____

2. "<u>Don't</u> drink water from the spring," my <u>sister</u> warned, "<u>Unless</u> you want to get sick."

   _____

3. On <u>Friday</u>, <u>April</u> 24, I will be in Minneapolis for a meeting of the <u>aclu</u> (American Civil Liberties Union).

   _____

4. My father, John S. Haynes, <u>sr.</u>, will retire next <u>spring</u> after thirty years with the <u>NYPD</u> (New York Police Department).

   _____

5. Susan Cordova, <u>PhD.</u>, teaches <u>biology 340</u> on <u>Wednesday</u> evenings.

   _____

6. "Of course I'll be there," Maria answered, "<u>if</u> the <u>event</u> benefits the <u>children's aid society</u>."

   _____

ANSWERS ARE ON PAGE 261.

≡ PRE-GED Practice ≡
OTHER CAPITALIZATION RULES

Read each sentence. Then choose the best correction for each sentence.

1. **The coach, Joe Stearns, EdD., recommended a book on Physical Fitness.**

    (1) change *coach* to *Coach*
    (2) change *EdD.* to *edd*
    (3) change *book* to *Book*
    (4) change *Physical Fitness* to *physical fitness*
    (5) no correction is necessary

2. **"Raoul always wakes up early," said his wife, "and no one else gets any sleep after that, even on weekends."**

    (1) change *said* to *Said*
    (2) change *wife* to *Wife*
    (3) change *and* to *And*
    (4) change *weekends* to *Weekends*
    (5) no correction is necessary

3. **Bill's Rusty Spoon Restaurant was closed before the Memorial Day holiday by an administrator for the department of health.**

    (1) change *Restaurant* to *restaurant*
    (2) change *Memorial Day* to *memorial day*
    (3) change *administrator* to *Administrator*
    (4) change *department of health* to *Department of Health*
    (5) no correction is necessary

4. **Dr. Debra Samrit, a psychiatrist from the Northwest side of Denver, gave a lecture on guilt.**

    (1) change *psychiatrist* to *Psychiatrist*
    (2) change *Northwest* to *northwest*
    (3) change *lecture* to *Lecture*
    (4) change *guilt* to *Guilt*
    (5) no correction is necessary

5. **"Vote for me," the Senator shouted. "There will be more jobs in this state by next May."**

    (1) change *the* to *The*
    (2) change *Senator* to *senator*
    (3) change *There* to *there*
    (4) change *May* to *may*
    (5) no correction is necessary

ANSWERS ARE ON PAGE 261.

USING END PUNCTUATION

A sentence can be ended in three ways: with a period, a question mark, or an exclamation point.

A **period** is used to end a sentence that gives information or states a feeling or wish.

The Riveras will arrive tomorrow.

A **question mark** is used to end a question.

Why does Mary Ann always work late?

An **exclamation point** is used to end a sentence that shows strong excitement or emotion.

Help!
Please hurry, Doctor!

Pay special attention to how end punctuation is used in quotations.

The period always goes inside the quotation marks.

Incorrect: "Elephants," he said, "can be dangerous".
Correct: "Elephants," he said, "can be dangerous."

The question mark and exclamation point can go either inside or outside the quotation marks. To decide which, look at the meaning of the sentence. If the quotation is itself a question, put the question mark inside the quotation marks.

Incorrect: "Is that elephant loose," Shawna asked?
Incorrect: "Is that elephant loose" Shawna asked?
Correct: "Is that elephant loose?" Shawna asked.

Sometimes a quotation is part of a sentence that is a question. Then put the question mark outside the quotation marks.

Incorrect: Did Charise say, "That elephant is loose?"
Incorrect: Did Charise say, "That elephant is loose."?
Correct: Did Charise say, "That elephant is loose"?

When using exclamation points with quotation marks, follow the same rule. If the quotation is an exclamation, put the exclamation point inside the quotation marks. If the quotation is not an exclamation but is part of a sentence that is, put the exclamation point outside the quotation marks.

Incorrect: Kim Soon said, "Run for your life"!
Incorrect: Kim Soon said, "Run for your life."!
Correct: Kim Soon said, "Run for your life!"

Hint: Never use more than one kind of end punctuation.

USING ABBREVIATIONS AND INITIALS

In addition to ending sentences, periods are used in abbreviations and with initials.

Dec. 3 (December 3)
C.S. Lewis
Badger Co. (Badger Company)

When an abbreviation comes at the end of a sentence, use only one period.

Incorrect: Pedro works at Celltine, Inc..
Correct: Pedro works at Celltine, Inc.

EXERCISE 3

Directions: Write the correct punctuation in the blanks in each sentence. Use either a period, question mark, or exclamation point.

Example: Will a week from tomorrow be Feb_._23_?_

1. Mrs___ Rachet completed the annual report___

2. Look out for that bus___

3. Her address is 321 Lake St___

4. Did he pick the winning lottery number___

5. "Did he already spend all the money___" Georgia asked___

6. As the ladder slipped, Lynn screamed, "Help___"

7. "Who was that masked man___" the salesperson asked___

8. My uncle named his new business the Rivets Co___

9. "Quick___" shouted the police officer over his car radio___

10. As she looked all over the house, Maxine moaned, "Where are my keys___"

11. Wow___ That's the best news I've ever heard___

12. "What's your favorite movie___" Derrick asked___

ANSWERS ARE ON PAGE 261.

≡ PRE-GED Practice ≡
USING END PUNCTUATION

Read each sentence. Then choose the best correction for each sentence.

1. **"Is Mark's new company located in Philadelphia," Julie asked.**

    (1) change *Philadelphia,"* to *Philadelphia."*
    (2) change *Philadelphia,"* to *Philadelphia"?*
    (3) change *Philadelphia,"* to *Philadelphia?"*
    (4) change *asked.* to *asked?*
    (5) no correction is necessary

2. **When the engine caught on fire, Sachi yelled, "Get out of the car now"!**

    (1) change *yelled,* to *yelled!*
    (2) change *now"!* to *now."*
    (3) change *now"!* to *now!".*
    (4) change *now"!* to *now!"*
    (5) no correction is necessary

3. **When Trivits, Inc., didn't hire her, Mercedes wanted to know what she had to do to get a job?**

    (1) change *Inc.,* to *Inc,*
    (2) change *job?* to *job.*
    (3) change *job?* to *job!*
    (4) change *job?* to *job!.*
    (5) no correction is necessary

4. **On Feb. 29, Suzanne took the day off. The next day, she innocently asked her boss, "Wasn't that a holiday?"**

    (1) change *Feb.* to *Feb*
    (2) change *off.* to *off!*
    (3) change *boss,* to *boss?*
    (4) change *holiday?* to *holiday.*
    (5) no correction is necessary

5. **Who said, "I want to play basketball?"**

    (1) change *said,* to *said?*
    (2) change *said,* to *said.*
    (3) change *basketball?"* to *basketball"?*
    (4) change *basketball?"* to *basketball."?*
    (5) no correction is necessary

ANSWERS ARE ON PAGE 262.

COMMA

The comma has two main uses. The first is for separating clauses in compound and complex sentences. (You may want to review compound and complex sentences in Chapter 4.) The second use is in separating items in the sentence—such as interrupting phrases and items in a series.

COMMAS IN COMPOUND SENTENCES
Commas with Conjunctions

Remember, a **compound sentence** is made up of two simple sentences, or independent clauses, that are joined together. The most common way of joining clauses is by using a comma plus one of these conjunctions: *and, or, nor, but, for, so,* and *yet.*

The shark swam toward the shore, *but* the swimmers didn't notice.

When clauses are joined using a conjunction, place a comma before the conjunction. Never join independent clauses using only a comma.

Incorrect: It rained hard all week, the rivers rose out of their banks.
Incorrect: It rained hard all week and the rivers rose out of their banks.
Correct: It rained hard all week, and the rivers rose out of their banks.

Commas with Conjunctive Adverbs

A second way of joining independent clauses is by using a **conjunctive adverb**. These are words such as *however, furthermore, nevertheless, for example,* and *moreover.*

The snow piled up three feet high; *however,* the snowplows had the roads open by noon.

Notice that a semicolon comes before the conjunctive adverb and a comma follows it.

COMMAS IN COMPLEX SENTENCES

Complex sentences are made up of one main, or independent clause, and one or more dependent clauses. A dependent clause is joined to the main clause by a conjunction such as *when, after, because, if,* and *although.*

> After Kyoko heard the news, she leaped from her chair.
>
> She couldn't believe her good luck because she had never won anything.

Notice that when the dependent clause comes at the beginning of the sentence, it is followed by a comma. When the dependent clause comes at the end of the sentence, no comma is used.

Commas with Quotations

Use a comma to separate a direct quotation from the rest of a sentence.

> Juan said, "I'm joining a softball team."
>
> "Maybe you'll be called up to the majors," Stan joked.

If a quotation comes first in a sentence, and if it is a question or an exclamation, do not use a comma to separate the quotation from the rest of the sentence.

> Incorrect: "When can I play?", Juan asked.
> Incorrect: "When can I play," Juan asked.
> Correct: "When can I play?" Juan asked.

Commas with Interrupting Phrases

An interrupting phrase is not a necessary part of a sentence. It simply gives additional information. Three types of interrupting phrases should be set off from the rest of the sentence by commas.

1. Renaming Phrases

In Chapter 3, you learned about phrases that rename the subject or object of a sentence. These interrupters should be set off with commas.

Manuel Suarez, *the man behind the desk,* is an accountant.

The phrase *the man behind the desk* renames or further identifies Manuel Suarez. Set it off with commas.

2. Direct Address

When a sentence is directed to a specific person, the person's name should be set off with commas.

Please hand me that book, *Maria.*
If you will go with me, *Amy,* I will buy your dinner.

3. Extra Information

Some words and phrases interrupt a sentence to give added information. These should be set off with commas.

Lydia, *in fact,* refused to accept the gift.
Nevertheless, we must keep making an effort.

When the phrase is in the middle of the sentence, put commas on both sides of it. When the phrase begins or ends a sentence, separate it with one comma.

One common type of interrupting phrase is made up of a subject and a verb such as *believe, think,* or *know.* Set them off with commas.

The plan, *I believe,* is a good one.

Phrases such as *in fact* and *of course* and phrases used to show contrast are also interrupters. Set them off with commas.

Sandy Davis is, *in fact,* my mother's cousin.
Rene will work on Thursday, *not on Friday.*

Before setting off a phrase with commas, be sure the phrase is not essential to the meaning of the sentence.

Incorrect: I think, that Mike should become a professional musician.

Correct: Mike, I think, should become a professional musician.

Correct: I think that Mike should become a professional musician.

In the first sentence, *I think* is part of the main clause. No commas should be used. In the second sentence, *I think* is an interrupter. It is not necessary to the meaning of the sentence. Use commas to set it off.

Commas with a Series

When more than two nouns or verbs, or more than two adjectives or adverbs are used in a series, separate them with a comma. The final item in the series of nouns or verbs is usually introduced by a conjunction, such as *and.* A comma should be used before the conjunction.

That *big, ugly, ill-tempered* dog is a nuisance.
We had *hot dogs, baked beans, and salad.*

Commas should also be used to set off phrases, or even clauses, that are written as a series.

Andrew *grabs the ball, dribbles to his left, pulls up, and shoots.*

Commas with Addresses, Dates, and Greetings

Use a comma to separate parts of an address or of a date.

20 Stanford Street, Dayton, Ohio 66660
November 7, 1995

Notice, no comma is used to separate these items:

- the month and day
- the house number and street name
- the state and zip code
- the month and year when no date is given

Also use a comma after the greeting and closing in an informal letter.

8122 Thompson Avenue
Anderson, Indiana 55201
December 7, 1995

Dear family and friends,

    We are having a get-together to celebrate the holiday season on Saturday, December 21 any time after 7 P.M. Feel free to bring your favorite snack, dessert, or drink. Please R.S.V.P. by December 14. We look forward to seeing you in a few weeks.

Sincerely,

Christine and Alan

Christine and Alan

EXERCISE 4

Directions: If a comma is missing from a sentence, add it. If a comma is not needed, cross it out.

Example: Fran, will you please come here/and help me?

1. When Akiko came by the office she fixed the copy machine.

2. The little boy asked "How can I get home from here?"

3. On January 3, the Bombers will play at Johnson Field, Omaha Nebraska.

4. It was in fact the best cheesecake she had ever had.

5. Jim picked up the trash can and a rat came flying out.

6. Why don't you wear your yellow sweater Tomás?

7. This exercise program is easy for me; moreover I have lost ten pounds.

8. Yolanda the woman who got me this job has now quit.

9. Mr. Chung hurriedly left his house, after getting the telephone call.

10. "Gina will pick you up in an hour" the woman replied.

ANSWERS ARE ON PAGE 262.

OTHER TYPES OF PUNCTUATION

COLON

Use a colon after a complete thought that introduces a list. Do not use a colon if the introduction to the list is not a complete thought.

Incorrect: We packed: apples, cheese, and a loaf of bread.
Correct: We packed the following items: apples, cheese, and a loaf of bread.
Correct: We packed apples, cheese, and a loaf of bread.

Use a colon after the greeting in a formal or business letter.

Dear Sir or Madam:

Use a colon to separate the hour from minutes in written time.

It is now 6:45.

SEMICOLON

A semicolon is used in two ways in forming compound sentences. When the clauses in a compound sentence are linked using a conjunctive adverb, place a semicolon before the adverb.

David is a good tennis player; however, he has never beaten Christy.

Closely related clauses in a compound sentence can also be linked without using either a conjunction or a conjunctive adverb. Use the semicolon by itself to show the two clauses are independent.

It is a beautiful day; I should be spending it outdoors.

A semicolon can also be used to separate items in a series when there are already commas within the items.

The contestants in the dog show were Fido, a brown mutt; Fifi, a French poodle; and Farley, a golden retriever.

QUOTATION MARKS

Use quotation marks to show the exact words of a speaker.

"Stop yelling," Michael said, "or we will go home."

If the sentence is only a statement about what someone says, don't use quotation marks.

Michael said that we should stop yelling or we will go home.

Be alert to the use of other punctuation with quotation marks.

- Place commas and periods inside quotations.

- Place question marks and exclamation points outside quotation marks if the entire sentence is a question or exclamation.

- Place question marks and exclamation points inside quotation marks only if the quotation itself is a question or exclamation.

APOSTROPHE

The apostrophe has two main uses. The first of these is to show possession. When used for possession, an apostrophe shows that one thing belongs to another.

Piri's cat is more ferocious than any dog on the street.

The second use for apostrophes is to form contractions. A **contraction** is one word that is made up of two words with one or more letters left out. The apostrophe is used in place of the missing letters. See the examples on the next page.

COMMON CONTRACTIONS

isn't	→	is not	can't	→	cannot
doesn't	→	does not	we'll	→	we will
wouldn't	→	would not	let's	→	let us
they're	→	they are	I'm	→	I am
they'd	→	they had or they would	She's	→	she is or she has
			you've	→	you have
won't	→	will not	there's	→	there is or there has
hasn't	→	has not			

Two common contractions sometimes cause problems. *It's* is a contraction meaning "it is" or "it has." Don't confuse *it's* with *its,* which is a possessive pronoun.

Incorrect: That cat must be controlled by *it's* owner.

Correct: *It's* a cat without fear.

Correct: It knows *its* teeth and claws are sharp.

Who's is a contraction meaning "who is" or "who has." Do not confuse *who's* with *whose,* which is a possessive pronoun.

Incorrect: *Who's* dog wandered onto Piri's street?

Correct: I like the one *who's* got scratches on its nose.

Correct: I know *whose* dog it is.

EXERCISE 5

Directions: Write the correct punctuation in the blanks provided. Watch for blanks that need two kinds of punctuation.

Example: Which would you prefer __:_ a soft drink __,_ a glass of water __,_ or a cup of coffee __?_

1. Teresa really wanted to go to Mexico ___ nevertheless ___ she agreed to spend her vacation at the lake.

2. At the supermarket, we ran into our old neighbors ___ the Okaras ___ who lived next door ___ Jill and Sean ___ the ones who gave noisy parties ___ and Marianne ___ our babysitter.

3. Keisha cried ___ He forgot my birthday ___ then he went to a hockey game ___

4. Paulo wished he could remember everything ___ however ___ he was already forgetting the details.

5. He gave these reasons for moving ___ a bigger yard ___ more bedrooms ___ lower taxes ___ and a better school district.

6. It is now 7 ___ 00 and Stan just got here ___ nevertheless ___ we're still going to the game.

7. Jan yelled to her brother ___ Who's going to feed the dog ___

8. Dear Madam ___

I bought a SlimMachine because I wanted to lose weight ___ It broke the first day I used it ___ Please refund my money ___

> Sincerely ___
> John Arocha

9. We're looking for a new car ___ the one we have is worn out.

10. I want a job downtown ___ not one out in the suburbs.

ANSWERS ARE ON PAGE 262.

JOURNAL WRITING

Write a journal entry for today. In two or three paragraphs, tell what you did, who you saw, and where you went. As you write, correctly use as many kinds of punctuation as you can. When you're finished, proofread your writing. Pay special attention to your punctuation.

≡ PRE-GED Practice ≡
CAPITALIZATION AND PUNCTUATION

Read each sentence. Then choose the best correction for each sentence.

1. **James said in surprise, "How did you get here so quickly?".**

   (1) change *surprise, "How* to *surprise: "How*
   (2) change *surprise, "How* to *surprise "How*
   (3) change *quickly?".* to *quickly?"*
   (4) change *quickly?".* to *quickly"?*
   (5) no correction is necessary

2. **When Annie reached home, she found the door wide open. It's lock was broken. She ran to the neighbor's house and telephoned the police.**

   (1) change *home,* to *home;*
   (2) change *home,* to *home*
   (3) change *It's* to *Its*
   (4) change *house and* to *house, and*
   (5) no correction is necessary

3. **"Who's the best cook," Jerome asked, "Harry or Barbara?"**

   (1) change *Who's* to *Whose*
   (2) change *cook,"* to *cook?"*
   (3) change *asked,* to *asked.*
   (4) change *Barbara?"* to *Barbara"?*
   (5) no correction is necessary

4. **Lupita plays three sports, tennis, basketball, and softball. She won't say which she likes best, but she's a great softball player.**

   (1) change *sports,* to *sports:*
   (2) change *won't* to *wont'*
   (3) change *best,* to *best*
   (4) change *best,* to *best;*
   (5) no correction is necessary

5. **That movie was great, I'd love to see it again. I can't remember the star's name; nevertheless, I think she's great.**

   (1) change *great,* to *great;*
   (2) change *can't* to *ca'nt*
   (3) change *name;* to *name,*
   (4) change *nevertheless,* to *nevertheless;*
   (5) no correction is necessary

6. **The people of the state of Colorado are in fact satisfied with who's running their government.**

   (1) capitalize *state*
   (2) begin *Colorado* with a small letter
   (3) place commas before and after *in fact*
   (4) change *who's* to *whose*
   (5) no correction is necessary

7. **"The person who's lucky enough to pick the winning number," shouted the host, "Will be the proud owner of this new car!"**

   (1) change *who's* to *whose*
   (2) change *number,"* to *number",*
   (3) change *"Will* to *"will*
   (4) change *car!"* to *car"!*
   (5) no correction is necessary

8. **The three greatest poets of ancient times were Homer, Virgil, and Ovid.**

   (1) change *were Homer,* to *were: Homer,*
   (2) add a comma after *were*
   (3) change *Homer, Virgil, and Ovid* to *Homer, Virgil and Ovid*
   (4) change *Homer, Virgil, and Ovid* to *Homer; Virgil; and Ovid*
   (5) no correction is necessary

9. **Dad, will you tell me a story about your Uncle, the one who went gold prospecting in Alaska?**

   (1) change *Dad,* to *Dad*
   (2) change *Uncle* to *uncle*
   (3) remove the comma after *Uncle*
   (4) change the question mark to an exclamation point
   (5) no correction is necessary

10. **The old saying that money does'nt grow on trees is a good one to remember.**

    (1) place quotation marks before *money* and after *remember.*
    (2) change *money* to *Money*
    (3) change *does'nt* to *doesn't*
    (4) change the period to an exclamation point
    (5) no correction is necessary

11. **Whenever Renee and Julie eat out, they choose the french restaurant.**

    (1) remove the comma after *out*
    (2) replace the comma after *out* with a semicolon
    (3) change *out, they* to *out, and they*
    (4) change *french* to *French*
    (5) no correction is necessary

12. **"When is Judy due to have her baby," asked Jack, "and what will they choose for a name"?**

    (1) change *baby,* to *baby?*
    (2) change *Jack, "and* to *Jack. "And*
    (3) change *Jack, "and* to *Jack, "And*
    (4) change *name"?* to *name?"*
    (5) no correction is necessary

13. **Sumari is going on a bicycle trip this Fall, and she plans on camping out.**

    (1) change *Fall* to *fall*
    (2) change the comma after *Fall* to a semicolon
    (3) add a comma after *and*
    (4) change the period to a question mark
    (5) no correction is necessary

14. **The administrator of the Department of Natural Resources has an important job; he manages the state's public lands.**

    (1) capitalize *administrator*
    (2) change *Department of Natural Resources* to *department of natural resources*
    (3) change the semicolon to a comma
    (4) change the semicolon to a colon
    (5) no correction is necessary

15. **When Dr. Mendez announced her retirement, the Doctors at the hospital organized a party.**

    (1) change *Dr. Mendez* to *dr. Mendez*
    (2) change the comma to a semicolon
    (3) add a conjunction after the comma
    (4) change *Doctors* to *doctors*
    (5) no correction is necessary

16. **Is your date of birth June, 12, 1961, or am I confusing you with Phil? I know his birthday is in June.**

    (1) remove the comma after *June*
    (2) remove the comma after *1961*
    (3) change the comma after *1961* to a semicolon
    (4) add a comma after *I know*
    (5) no correction is necessary

17. **The schedule couldn't be changed, because many of the club members are from out of town.**

    (1) change *couldn't* to *could'nt*
    (2) remove the comma after *changed*
    (3) change the comma to a semicolon
    (4) add a comma after *because*
    (5) no correction is necessary

18. **When you consider how much money the club raised, I suppose, that all your work was worthwhile.**

    (1) remove the comma after *raised*
    (2) change the comma after *raised* to a semicolon
    (3) remove the comma after *suppose*
    (4) change *your* to *you're*
    (5) no correction is necessary

19. **Curtis couldn't decide which to visit first; the National Gallery, the Washington Monument, or the men's room.**

    (1) change the semicolon to a colon
    (2) change *National Gallery* to *national gallery*
    (3) change all the commas to semicolons
    (4) change *men's* to *mens'*
    (5) no correction is necessary

20. **Most of the program's fund's come from federal taxes, local charities, and donations from businesses.**
    (1) change *program's* to *programs'*
    (2) change *fund's* to *funds*
    (3) add a colon after *come*
    (4) change all the commas to semicolons
    (5) no correction is necessary

21. **As the building was about to collapse, a firefighter yelled, "Quick! Put this towel over your face and jump"!**
    (1) remove the comma after *collapse*
    (2) remove the comma after *yelled*
    (3) replace the exclamation point after *Quick* with a comma
    (4) change *jump"!* to *jump!"*
    (5) no correction is necessary

22. **Students who apply to this Junior College are given credit for the following: high school courses, work experience, and military service.**
    (1) change *Junior College* to *junior college*
    (2) add a comma after *College*
    (3) remove the colon after *following*
    (4) change the commas to semicolons
    (5) no correction is necessary

23. **"Why doesn't he scold the girls when they don't eat they're breakfast?" asked Jane.**
    (1) add a comma after *girls*
    (2) change *don't* to *dont'*
    (3) change *they're* to *their*
    (4) replace the question mark with a comma
    (5) no correction is necessary

24. **The stranger handed the girl's mother a torn envelope and a rusty key when she asked him what he wanted?**
    (1) change *girl's* to *girls*
    (2) capitalize *mother*
    (3) add a comma after *key*
    (4) change the question mark to a period
    (5) no correction is necessary

25. **Raoul spends most of his time in the science lab, as a result, his grade for Biology 100 will improve this spring.**
    (1) change the comma after *lab* to a semicolon
    (2) remove the comma after *result*
    (3) change *Biology 100* to *biology 100*
    (4) change *spring* to *Spring*
    (5) no correction is necessary

ANSWERS ARE ON PAGE 263.

These patterns of organization are used in most writing situations:

- time order
- cause-and-effect order
- comparison-and-contrast order
- simple listing

Comparing My Two Brothers

Remi	Regis
short	tall
weighs 150	weighs 170
brown hair	blond hair
loud	quiet
comical	serious

6 Patterns of Organization

You know how to write a good sentence. You can make subjects and verbs agree and keep the tenses clear. Your pronoun references make sense and you've got punctuation mastered. However, there is still more to good writing.

What's wrong with the following paragraph?

You can buy good pizzas, but the ones you make at home can be even better. Some people like grated cheeses. When you've got your pizza loaded up, put it in the oven at 350°F for about 12-15 minutes. Add your favorite ingredients. Pour on the tomato sauce and spread it around. Spread out the pizza dough on a well-greased baking sheet. Myself, I like sliced cheese. Pile on the ingredients; the more the better. Add the cheese.

Although the sentences are correctly written, the paragraph doesn't make much sense. The ideas are not written in correct time order, and so you don't get a clear idea about how to make a pizza.

Here's one important rule to remember about writing a paragraph.

A good paragraph must be well organized.

There are four basic ways to organize writing. One of these **patterns of organization** will bring order to almost any writing.

- time order

- cause-and-effect order

- comparison-and-contrast order

- simple listing

TIME ORDER

When you organize ideas in **time order**, you tell about them in the order they occur.

WHEN TO USE TIME ORDER

Time order is one of the easiest organization patterns to use. Simply tell about events in the order they happen. Time order is very useful for telling a story or explaining to someone how to do something, such as making a pizza.

WHEN TO USE TIME ORDER
Uses
1. To list steps in a process
2. To explain how something works
3. To describe a routine
4. To tell about an event
Examples
How do you make a pizza?
How does an electric switch work?
How do you spend Sunday morning?
What happened in the accident?

Organizing Details in Time Order

Organize details in time order in two steps. First make a list of all the details you want to tell about. Then go back and number the details in the order they happen. Here's how the details of the confused paragraph that opened this chapter might be organized.

How to Make a Pizza

1. Grease a baking sheet.
2. Spread out the pizza dough on the baking sheet.
3. Pour on tomato sauce.
4. Spread the tomato sauce around.
5. Add the cheese.
6. Add your favorite ingredients.
7. Bake it at 350° for about 12–15 minutes.

Using the ordered list as a guide, the paragraph might be written like this:

You can buy good pizzas, but the ones you make at home can be even better. First, spread out the pizza dough on a well-greased baking sheet. Then pour on the tomato sauce and spread it around. Next, add the cheese. Some people like grated cheeses. Myself, I like sliced cheese. It covers better. Next, add your favorite ingredients. Pile them on; the more the better. When you've got your pizza loaded up, put it in the oven at 350°F for about 12-15 minutes.

This paragraph makes sense. Anyone can follow the directions step by step and make a pizza.

Besides putting the details in time order, the writer has added **transition words**. These are words such as *first, next, then, after,* and *when.* Transition words give the reader clues about the order of events. They make the writing even clearer.

EXERCISE 1

Directions: Number the items in each list in time order. The items in List 1 have been done for you.

1. Getting ready for work
   - _(2)_ I take a quick shower.
   - _(4)_ I eat breakfast.
   - _(3)_ I get dressed.
   - _(5)_ I leave the house.
   - _(1)_ The alarm goes off.

2. Making pancakes
   - _5_ Flip the pancakes.
   - _2_ Add 1/3 cup of milk.
   - _1_ Measure the mix into a bowl.
   - _4_ Pour the mixture onto griddle.
   - _3_ Mix well.

3. How to plant a tree
   - _2_ Put the tree in the hole.
   - _5_ Give the newly planted tree plenty of water.
   - _4_ Holding the tree straight, fill the hole with dirt.
   - _1_ Dig a hole.
   - _3_ Spread the roots out in the hole.

4. Wars in American history
   - _3_ World War I
   - _5_ Vietnam War
   - _1_ American Revolution
   - _2_ Civil War
   - _4_ World War II

ANSWERS ARE ON PAGE 263.

CAUSE-AND-EFFECT ORDER

When you use **cause-and-effect order**, you tell what happened because of something else.

WHEN TO USE CAUSE-AND-EFFECT ORDER

Cause-and-effect order is useful whenever you want to tell why something happened or what will happen. You might choose cause-and-effect order to tell what happened at work the day twelve inches of snow fell in two hours. You might use it to tell what will happen because the star center of a basketball team is injured.

WHEN TO USE CAUSE-AND-EFFECT ORDER

Uses

1. To explain why an event happened
2. To explain the results of an event
3. To predict what will happen because of some event

Examples

Why did a local business close down and lay off 300 workers?
What happened because the Mississippi overflowed its banks?
What will happen now that a new industry is moving to town?

Organizing Details in Cause-and-Effect Order

There are two ways to organize ideas in cause-and-effect order. You might look at an **effect**, or result, and then explain what caused it. Or you might look at a **cause**, or situation, and tell what effects it has had or will have.

It's important to remember that one cause can have many effects. Likewise, one effect can have many causes.

Often, you will have a string of cause-and-effect events. One event will have an effect. That effect will cause something else to happen, which causes something else to happen, and so on.

---

cause → effect

cause → effect

cause → effect

cause → effect

Usually cause-and-effect order also follows time order. That is, you tell about the events in the order they happened. Telling when events happened is often helpful in explaining how one event caused another.

Recognizing True Cause-and-Effect Details

Be alert to one common mistake in using cause-and-effect order. Don't think one event caused another just because it happened first. Read the following passage. What cause-and-effect relationship does it give?

The hockey team was on the road for six games. The star player scored seven goals on the trip. The team returned home, so the player broke his leg in practice. He will be out for the season.

This passage contains one cause-and-effect relationship: the player broke his leg, so he will be out for the season. The star didn't break his leg because the team returned home. The word *so* incorrectly suggests a cause-and-effect relationship. When you organize information in cause-and-effect order, be sure the facts are correctly related.

The following is a list of ideas about the effects of higher costs for new cars. Cross out one topic that is not a true effect.

1. People will keep their cars longer.

2. People still want new cars even if they can't afford them.

3. Mechanics have more business because they must keep older cars running longer.

4. To save money, people may buy less well-equipped new cars.

You should have crossed out item 2. It may be true that people still want new cars even if they can't afford them, but it is not an effect of higher-priced cars.

EXERCISE 2

Directions: Put a check in front of the correct answer for each question that follows.

1. Which of the following is NOT a cause of air pollution?

___ (1) exhaust fumes from cars and trucks

✓ (2) electric cars are not practical

___ (3) factories that exhaust smoke out of smokestacks

___ (4) burning leaves and trash

2. Which of the following is NOT a cause of homelessness?

___ (1) Many factories and other businesses have laid off workers.

___ (2) Some people do not have enough money saved to support themselves or their families while they look for a new job.

___ (3) Single occupancy hotels have been torn down and replaced with buildings that charge higher rents for their apartments.

✓ (4) Every big city in America now has more homeless people on the streets than ever before.

ANSWERS ARE ON PAGE 263.

192 PRE-GED WRITING SKILLS

EXERCISE 3

Directions: List two causes and two effects for each problem listed below.

Causes

people are allowed to have guns in their homes

crime is in the family

Effects

easier access to weapons that cause violent crimes

cycle that continues

Violent Crime

Causes

parents never taught

discrimination against races

Effects

children are not taught and the cycle continues

those races were never allowed to be educated

Lack of Basic Educational Skills

ANSWERS ARE ON PAGE 264.

COMPARISON-AND-CONTRAST ORDER

When you use **comparison-and-contrast order**, you show how one item is similar to and how it is different from another item.

WHEN TO USE COMPARISON-AND-CONTRAST ORDER

Comparison-and-contrast order is helpful whenever you want to tell how two things are alike or different. For example, you might use this organization to make a decision about two job offers.

You might ask yourself how far you want to travel to get to a job. Do you want to work near your home or are you willing to make a longer commute to and from work? What amount of training or educational experience does each job require? Is there a difference in pay between the two jobs?

You might also ask yourself what type of work you will be expected to do on each job. Is there a difference in benefits such as number of vacation and sick days and insurance coverage? Using comparison and contrast will help you make this kind of decision more easily.

WHEN TO USE COMPARISON-AND-CONTRAST ORDER

Uses

1. To describe similarities and differences
2. To explain advantages and disadvantages

Examples

How was this year's vacation like the one you took last year?

Which candidate for mayor will do the most for the city?

Whole-to-Whole Pattern

When you use ***whole-to-whole organization***, you say everything you want to say about one subject. Then you say everything about the other subject. Here's how a writer used this pattern to compare the restaurants.

Jake's Grill has the best barbecue in the city. The food is fresh, hot, and spicy, and there's lots of it. Jake's doesn't have the greatest atmosphere. It has tile floors, bare tables, and bright lighting. Of course, the food's cheap, so who's complaining? If you want atmosphere, go to Chez Paris. The French food is good, fresh, and mildly spicy, but the servings are small. Chez Paris has all the atmosphere you could want, though. The dining room is elegant. It has soft lighting, and classical music plays in the background. If you want to impress someone, Chez Paris is the place, but it is expensive.

Point-by-Point Pattern

You can also organize your writing by using a ***point-by-point pattern***. With this organization, you tell one thing about one subject. Then you compare the same point of the other subject. After that, you tell about the next point, and so on. Here's how the writer compared the restaurants using the point-by-point pattern.

Both Jake's Grill and Chez Paris have good food. Jake's has the best barbecue in town. Chez Paris has French cooking. The food at Jake's is fresh, hot, and spicy, and the helpings are huge. Chez Paris offers good food that's fresh and mildly spicy. The servings, however, are small. Don't go to Jake's for the atmosphere. It has tile floors, bare tables, and bright lights. Chez Paris has an elegant dining room. It is softly lit, and classical music plays in the background. The atmosphere makes Chez Paris expensive, however. Jake's is cheap.

Planning a Comparison-and-Contrast Paragraph

A chart is a useful way to organize ideas when using comparison-and-contrast order. Set it up in columns like the ones shown below.

Items to Discuss	Jake's Grill	Chez Paris
Type of food	American barbecue	French
Quality of food	fresh, hot, very spicy, very filling	fresh, mild spices, small servings
Atmosphere	plain, tile floors, bright lighting, no tablecloths	elegant dining room, classical music, soft lighting
Price	cheap	expensive

EXERCISE 4

Directions: Complete the comparison-and-contrast chart below about dogs and cats.

Items to Discuss	Dogs	Cats
Care	have to be fed, watered, cared for daily	*have to fed but pretty much take care of themselves*
Behavior	usually like people and other dogs, like to play and run	*keep to themselves and dont really like to play*

ANSWERS ARE ON PAGE 264.

EXERCISE 5

Directions: Compare and contrast two friends. Tell how they are alike and how they are different.

Friend 1: Lindsay

Friend 2: Arianna

How are they alike?

like to talk on the phone and hang
out; have a sister; live in suburbs;
live in a court

How are they different?

brown-skinned; short hair; short	**Their looks**	light-skinned; long hair; tallish
stares at the walls; doesn't like to party stepfather and mother	**Their interests** **Their families**	volleyball; boys; computer; parties mother and father; older brother
Randallstown;	**Type of home**	Howard county; big house
public school edu.	**Type of work**	Private school edu.

ANSWERS WILL VARY.

SIMPLE LISTING

When you use **simple listing**, you may not organize details in a specific order. A list gives examples or characteristics to support a main idea.

WHEN TO USE LISTING

Use listing when you want to give examples of an idea. For instance, you might want to tell a friend what to see when visiting your town. You might mention the zoo, museums, riverfront, shopping malls, and other sights. You could tell something about each one, but it doesn't matter which you tell about first. Your main idea is to say there are a lot of good things to do.

WHEN TO USE LISTING

Uses

1. To give examples to support a main idea

2. To list characteristics of an item

3. To break a large group into smaller categories

Examples

What are some good movies to watch on a big screen?

What skills does a boxer need to become a world champion?

How many kinds of musical instruments are there?

Ordering Details on the List

No specific order is necessary in organizing the items on a list. Sometimes, however, you may want to create an order. You might organize items by size, by color, by age, by how unusual they are, or by some other characteristic you choose. In the following example, the writer lists the evils of picnicking from bad to worst.

I have never liked picnics. The weather is always hot. Cold drinks are never cold enough. The wind blows paper plates and potato chips off the table. Insects gang up on me. Ants always find the food, and gnats fly into my ears. Wasps just wait for me to sit on them. Worst of all are the mosquitoes. No matter how fast I swat them, I always go home scratching every imaginable part of my body.

In this paragraph, the writer organizes the list from tiny to huge.

I love all kinds of dogs, except Chihuahuas. They're too small. I want a dog that can at least see the top of the coffee table. Airedales are fun and very intelligent. German shepherds are even better. You can have a lot of fun walking one of those. They're big and strong and have great personalities. For my money, though, the biggest are the best. Give me a Great Dane any day. That's a dog you can enjoy.

EXERCISE 6

Part A

Directions: Write a paragraph listing what you like—or dislike—about your home. You might want to begin by making a simple list of ideas. Think about the location, neighbors, cost of rent, and convenience.

List of Ideas

_____

_____

_____

_____

Part B

Directions: Look at your list. Is there some way you can organize the details? Now write your paragraph.

Paragraph

_____

_____

_____

_____

_____

_____

_____

ANSWERS WILL VARY.

JOURNAL WRITING

Think of a story you like to remember about yourself, friends, or family. Write three paragraphs telling the story. Before you begin, think which organization pattern will work best for your story. Then make a list or chart to organize your ideas. When you've finished writing, review your work. Did you use the best organization plan? What other organization plan might you have used?

≡ PRE-GED Practice ≡
PATTERNS OF ORGANIZATION

Choose the best answer to each question.

1. **Use time order when you want to**
   - (1) describe an event
   - (2) explain the results of an event
   - (3) show how two activities are alike
   - (4) predict what will happen next
   - (5) give examples of a type of activity

2. **Use comparison-and-contrast organization when you want to**
   - (1) break a large group into smaller categories
   - (2) explain how something works
   - (3) predict what will happen next
   - (4) explain the advantages and disadvantages of a choice
   - (5) tell a joke

3. **Use cause-and-effect organization when you want to**
   - (1) show how two vacuum cleaners are alike and different
   - (2) tell how to make biscuits
   - (3) explain how lack of oil in the engine led to engine damage
   - (4) give examples of violence on television
   - (5) explain how to make a copier work

4. **Use simple listing when you want to**
   - (1) tell how your uncle came to the United States
   - (2) give instructions for growing roses
   - (3) give examples of your son's poor study habits
   - (4) decide which movie will be the best to see
   - (5) explain how the lawn mower works

Questions 5–7 refer to the following paragraph.

(1) Gray wolves once lived across most of the United States. (2) When Europeans first came to America in the sixteenth century, they began changing the land. (3) Settlers turned forests into fields and prairies into towns. (4) Wolves no longer had a place to live and were pushed farther west. (5) They still survived, though, for a while. (6) Settlers kept moving west, however. (7) In the nineteenth century, people had settled the entire country. (8) They decided to get rid of wolves altogether. (9) As a result, wolves are now gone from most states. (10) People poisoned and shot wolves on sight.

5. **This paragraph uses two kinds of order, cause-and-effect order and**
   - (1) comparison-and-contrast order
   - (2) feature-by-feature order
   - (3) whole-to-whole order
   - (4) simple listing
   - (5) time order

6. **One reason the wolves disappeared is that**
   - (1) settlers changed the land
   - (2) forests were cut down
   - (3) wolves no longer had a place to live
   - (4) wolves were shot and poisoned
   - (5) all of the above

7. One sentence is not in correct order. To correct the order

  (1) move sentence 1 to the end of the paragraph
  (2) move sentence 3 after sentence 4
  (3) move sentence 4 after sentence 5
  (4) move sentence 6 before sentence 3
  (5) move sentence 9 after sentence 10

Questions 8–10 refer to the following paragraph.

(1) Buying a house is expensive. **(2)** You need thousands of dollars to put down on the house. **(3)** Even then, you must borrow thousands of dollars more. **(4)** Then each month for fifteen or thirty years, you have to make monthly payments to pay off the loan. **(5)** In addition, you have to pay taxes on the house. **(6)** You don't have to pay taxes on an apartment. **(7)** If something on your house needs repairing, you have to pay for it. **(8)** Eventually, however, you will own the house. **(9)** If you rent an apartment, you may make a small deposit when you move in. **(10)** After that you make a monthly rent payment, which is probably smaller than the cost of a house payment. **(11)** Repairs are usually paid for by the building's owner. **(12)** As long as you live in an apartment, you'll be making rent payments.

8. This paragraph is organized using

  (1) cause-and-effect order
  (2) time order
  (3) comparison-and-contrast order with a feature-by-feature pattern
  (4) comparison-and-contrast order with a whole-to-whole pattern
  (5) simple listing

9. One sentence is out of order. To fix the organization, move sentence

  (1) 2 to follow sentence 5
  (2) 5 to follow sentence 8
  (3) 6 to follow sentence 10
  (4) 8 to follow sentence 10
  (5) 9 to follow sentence 3

10. An example of a cause-and-effect relationship is

  (1) sentence 2
  (2) sentence 5
  (3) sentence 7
  (4) sentence 11
  (5) there are no cause-and-effect relationships in this passage

ANSWERS ARE ON PAGE 264.

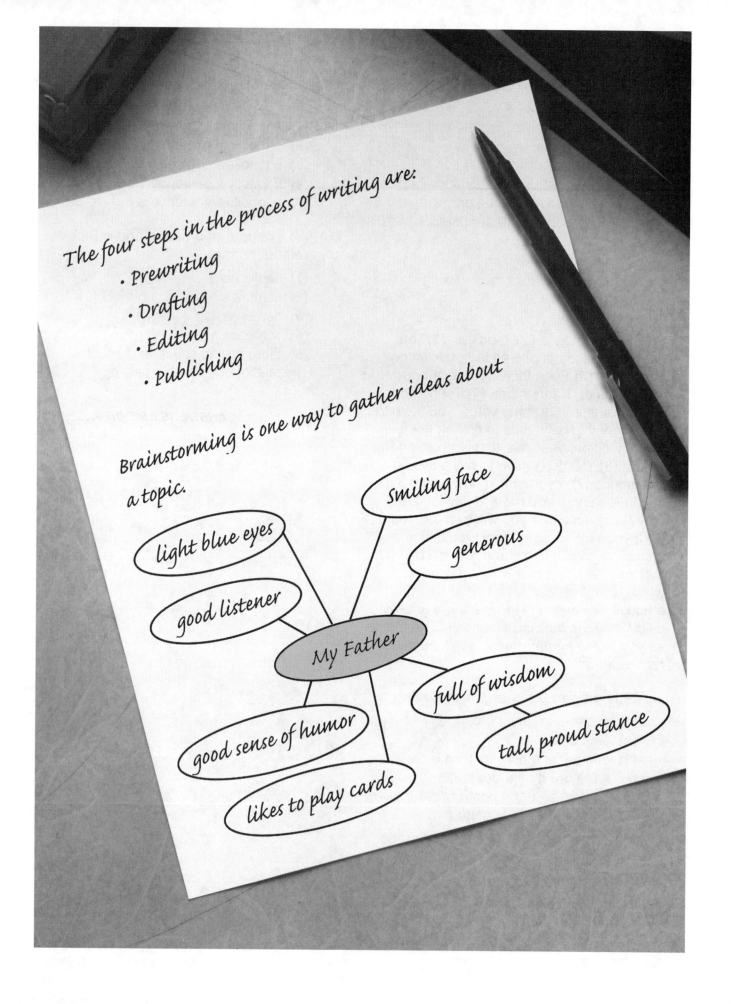

The four steps in the process of writing are:

- Prewriting
- Drafting
- Editing
- Publishing

Brainstorming is one way to gather ideas about a topic.

smiling face

light blue eyes

generous

good listener

My Father

full of wisdom

good sense of humor

tall, proud stance

likes to play cards

7 Process of Writing

Often, the hardest part of writing is getting started. You may know what your topic is. You may even know what information to include. Nevertheless, putting the first words down on paper can seem impossible. What do you say first? What's most important? How can you get your reader interested? How can you make your reader understand?

PREWRITING

Fortunately, there is a way to get past these first problems in writing. It is the ***prewriting*** process. This process will help you develop and organize ideas and prepare to write.

STEPS IN PREWRITING

1. Thinking about what you are writing
2. Brainstorming (listing ideas)
3. Organizing ideas

THINKING ABOUT WHAT YOU ARE WRITING

Answer the following questions about your writing. Your answers will help you see more clearly what you are trying to do and how to go about doing it.

- What am I writing about?

- Who is going to read my writing?

- What is the purpose for my writing?

For example, imagine that a writer wants to write about how her neighborhood turned a vacant lot into a playground. The lot was overgrown with weeds. There was trash, broken glass, and an abandoned car in the lot. Neighborhood kids played in the lot because there wasn't a park nearby. People in the neighborhood worked together to make it into a playground. Here's how the writer answered the questions about her topic.

- *What am I writing about?*
  (a neighborhood project to turn a vacant lot into a playground)

- *Who is going to read my writing?*
  (the editor and readers of our local newspaper)

- *What is my purpose?*
  (tell how my neighborhood turned an ugly lot into a place for kids to play)

The writer did not do research to answer these questions. She simply thought about why she was writing. Answering the questions made the writing process more concrete. She knew what she had to do.

BRAINSTORMING

Brainstorming is a way of gathering ideas to write about. When you brainstorm, you jot down every idea that comes to mind about your topic. You don't worry about spelling or writing in complete sentences. You don't even think whether an idea is good or bad. All you're trying to do is to get ideas.

On the next page is a cluster map the writer came up with by brainstorming about the vacant lot.

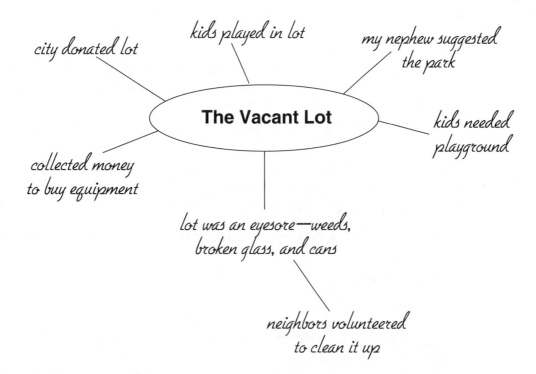

EXERCISE 1

Directions: Brainstorm for ideas about each of the following topics. Spend a few minutes on each. You will be using one of these lists later on for a piece of writing, so save your work.

1. My best vacation

2. My oldest friendship

3. What I'll be doing five years from today

4. An exciting sports event

5. Someone I admire

6. My favorite restaurant

7. A dream come true

ANSWERS WILL VARY.

ORGANIZING

The third step in prewriting is organizing information. Look at the list of ideas you brainstormed. Decide what ideas you want to include. Then add any new ideas that you think of.

Next decide on a pattern of organization. You might choose time order, cause-and-effect, comparison-and-contrast, simple listing, or any other order that makes sense. If you need a review of patterns of organization, turn to Chapter 6. When you have chosen a pattern, number your ideas in the order you will write about them.

Look how the person writing about the vacant lot organized her list.

The Vacant Lot

4. city donated lot
2. kids played in lot full of glass and trash
   ~~my nephew suggested the park~~
3. kids needed playground
5. neighbors volunteered to clean it up—city provided trash truck
1. lot was an eyesore—weeds, broken glass, and cans
6. collected money from local businesses to buy equipment
7. put in basketball court, playground equipment

Notice the changes the writer made. She crossed out one idea and added to some of her other ideas. Then she numbered them in a time order. She wanted to tell about the park in the order in which events happened.

EXERCISE 2

Directions: Choose one of your lists from Exercise 1 on page 205. Make any changes you wish to the list. You can add new ideas or scratch out ideas you don't want to use. Then number the ideas in the order you want to write about them.

Keep in mind that you'll be using this work later, so be sure to save it.

ANSWERS WILL VARY.

DRAFTING

Now that you have completed prewriting, you are ready to put your ideas down on paper. This is done most easily if you do it in stages, just like prewriting. There are two steps in **drafting**: the rough draft and the revised draft.

ROUGH DRAFT

The purpose of the rough draft is to turn your list of ideas into sentences and paragraphs. Don't worry too much about grammar or spelling. You can fix those mistakes later. Just try to get your ideas down in the proper order. Use your list as a guide, but if you think of new ideas or want to change the order of ideas, go ahead.

Your writing will have three parts: an introduction, a body, and a conclusion.

Introduction

The **introduction** does three things. First, it tells what the topic is. Second, it gives the main idea, or point, of the writing. Third, it gives the reader some idea of what will be discussed.

When the writer began drafting the story of the vacant lot, she wrote this introduction. Notice how she achieved the three goals of an introduction.

> There used to be a vacant lot down the street. It was filled with trash, broken glass, and cans. Besides being an eyesore, it was dangerous. Kids played there. They often cut themselves on broken glass and rusty cans. Finally, people got together and did something. Now it's a park and playground for neighborhood kids.

Here are some hints that will help you write a good introduction.

1. State your main idea clearly. If your readers know what to expect, they will understand your ideas better. Also, if you clearly state your main idea, you can look back at it as you write. You can see if what you say in the body supports your main idea.

2. Give your readers an idea of the content and organization. Then your readers won't become confused by how you present your ideas. If you can't explain the content and organization, you may not be quite ready to begin writing. Go back to Step 1 of prewriting.

3. Get your readers interested so they will keep reading. There are many ways to do this. You could begin with an odd or interesting fact. You could explain why your information is important. The first introduction to "The Vacant Lot" uses this method. You could begin with a question. Here's how a question could be used to introduce "The Vacant Lot."

What do you do with a vacant lot? Our neighborhood had that problem. One lot was empty and ugly. Everyone talked about it. No one knew what to do with it. Then one day, we found the answer. We would turn the lot into a playground.

EXERCISE 3

Directions: Write an introduction. Use your list of ideas from Exercises 1 and 2 as a guide. Write on every other line so you will have room to revise later.

When you're finished, check your writing. Make sure it gives the topic and main idea. It should also give your readers an idea of the content and organization, and it should get them interested.

ANSWERS WILL VARY.

Body

In the introduction, you told what your main idea is. In the **body** of your writing, you give the details and facts that explain the main idea.

Use your numbered list of ideas as a guide while writing the body. If new ideas occur to you, add them as you go. Start a new paragraph for each big idea or topic you want to explain.

Here is the body of "The Vacant Lot." Compare the development of ideas to the original list. Also notice how the ideas were divided into paragraphs. The first paragraph tells about the lot the way it was. The second paragraph is about how the neighborhood changed it.

Just a year ago, the lot was covered with weeds. Kids played in the lot. It was dangerous, though, because of the trash. Broken glass and cans were lying around. However, kids didn't have any other place to play unless they wanted to play in the street.

We turned the lot into a playground. A group met with people from the city. They talked the city into donating the land. Other people talked local businesses into donating playground equipment and money. We put in a basketball court and some playground equipment. Then everyone in the neighborhood pitched in to clean up the lot. The city provided a trash truck to haul the junk away.

As you write, look back at your introduction from time to time. Check that you are giving the information you said you wanted to include.

EXERCISE 4

Directions: Now begin the body of your writing. Continue to use the list of ideas from Exercise 2 as your guide in writing. Add details as you think of them. Create new paragraphs for each big idea. Write on every other line so you will have room to revise later.

ANSWERS WILL VARY.

Conclusion

Your ***conclusion*** is the ending for your writing. It's not new information. It is a wrap-up of what you have already said. The length of your conclusion depends on the length of the whole piece of writing. It might be one or two sentences or one or more paragraphs. There are many ways to write a conclusion. Here are two ideas.

You can summarize what you have said. Your conclusion will be a reminder for your reader. It says again, in a different way, the main idea you gave in your introduction. Here is how the writer of "The Vacant Lot" might have used a summary as her conclusion.

Working together, our neighborhood got rid of an eyesore. In the process, we've given kids a safe place to play.

Another way to end your writing is to tell your reader the broader truth of what you've said. "The Vacant Lot" might have been ended like this:

The vacant lot had been a problem in our neighborhood for years. No one knew what to do with it. We found the answer when we stopped looking at the lot only as a problem. Instead, we looked on it as an opportunity. Now we have a great new park for our kids.

This conclusion says the story is not just about getting rid of a vacant lot or building a playground. It's about turning problems into opportunities.

EXERCISE 5

Directions: Complete the draft you worked on in Exercises 2, 3, and 4 by writing a conclusion. Write on every other line so you will have room to revise later. Before you start, read the introduction and body you have already completed, just to refresh your memory.

ANSWERS WILL VARY.

REVISED DRAFT

Now your rough draft is complete. The next step in the writing process is revision. During **revision**, you make changes to improve your writing. You can change the order of ideas, rewrite sentences or paragraphs, make different word choices, or cut out ideas that you no longer think are important. Take as much time as you want during this stage. You are finished when you are happy with your work. Here are a few specific things to look for.

Improve Word Choices

While writing your rough draft, you were thinking mainly about getting your ideas down on paper. You didn't spend a lot of time choosing the right words. During revision, read each sentence carefully. Ask yourself if you have chosen the best words to say exactly what you mean. More precise words will make your writing clearer and more interesting.

Improve Links Between Paragraphs

When you wrote your rough draft, you started a new paragraph for each big idea. Now check that your reader will see how the ideas in each paragraph are linked.

One way to improve the links between paragraphs is by starting paragraphs with transition words. These are words such as *furthermore, then, on the other hand, as a result, in addition,* and *another advantage is.* Transition words show that ideas are connected.

Add Details and Examples

Ask yourself if your ideas are clear. Can your reader picture what you are saying? If not, your writing might need more details or examples. Use facts, descriptive words, or examples to support what you are saying.

Below is a revised draft of "The Vacant Lot." Notice how the writer has improved word choices, added details, and made the links between paragraphs stronger.

THE VACANT LOT

What do you do with a vacant lot? Our neighborhood had that problem. One lot was empty and ugly. Everyone talked about it. No one knew what to do with it.

Then one day, we found the answer. We would turn the lot into a playground. The lot was covered with weeds. Children played in the lot. It was dangerous, though, because broken glass and cans were lying around. However, children didn't have any other place to play unless they wanted to play in the street.

A group met with people from the city. They talked the city into donating the land. Other people talked local businesses into donating playground equipment and money. Then everyone in the neighborhood pitched in to clean up the lot. The city provided a trash truck to haul the junk away. We put in a basketball court and some playground equipment.

Working together, our neighborhood got rid of an eyesore. In the process, we've given children a safe place to play.

EXERCISE 6

Directions: Revise your draft. Look for ways to make your ideas clearer. You might want to change words, put ideas in a different order, or add transitions. Keep changing your draft until you are happy with your writing.

ANSWERS WILL VARY.

EDITING

After you have finished your revised draft, the next step is editing. **Editing** is proofreading your writing for mistakes in grammar, punctuation, capitalization, and spelling. Follow these steps during editing.

1. Read your writing out loud. Listen for words or sentences that sound wrong or awkward. Mark these places. You can come back and figure out what is wrong after you have finished reading aloud.

2. Look at each sentence by itself. Look for anything that is wrong. Be especially alert for fragments and run-ons.

3. Read your writing several times. Each time, look for a certain kind of error. Choose two or three mistakes you sometimes make. For example, if you have trouble with using commas, look closely at all the commas. If you have trouble with pronoun agreement, look at the pronouns.

EXERCISE 7

Directions: Edit your draft. Look for errors in spelling, grammar, capitalization, and punctuation. Then make a clean copy of your writing. You may want to read your finished draft one more time to make sure you have not made an error while copying it.

ANSWERS WILL VARY.

PUBLISHING

The final step in the writing process is publishing. ***Publishing*** is sharing your writing with others. You might ask friends or your family to read it. When they are finished, ask them what they think. Do they agree with what you have said? Do they understand your ideas? Don't hesitate to ask questions. Also, don't worry if they don't agree. After all, your reason for writing was to make your readers think about what you are interested in. Sharing your ideas is what writing and publishing are all about.

 ### JOURNAL WRITING

Think about the writing process you have just completed. What did you enjoy about it? What was difficult for you? If you were to do this writing a second time, what would you do differently? Think about these questions for a few minutes. Then write two or three paragraphs about your writing experience.

PROCESS OF WRITING

Choose the best answer to each question.

1. Brainstorming is part of what step in the writing process?

(1) prewriting
(2) drafting
(3) editing
(4) proofreading
(5) publishing

2. During what step in the writing process do you pay most attention to grammar?

(1) prewriting
(2) rough drafting
(3) revising
(4) editing
(5) publishing

3. The three parts of most pieces of writing are the body, the conclusion, and the

(1) rough draft
(2) introduction
(3) revision
(4) summary
(5) opening

4. When writing the rough draft, your main task is to

(1) correct errors in grammar, punctuation, and spelling
(2) organize your ideas
(3) decide on a main point
(4) get your ideas down on paper
(5) proofread

5. The first place the main idea should be stated is in the

(1) introduction
(2) conclusion
(3) body
(4) revision
(5) summary

6. The conclusion should

(1) introduce the main idea
(2) remind the reader of the main idea
(3) give details to support the main idea
(4) provide new information about the topic
(5) explain the organization of the writing

7. Which of the following is a way of publishing writing?

(1) having a friend read it
(2) getting it printed in a newspaper
(3) mailing it to an aunt to read
(4) reading it aloud to your brother
(5) all of the above

Questions 8–15 refer to the following passage.

(1) Usually grandparents pass along quilts or dishes to their grandchildren. (2) My sister Ann and I got something different. (3) Grandfather Cox left us his cabin.

(4) Grandfather cut the logs himself. (5) He used a hand saw and an ax. (6) That fall the weather was rainy. (7) When the logs were cut down Grandfather hauled them to the building site, pulling them behind an old mule named Bill.

(8) Grandfather and Great-Uncle Samuel built the cabin. (9) It was Grandfather's get-away-from-it-all cabin. (10) It only had one room and a front part, but that cabin became Grandfather's second home. (11) He called it his fishing cabin. (12) It was more than that, however.

(13) When Grandfather died, my dad had gotten the cabin. (14) Now Ann and I call it ours. (15) We go there often, and we love it. (16) I plan on leaving it to my children.

8. **What is the main idea of this passage?**

   (1) how the writer inherited the cabin
   (2) how Grandfather built the cabin
   (3) the importance of the cabin in the family
   (4) the kinds of gifts grandparents leave their children
   (5) what makes a good fishing cabin

9. **What pattern of organization is used?**

   (1) time order
   (2) simple listing
   (3) comparison-and-contrast
   (4) feature-by-feature
   (5) cause-and-effect

10. **The connection between paragraphs two and three could be improved by which of the following changes?**

    (1) get rid of sentence 7
    (2) begin sentence 8 with *Then*
    (3) begin sentence 8 with *As soon as*
    (4) combine the paragraphs; separate paragraphs are not needed
    (5) no correction is necessary

11. **Which change would improve the order of details?**

    (1) put sentence 4 after sentence 6
    (2) put sentence 9 before sentence 7
    (3) put sentence 9 after sentence 12
    (4) put sentence 15 before sentence 12
    (5) no correction is necessary

12. How should sentence 7 be corrected?

(1) add a comma after *down*
(2) change *site* to *sight*
(3) change *hauled* to *had hauled*
(4) add a comma before *Bill*
(5) no correction is necessary

13. What sentence should be gotten rid of during revision?

(1) sentence 3
(2) sentence 6
(3) sentence 8
(4) sentence 12
(5) no correction is necessary

14. How should sentence 10 be corrected?

(1) change *front part* to *porch*
(2) change the comma to a semicolon
(3) change *but* to *and*
(4) change *Grandfather's* to *grandfather's*
(5) no correction is necessary

15. How should sentence 13 be corrected?

(1) remove the comma after *died*
(2) change *my* to *mine*
(3) change *dad* to *Dad*
(4) change *had gotten* to *got*
(5) no correction is necessary

ANSWERS ARE ON PAGE 264.

Knowing word parts, spelling patterns, and vowel combinations will help you become a better speller.

Some of the most commonly misspelled words include:

bookkeeper

fundamentally

courteous

anonymous

embarrass

February

Wednesday

maneuver

leisure

unforgettable

noticeable

proceed

8 Spelling

Spelling is not the most important part of writing. Even if some words are spelled incorrectly, your reader will probably still understand your meaning. Bad spelling, however, makes your writing, and you, look bad. That's not necessary because you can get spelling right.

WORD PARTS

Thinking about the parts of words is one step toward good spelling. Look at the word *misunderstanding*. If you try to memorize the spelling letter by letter, you have a lot to remember—sixteen letters. Instead, think of it as having three parts.

Prefix	Root word	Suffix
mis	understand	ing

A ***root word*** is the main word. It is the word without anything else added. The root word can stand by itself. A ***prefix*** is a word part that is added to the beginning of a root word. A ***suffix*** is a word part that is added to the end of a root word. Prefixes and suffixes do not stand by themselves. They are used to change the meaning of a root word.

Misusing prefixes and suffixes can cause spelling errors. By learning the most common word parts, you can avoid many spelling errors.

COMMON PREFIXES

Prefix	Meaning	Example
anti	against	anticrime
con, com, col, cor, co	together, with	context, correlate
dis	not, apart	dishonest
in, im, ir, il, non, un	not	impossible, unlikely
inter	between	international
mis	wrongly, bad	misbehave
pre	before	preview
pro	for, in front of	prolabor
re	again	renew
trans	across	transatlantic

COMMON SUFFIXES

Suffix	Meaning	Example
able, ible	able to be	readable
al	relating to	musical
ance, ence	state of	dependence
er, or, ar, ist	someone or something that does an action	manager, conductor, geologist
ful, ous	full of, having	careful, furious
ic	nature of	poetic
ish	having the quality of	foolish
ity	state or quality	sincerity
ive	tending toward	descriptive
ly	in a certain way	happily
ment	act of, result of	encouragement
tion, sion	act of, process of	separation, decision

EXERCISE 1

Directions: Write the parts of each word in the blanks. If a word does not have one of the parts, leave the blank empty.

	Prefix	**Root Word**	**Suffix**
Example: dishonorable	*dis*	*honor*	*able*
1. untruthful			
2. disappearance			
3. quickly			
4. prearrangement			
5. misconnection			
6. illogical			
7. singer			
8. replacement			
9. nonexistence			
10. courageous			

ANSWERS ARE ON PAGE 265.

SPELLING PATTERNS

ADDING PREFIXES

When you add a prefix to a root word, do not change the spelling of the prefix or the root word.

dis + believe ⟶ disbelieve
in + secure ⟶ insecure
mis + spell ⟶ misspell

ADDING SUFFIXES

When you add a suffix to a root word, the spelling is usually not changed.

finish + ing ⟶ finishing   danger + ous ⟶ dangerous
rude + ly ⟶ rudely   engage + ment ⟶ engagement

There are three exceptions to this guideline. Three rules will help you remember them.

1. The root word ends with a silent *e* and the suffix begins with a vowel. In most cases, drop the silent *e*.

care + ing ⟶ caring   adventure + ous ⟶ adventurous

There are some exceptions to this rule. You'll need to memorize them. In words in which the consonant *c* is pronounced *s* or when *g* is pronounced *j*, keep the silent *e*.

trace + able ⟶ traceable   courage + ous ⟶ courageous
advantage + ous ⟶ advantageous   peace + able ⟶ peaceable
notice + able ⟶ noticeable   change + able ⟶ changeable

> **Note:** If the suffix begins with a consonant, keep the silent *e*. No spelling change is needed.

care + less ⟶ careless   require + ment ⟶ requirement

2. The root word ends in a *y* preceded by a consonant. Change the *y* to an *i* before adding the suffix.

merry + ment → merriment   angry + ly → angrily
satisfy + ed → satisfied   happy + ness → happiness

Note: If the suffix begins with an *i* do not change the spelling of the root word.

carry + ing → carrying   thirty + ish → thirtyish

3. The final consonant of the root word may have to be doubled before adding a suffix. Double the consonant if all of the following are true:

- The root word ends with a single consonant (other than *w* or *x*) and is preceded by a single vowel.

- The accent, or emphasis, of the root word is on the last syllable or the root word has only one syllable.

- The suffix begins with a vowel.

plan + ing → planning   refer + ed → referred
occur + ence → occurrence   commit + ed → committed

Here are some examples of words that do not double their final consonant.

quarrel + ing → quarreling   infer + ence → inference
equip + ment → equipment   review + ing → reviewing

COMPOUND WORDS

A ***compound word*** is a single word that is made by combining two or more words. Do not change the spelling of any of the words when forming the compound.

zoo + keeper → zookeeper   star + gazer → stargazer

EXERCISE 2

Directions: A word in each of the following sets of words may be spelled incorrectly. If a word is misspelled, write it correctly in the blank. If none of the words is misspelled, write *C* in the blank.

Example: immature   ilegal   irrelevant   subheading

   illegal

1. bicycle   dissapprove   inject   misplace

_____

2. commitment   committing   infering   intended

_____

3. arrangement   improvised   removable   valueable

_____

4. hateful   truest   encouragment   pursuing

_____

5. bookcase   desktop   roadblock   bookeeper

_____

6. careless   added   creative   skiing

_____

7. openning   becoming   relaxing   laughable

_____

8. reuse   maladjusted   immobile   irresponsible

_____

9. defineable   ageless   supplier   changeable

_____

10. prohibited   emitting   rejected   limitted

_____

ANSWERS ARE ON PAGE 265.

≡ PRE-GED Practice ≡
SPELLING PATTERNS

Choose what correction should be made to each sentence below. If you think the sentence is correct, choose (5).

1. **After Raymond finished reviewing the article, the librarian replaced the reference book. It belonged on the top bookshelf.**

   (1) change *reviewing* to *reviewwing*
   (2) change *replaced* to *replacied*
   (3) change *reference* to *referrence*
   (4) change *bookshelf* to *bookkshelf*
   (5) no correction is necessary

2. **My preference is not to talk about the occurrence. I was never so embarrased as when I couldn't find my car. My boss and I walked all over that lot, and I felt totally foolish.**

   (1) change *preference* to *preferrence*
   (2) change *occurrence* to *occurence*
   (3) change *embarrased* to *embarrassed*
   (4) change *foolish* to *foollish*
   (5) no correction is necessary

3. **When Rachel remodeled her kitchen, she thoughtfully listed all her requirments. At the top of her list was a dishwasher.**

   (1) change *remodeled* to *remodelled*
   (2) change *thoughtfully* to *thoughtfuly*
   (3) change *requirments* to *requirements*
   (4) change *dishwasher* to *dishewasher*
   (5) no correction is necessary

4. **I immediately began studing when I got home. I was careful to reread every page. I sincerely hope I do well on the test.**

   (1) change *immediately* to *imediately*
   (2) change *studing* to *studying*
   (3) change *careful* to *carful*
   (4) change *sincerely* to *sincerly*
   (5) no correction is necessary

5. **Tanya is an excellent typeist. She makes a noticeable difference in the office. I don't think she is accustomed to working such long hours, however.**

   (1) change *typeist* to *typist*
   (2) change *noticeable* to *noticable*
   (3) change *difference* to *differrence*
   (4) change *accustomed* to *accustommed*
   (5) no correction is necessary

ANSWERS ARE ON PAGE 266.

LETTER COMBINATIONS

THE *i* PLUS *e* COMBINATION

An old rhyme will save you from lots of spelling errors if you keep it in mind.

I before *e* except after *c* or when sounding like *a* as in *neighbor* and *weigh*.

I before *e* . . .

believe   friend   niece   relief

except after *c* . . .

receive   ceiling   receipt   conceit

or when sounding like *a* as in *neighbor* and *weigh*.

eight   sleigh   reign   vein

There are only a few exceptions to the rule.

weird	either	height	foreign	protein
seize	neither	leisure	their	species

CEDE, CEED, SEDE

Remember how to spell words that end with the "seed" sound by remembering the exceptions.

1. Only one word ends with *sede: supersede*.

2. Only three words end with *ceed: exceed, proceed, succeed*.

3. All other words that end with the "seed" sound are spelled *cede: precede, concede, recede*, and *secede*, for example.

EXERCISE 3

Directions: A word in each of the following sets of words may be spelled incorrectly. If a word is misspelled, write it correctly in the blank. If none of the words is misspelled, write *C* in the blank.

Example: belief   cheif   neighbor   weight

chief

1. intercede   exceed   succede   precede

   _____

2. relieve   deciet   species   conceived

   _____

3. breif   efficient   foreign   field

   _____

4. science   achievement   sleigh   wierd

   _____

5. preceed   recede   concede   proceed

   _____

6. hygiene   conscience   niether   ceiling

   _____

7. piece   retrieve   weight   yeild

   _____

ANSWERS ARE ON PAGE 266.

COMMONLY MISSPELLED WORDS

The following list is made up of some of the most frequently misspelled words. Many of them follow basic spelling rules you have already learned. These words are followed by a page number that refers to the spelling hint. Others words do not follow specific rules and you must memorize them.

absence	campaign	disappoint
accept	carriage	diseased
accurate	ceiling (225)	dissatisfied (221,
acknowledge	cemetery	222)
acquaintance	changeable (221)	earnest
acquire	chocolate	ecology
actually (221)	college	education
admission	commitment	efficient
advantageous	committee	eighteen
aggressive	community	embarrass
agreeable (221)	conceivable (221, 225)	engineer
aisle	connoisseur	enough
already	conscience	enthusiasm
amateur	consciousness	environment (221)
analyze	convenience	equipment (221)
anonymous	cooperative	excellence
anxious	corporation	exceptional
apologize	correspond	exercise
arrangement (221)	courteous	exhibit
article	criticize	extremely (221)
associate	curriculum	familiar
athlete	customer	famous
attendance	deceit (225)	favorite
audience	definite	February
average	delicious	fierce (225)
baggage	delivery	foreign
banana	dependent	fortunate
beautiful	descendant	forty
beginning (222)	desert	fourteen
believe (225)	desirable (221)	frequently (221)
bookkeeper (222)	desperate	fulfillment (221)
bought	dessert	fundamentally (221)
bouquet	develop	gaiety
breathe	development (221)	gauge
burial	devise	generous
business	diligent	genuine
calendar	disappear	government (221)

grammar
guidance (221)
happened (222)
harassment
headache (222)
height
hereafter (222)
honorable (221)
icy
immediately (221)
improvement (221)
incidentally (221)
independence
independent
individual
instructor
insurance
intellectual
intelligent
interrupt
irrelevant
jewelry
judgment
junior
knives (28)
knowledge
language
league
leisure
liquor
losing (221)
luxury
machinery
maintenance
management (221)
maneuver
manufacture
marriage
mechanical
message
mischievous (225)
misspelling (221)

mysterious
naturally (221)
necessary
neither
nephew
niece (225)
ninth
noticeable
obedience
occasional
occurring (222)
officially (221)
omitted (222)
opportunity
original
outrageous (221)
parallel
particular
permanent
permission
physician
picnicking
pleasant
possession
precious
prevalent
privilege
procedure
proceed (225)
quietly (221)
quite
receipt (225)
receive (225)
recipe
referred (222)
relieve (225)
remember
resourceful (221)
responsibility
restaurant
rhyme
rhythm

safety
scenery
schedule
school
science
secretary
seize
separate
siege (225)
signature
society
standard
straight
studying (222)
succeed (225)
supersede (225)
temperature
territory
themselves (39)
therefore
thorough
tomorrow
tragedy
truly
twelfth
unforgettable (222)
unfortunately (221)
unnatural (221)
usually (221)
vacuum
valuable (221)
varied (222)
vegetable
vehicle
versatile
village
villain
volunteer
weather
Wednesday
weird

JOURNAL WRITING

Why do you want to pass the GED Test or take college-level classes? What will it mean to you? Think about your answer for a few minutes. Then answer the questions by writing three paragraphs in your journal. When you are finished, check your spelling carefully. If there are any words you are unsure of, think if there are any rules that apply. If not, check the words in a dictionary. You might want to begin a list of words that give you spelling trouble. Review the list every day or two until you have mastered the words. Then start a new list.

≡ PRE-GED Practice ≡
SPELLING

Read each sentence. Then choose the best correction for each sentence. If you think the sentence is correct, choose (5).

1. **Our new eraseable ink pen is capable of writing under water. If management is agreeable, I'll prove it on network TV.**

    (1) change *eraseable* to *erasable*
    (2) change *capable* to *capible*
    (3) change *management* to *managment*
    (4) change *agreeable* to *agreeble*
    (5) no correction is necessary

2. **You are mistaken if you think the Timberwolves' loss was dissappointing to me. I've never been extremely fond of the team.**

    (1) change *mistaken* to *misstaken*
    (2) change *dissappointing* to *dissappointting*
    (3) change *dissappointing* to *disappointing*
    (4) change *extremely* to *extremly*
    (5) no correction is necessary

3. **The talk show host was in a mischievous mood. Failling to understand that the joke was on her, the guest proceeded to bow deeply.**

    (1) change *mischievous* to *mischeivous*
    (2) change *Failling* to *Failing*
    (3) change *proceeded* to *proceded*
    (4) change *proceeded* to *proseded*
    (5) no correction is necessary

4. **Lupita received her first issue of Science America almost immediately after she placed her order. What efficeint service!**

    (1) change *received* to *recieved*
    (2) change *Science* to *Sceince*
    (3) change *immediately* to *immediatly*
    (4) change *efficeint* to *efficient*
    (5) no correction is necessary

5. "If you procede with harassing the umpire," the manager warned her, "you will succeed in getting tossed out of the game."

   (1) change *procede* to *proceed*
   (2) change *harassing* to *harasing*
   (3) change *succeed* to *succede*
   (4) change *tossed* to *tosed*
   (5) no correction is necessary

6. The weather is unsettled, but don't be discouraged from going picnicking. It's irelevant to me if you get soaked.

   (1) change *unsettled* to *unsettlled*
   (2) change *discouraged* to *discouragged*
   (3) change *picnicking* to *picnicing*
   (4) change *irelevant* to *irrelevant*
   (5) no correction is necessary

7. The dogcatcher watched helplessly as the fierce dog leaped the fence and escaped.

   (1) change *dogcatcher* to *dogecatcher*
   (2) change *helplessly* to *helplesslly*
   (3) change *fierce* to *feirce*
   (4) change *leaped* to *leapped*
   (5) no correction is necessary

8. The amateur climber couragously accepted the challenge.

   (1) change *amateur* to *amatuer*
   (2) change *amateur* to *amature*
   (3) change *couragously* to *courageously*
   (4) change *accepted* to *acepted*
   (5) no correction is necessary

9. During both halfs the team performed well. Players were resourceful and aggressive, but they lost.

   (1) change *halfs* to *halves*
   (2) change *performed* to *performmed*
   (3) change *resourceful* to *resourcful*
   (4) change *aggressive* to *aggresive*
   (5) no correction is necessary

10. The burial of the lizard at the pet cemetary was a sad occasion.

   (1) change *burial* to *buryal*
   (2) change *burial* to *burieal*
   (3) change *cemetary* to *cemetery*
   (4) change *occasion* to *occassion*
   (5) no correction is necessary

11. **Does Shandra realyze that she definitely won't receive the promotion without succeeding on the GED?**

    (1) change *realyze* to *realize*
    (2) change *definitely* to *definitly*
    (3) change *receive* to *recieve*
    (4) change *succeeding* to *succeding*
    (5) no correction is necessary

12. **The police retrieved the stolen valuables. Neither theif was captured.**

    (1) change *retrieved* to *retreived*
    (2) change *valuables* to *valueables*
    (3) change *neither* to *niether*
    (4) change *theif* to *thief*
    (5) no correction is necessary

13. **The scientist had two theorys about how ancient societies educated their children.**

    (1) change *scientist* to *sceintist*
    (2) change *theorys* to *theories*
    (3) change *ancient* to *anceint*
    (4) change *societies* to *societys*
    (5) no correction is necessary

14. **The nightwatchman glanced nervously outside. Both streetlights proceeded to flicker and go out.**

    (1) change *nightwatchman* to *nightewatchman*
    (2) change *nervously* to *nervouslly*
    (3) change *streetlights* to *streettlights*
    (4) change *proceeded* to *proceded*
    (5) no correction is necessary

15. **The sign said "Admitance Prohibited." During the rebellion, no one paid any attention.**

    (1) change *admitance* to *admittance*
    (2) change *prohibited* to *prohibitted*
    (3) change *rebellion* to *rebelion*
    (4) change *attention* to *attenttion*
    (5) no correction is necessary

16. **The magician was all business as he stood before the audience. He picked up the knives and hurled them at his assistant.**

    (1) change *business* to *busyiness*
    (2) change *audience* to *audeince*
    (3) change *knives* to *knifes*
    (4) change *hurled* to *hurlled*
    (5) no correction is necessary

17. **They chose to go skating on an icey cold day. Helen stood quietly on shore as Maria tested the safety of the ice.**

    (1) change *skating* to *skateing*
    (2) change *icey* to *icy*
    (3) change *quietly* to *queitly*
    (4) change *safety* to *safty*
    (5) no correction is necessary

18. **Jon lost consciousness when he saw the aggressive bear. Jon later admitted he was relieved to learn the bear was really another hiker.**

    (1) change *consciousness* to *consciousnness*
    (2) change *aggressive* to *agressive*
    (3) change *admited* to *admitted*
    (4) change *relieved* to *releived*
    (5) no correction is necessary

19. **Rosa actually preferred the new schedule. It was an improvement.**

    (1) change *actually* to *actualy*
    (2) change *preferred* to *prefered*
    (3) change *schedule* to *schdule*
    (4) change *improvement* to *improvment*
    (5) no correction is necessary

20. **The team owner claimmed the drop in attendance was of no significance. Do you have any confidence in what he says?**

    (1) change *claimmed* to *claimed*
    (2) change *attendance* to *attendence*
    (3) change *significance* to *significants*
    (4) change *confidence* to *confidance*
    (5) no correction is necessary

    ANSWERS ARE ON PAGE 266.

This Writing Skills Post-Test will allow you to check your readiness for the GED Writing Skills Test. Fill in your answers on the Post-Test Answer Grid below. Try to answer as many questions as possible. On the actual test, a blank will be counted as wrong, so make a reasonable guess at answers you are unsure of.

After you have completed this Post-Test, turn to the answer key and the evaluation chart on pages 242–244. Use the chart to see whether you are ready to take the actual GED Writing Skills Test. If not, the chart will tell you what areas you need to review further.

1 ① ② ③ ④ ⑤ **15** ① ② ③ ④ ⑤ **29** ① ② ③ ④ ⑤ **43** ① ② ③ ④ ⑤

2 ① ② ③ ④ ⑤ **16** ① ② ③ ④ ⑤ **30** ① ② ③ ④ ⑤ **44** ① ② ③ ④ ⑤

3 ① ② ③ ④ ⑤ **17** ① ② ③ ④ ⑤ **31** ① ② ③ ④ ⑤ **45** ① ② ③ ④ ⑤

4 ① ② ③ ④ ⑤ **18** ① ② ③ ④ ⑤ **32** ① ② ③ ④ ⑤ **46** ① ② ③ ④ ⑤

5 ① ② ③ ④ ⑤ **19** ① ② ③ ④ ⑤ **33** ① ② ③ ④ ⑤ **47** ① ② ③ ④ ⑤

6 ① ② ③ ④ ⑤ **20** ① ② ③ ④ ⑤ **34** ① ② ③ ④ ⑤ **48** ① ② ③ ④ ⑤

7 ① ② ③ ④ ⑤ **21** ① ② ③ ④ ⑤ **35** ① ② ③ ④ ⑤ **49** ① ② ③ ④ ⑤

8 ① ② ③ ④ ⑤ **22** ① ② ③ ④ ⑤ **36** ① ② ③ ④ ⑤ **50** ① ② ③ ④ ⑤

9 ① ② ③ ④ ⑤ **23** ① ② ③ ④ ⑤ **37** ① ② ③ ④ ⑤ **51** ① ② ③ ④ ⑤

10 ① ② ③ ④ ⑤ **24** ① ② ③ ④ ⑤ **38** ① ② ③ ④ ⑤ **52** ① ② ③ ④ ⑤

11 ① ② ③ ④ ⑤ **25** ① ② ③ ④ ⑤ **39** ① ② ③ ④ ⑤ **53** ① ② ③ ④ ⑤

12 ① ② ③ ④ ⑤ **26** ① ② ③ ④ ⑤ **40** ① ② ③ ④ ⑤ **54** ① ② ③ ④ ⑤

13 ① ② ③ ④ ⑤ **27** ① ② ③ ④ ⑤ **41** ① ② ③ ④ ⑤ **55** ① ② ③ ④ ⑤

14 ① ② ③ ④ ⑤ **28** ① ② ③ ④ ⑤ **42** ① ② ③ ④ ⑤

POST-TEST

In each of the following sets of words, there may be a misspelled word. If there is a misspelled word, mark the circle on the answer grid. If there is no misspelled word, choose (5).

1. (1) procede
   (2) exceed
   (3) recede
   (4) supersede
   (5) no error

2. (1) dissimilar
   (2) mispronounce
   (3) unecessary
   (4) immobilized
   (5) no error

3. (1) mystery
   (2) hereditary
   (3) cemetary
   (4) satisfactory
   (5) no error

4. (1) exaggerate
   (2) posession
   (3) dilemma
   (4) necessary
   (5) no error

5. (1) dictionaries
   (2) drugstore
   (3) refered
   (4) scratches
   (5) no error

6. (1) achievement
   (2) leisure
   (3) conceited
   (4) dishonored
   (5) no error

7. (1) reference
   (2) preferred
   (3) occuring
   (4) offered
   (5) no error

8. (1) admirable
   (2) truly
   (3) amusement
   (4) awarness
   (5) no error

The following sentences contain errors in capitalization and punctuation. Choose what correction should be made to each sentence. If you think the sentence is correct, choose (5).

9. **Maya and Tim have'nt yet sent out the invitations to the party they're planning.**

   (1) change *have'nt* to *haven't*
   (2) change *invitations* to *Invitations*
   (3) change *they're* to *theyr'e*
   (4) change the period to an exclamation point
   (5) no correction is necessary

10. **Floyd's Furniture Store sold three chairs, a bookcase, and two couches today but Floyd says business is bad.**

   (1) change *Floyd's Furniture Store* to *Floyd's furniture store*
   (2) remove the comma after *bookcase*
   (3) add a comma before *but*
   (4) change the period to a question mark
   (5) no correction is necessary

11. **The press release said that senator Salazar will, as usual, be in his home district in late summer.**

    (1) change *press release* to *Press Release*
    (2) change *senator* to *Senator*
    (3) remove the commas before and after *as usual*
    (4) change *summer* to *Summer*
    (5) no correction is necessary

12. **The supervisor of the volunteers asked whose responsible for the area east of Chatworth Lane.**

    (1) change *supervisor* to *Supervisor*
    (2) change *whose* to *who's*
    (3) change *east* to *East*
    (4) change *Lane* to *lane*
    (5) no correction is necessary

13. **Curtis's guest list includes the following: his Mother, the Atoles, and three neighbors.**

    (1) change *Curtis's* to *Curtis*
    (2) change the colon to a semicolon
    (3) change *Mother* to *mother*
    (4) change *neighbors* to *neighbors'*
    (5) no correction is necessary

14. **Because we needed to look at some old magazines, we asked if the Hinshaw Library was open on Sundays?**

    (1) remove the comma after *magazines*
    (2) change *Library* to *library*
    (3) change *Sundays* to *sundays*
    (4) change the question mark to a period
    (5) no correction is necessary

15. **I read in the newspaper, that a group of Greek singers will give a concert next Labor Day in Dayton, Ohio.**

    (1) remove the comma after *newspaper*
    (2) change *singers* to *Singers*
    (3) change *Labor Day* to *Labor day*
    (4) remove the comma after *Dayton*
    (5) no correction is necessary

16. **"Are you finished with that baseball book," asked Nancy, "Or are you still reading it?"**

    (1) change *baseball* to *Baseball*
    (2) change the comma after *book* to a question mark
    (3) change *Or* to *or*
    (4) change the question mark to a period
    (5) no correction is necessary

17. **Dr. Sanford's theory is that it is better to deal with a problem than to ignore it; I would rather ignore it.**

    (1) add a comma before *that*
    (2) add a comma after *problem*
    (3) change the semicolon to a colon
    (4) change the period to an exclamation point
    (5) no correction is necessary

The following sentences contain errors in grammar and usage. Choose what correction should be made to each sentence. If you think the sentence is correct, choose (5).

18. **Either William or his wife has took care of Yoko's baby more than I can remember.**

    (1) change *took* to *taken*
    (2) change *Yoko's* to *Yokos'*
    (3) change *more* to *most*
    (4) change *I* to *me*
    (5) no correction is necessary

19. **Patricia felt angrily when she learned that her friend had quit his job.**

    (1) change *angrily* to *angry*
    (2) change *she* to *her*
    (3) change *had quit* to *has quit*
    (4) change *his* to *their*
    (5) no correction is necessary

20. **Those neighbors who don't ever seem to sleep have went on a vacation to Finland.**

    (1) change *Those* to *Them*
    (2) change *who* to *that*
    (3) change *ever* to *never*
    (4) change *went* to *gone*
    (5) no correction is necessary

21. **Mrs. Stanovich, as well as her two sons, never run less than three miles a day.**

    (1) change *sons* to *son*
    (2) change *run* to *runs*
    (3) change *less* to *least*
    (4) change *miles* to *mile*
    (5) no correction is necessary

22. **The rules state that each runner must have their own number and be ready to begin at the starting line at noon.**

    (1) change *state* to *states*
    (2) change *have* to *has*
    (3) change *their* to *his or her*
    (4) change *begin* to *begins*
    (5) no correction is necessary

23. **Last week, not only Maria and also John wrote letters to their town newspaper complaining about poor police protection.**

    (1) change *and* to *but*
    (2) change *wrote* to *had written*
    (3) change *their* to *his or her*
    (4) change *poor* to *more poorer*
    (5) no correction is necessary

24. **In today's paper, there is several articles about community programs that have received much attention.**

    (1) change *today's* to *todays*
    (2) change *is* to *are*
    (3) change *have* to *has*
    (4) change *much* to *most*
    (5) no correction is necessary

25. **The governor feels strongly that solutions to the serious problems in this city must come from we citizens.**

    (1) change *strongly* to *strong*
    (2) change *serious* to *seriously*
    (3) change *this* to *those*
    (4) change *we* to *us*
    (5) no correction is necessary

26. **The efficiency expert who studied plant operations said the engine room should have more workers and fewest machines.**

    (1) change *who* to *which*
    (2) change *studied* to *studies*
    (3) change *more* to *most*
    (4) change *fewest* to *fewer*
    (5) no correction is necessary

27. **Neither Javier nor Craig know how many people have sent in their reservations.**

    (1) change *know* to *knows*
    (2) change *many* to *much*
    (3) change *have sent* to *had sent*
    (4) change *their* to *his or her*
    (5) no correction is necessary

28. **Laura was furious when she realized that she canceled her credit card before she was able to buy Toshio a birthday gift.**

    (1) change *furious* to *most furious*
    (2) change *realized* to *realizes*
    (3) change *canceled* to *had canceled*
    (4) change *was* to *is*
    (5) no correction is necessary

29. **The man whom you introduced me to last night called to ask if I would have dinner with him.**

    (1) change *whom* to *who*
    (2) change *introduced* to *had introduced*
    (3) change *would have* to *will have*
    (4) change *him* to *he*
    (5) no correction is necessary

30. **The manager can see scarcely no reason for my many absences, and she has told me so more often than I can recall.**

    (1) change *scarcely no* to *scarcely any*
    (2) change *my* to *mine*
    (3) change *many* to *much*
    (4) change *more* to *most*
    (5) no correction is necessary

31. **Of all the hairdressers' I have seen in the past five years, Antoinette is the one whom I like the most.**

    (1) change *hairdressers'* to *hairdressers*
    (2) change *past* to *passed*
    (3) change *whom* to *which*
    (4) change *most* to *more*
    (5) no correction is necessary

32. **Having recovered from a bad cold, Kathy now feels good enough to take care of her neighbor's child again.**

    (1) change *bad* to *badly*
    (2) change *feels* to *felt*
    (3) change *good* to *well*
    (4) change *her* to *hers*
    (5) no correction is necessary

33. **Bring those extra bags over to Kerry and I; we will be able to put them to good use.**

    (1) change *those* to *them*
    (2) change *I* to *me*
    (3) change *we* to *us*
    (4) change *good* to *gooder*
    (5) no correction is necessary

34. **Mrs. Armillo asked us who repairs our TV set, because hers often has wavy lines across the screen.**

    (1) change *asked* to *ask*
    (2) change *who* to *what*
    (3) change *hers* to *her's*
    (4) change *has* to *has got*
    (5) no correction is necessary

35. **After Todd will announce his plans to marry Danita, he bought a ring and planned a big engagement party.**

    (1) change *will announce* to *had announced*
    (2) change *bought* to *buys*
    (3) change *planned* to *had planned*
    (4) change *big* to *biggest*
    (5) no correction is necessary

36. **It bothers Ivan that he works more slowly than her although no one has complained to him about his performance.**

    (1) change *more slowly* to *most slowly*
    (2) change *her* to *she*
    (3) change *has complained* to *had complained*
    (4) change *him* to *he*
    (5) no correction is necessary

Choose the best correction for the underlined part of each sentence. If you think the original is best, choose (5).

37. **The belief that many experts think is true is that California will suffer another earthquake within ten years.**

    (1) It is true
    (2) Many experts believe
    (3) It is the distinguished opinion of these experts
    (4) The belief held by a majority of experts is beyond a doubt
    (5) The belief that many experts think is true is

38. **Since the rain had been so heavy. City officials advised people to beware of flash floods.**

    (1) heavy; city
    (2) heavy city
    (3) heavy; therefore; city
    (4) heavy, city
    (5) heavy. City

39. **Although she pretends to be mature, Anna still loves to read trashy novels, singing on a crowded bus, and to play hide-and-seek.**

    (1) novels, to sing on a crowded bus, and
    (2) novels; singing on a crowded bus; and
    (3) novels, she sings on a crowded bus, and
    (4) novels although singing on a crowded bus and
    (5) novels, singing on a crowded bus, and

40. **Postal authorities suggest stopping mail delivery <u>if going to be away</u> from home for a long period of time.**

    (1) if they are going to be away
    (2) because going to be away
    (3) if you are going to be away
    (4) when going to be away
    (5) if going to be away

41. **Officials say <u>the cost of the price of train fares</u> will increase next month.**

    (1) the cost of train fares
    (2) the cost of the train
    (3) trains
    (4) fares
    (5) the cost of the price of train fares

42. **<u>The soldier shared his dinner in full uniform with a stranger and her baby.</u>**

    (1) The soldier shared his dinner with a stranger and her baby in full uniform.
    (2) The soldier shared his dinner; in full uniform with a stranger and her baby.
    (3) The soldier in full uniform shared his dinner with a stranger and her baby.
    (4) The soldier shared his dinner in full uniform, with a stranger and her baby.
    (5) The soldier shared his dinner in full uniform with a stranger and her baby.

43. **The company is pleased with this year's <u>profits, instead they</u> are giving employees a bonus.**

    (1) profits; instead, they
    (2) profits; in fact, they
    (3) profits, in fact, they
    (4) profits; however, they
    (5) profits, instead they

44. **<u>Because we had planned to fly out today,</u> our flight was canceled.**

    (1) Because we had planned to fly out today
    (2) As a result, we had planned to fly out today,
    (3) Although we had planned to fly out today
    (4) Although we had planned to fly out today,
    (5) Because we had planned to fly out today,

45. **The apartment manager and the building owner both signed the letter; <u>he said that he was</u> sorry that the rent had to be raised.**

    (1) he said that they were
    (2) they said that he was
    (3) the letter said that the owner was
    (4) the letter said that he was
    (5) he said that he was

46. Christy was surprised when she heard that she had earned more money <u>than anyone</u> in her department.

(1) than anyone else
(2) from anyone else
(3) from any person
(4) than any person
(5) than anyone

47. <u>Blowing at more than 70 miles per hour, the wind knocked down trees and forced people to stay indoors.</u>

(1) The wind knocked down trees blowing at more than 70 miles per hour and forced people to stay indoors.
(2) The wind knocked down trees and forced people to stay indoors blowing at more than 70 miles per hour.
(3) The wind knocked down trees and forced people, blowing at more than 70 miles per hour, to stay indoors.
(4) After having been blown more than 70 miles per hour, the wind knocked down trees and forced people to stay indoors.
(5) Blowing at more than 70 miles per hour, the wind knocked down trees and forced people to stay indoors.

48. The lady arrived carrying an old basket, some dried <u>flowers, and with four</u> handmade dolls.

(1) flowers and with four
(2) flowers, and four
(3) flowers; and, four
(4) flowers; furthermore, with four
(5) flowers, and with four

49. <u>The lovely tablecloth was created by the work of an enormously talented son of mine.</u>

(1) My talented son designed the lovely tablecloth.
(2) The lovely tablecloth was designed by my talented son.
(3) My son made a tablecloth.
(4) A tablecloth was made by my son.
(5) The lovely tablecloth was created by the work of an enormously talented son of mine.

50. All afternoon the players <u>warmed up, practiced, and prepared</u> for the big game.

(1) warmed up; practiced; and prepared
(2) warmed up, were practicing, and were preparing
(3) were warming up, practiced, and got ready
(4) were warming up, practicing, and to get prepared
(5) warmed up, practiced, and prepared

Choose the best answer to each question.

51. **What kind of organization pattern would you use to tell about events that happened as a result of another event?**

    (1) time order
    (2) comparison-and-contrast organization
    (3) cause-and-effect organization
    (4) simple listing
    (5) whole-to-whole order

52. **What kind of organization pattern would you use to tell how to replace a leaking faucet?**

    (1) time order
    (2) comparison-and-contrast organization
    (3) cause-and-effect organization
    (4) simple listing
    (5) point-by-point order

53. **What kind of organization pattern would you use to explain why taking the train to work is better than driving a car?**

    (1) time order
    (2) comparison-and-contrast organization
    (3) cause-and-effect organization
    (4) simple listing
    (5) sequence-of-events order

54. **During which step in the writing process should you pay most attention to organizing your ideas?**

    (1) prewriting
    (2) drafting
    (3) revising
    (4) editing
    (5) publishing

55. **During which step in the writing process should you pay most attention to getting your ideas down on paper?**

    (1) prewriting
    (2) drafting
    (3) revising
    (4) editing
    (5) publishing

ANSWERS ARE ON PAGE 242.

POST-TEST

Post-Test Answer Key

1. (1) There are three words that end with *ceed: proceed, exceed,* and *succeed.*

2. (3) The prefix is *un* and the root word is *necessary.* Don't change either part when adding a prefix to a root word.

3. (3) There are different ways to spell the *ery* sound. You'll have to memorize words with this sound.

4. (2) No rule applies to this word; it must be memorized.

5. (3) Double the consonant if the suffix begins with a vowel.

6. (5)

7. (3) Double the final consonant of a root word when adding a suffix if the stress is on the last syllable of the root word, the root word ends with a single consonant other than *w* or *x,* and the suffix begins with a vowel.

8. (4) The two word parts are *aware* and *ness.* Do not change the spelling of either part.

9. (1) The apostrophe in a contraction replaces the missing letter. In this case, the missing letter is *o* in *not.*

10. (3) This is a compound sentence joined by the conjunction *but.* A comma is needed before the conjunction.

11. (2) *Senator* is used as the specific title of a person, so it should be capitalized.

12. (2) *Whose* shows possession. Here, the meaning is *who is,* so the word should be the contraction *who's.*

13. (3) In this sentence, *mother* is not used in direct address or as a substitute for a name, so it should not be capitalized.

14. (4) The sentence states that a question was asked, but is not itself a question, so no question mark is needed.

15. (1) Because the final clause is essential to the meaning of the sentence, it should not be preceded by a comma.

16. (3) The quotations are one sentence separated by *asked Nancy.* The beginning of the second part should not be capitalized.

17. (5)

18. (1) *Taken* is the correct past participle of the verb *take.* The helping verb *has* tells you to use the past participle.

19. (1) In this sentence, *felt* is used as a linking verb. Therefore, the adjective *angry* should be used.

20. (4) The helping verb *have* tells you to use the past participle. The correct past participle of the verb *go* is *gone.*

21. (2) The subject of the verb *runs* is the singular noun *Mrs. Stanovich.* The phrase *as well as her two sons* is not part of the subject. It adds extra information.

22. (3) *Their* is a plural possessive pronoun. In the original sentence it incorrectly refers to the singular noun *each runner.*

23. (1) *Not only* and *but also* go together to form a conjunction. *Not only . . . and also* is always incorrect.

24. (2) *There* cannot be the subject of a sentence. The subject is the plural noun *articles,* which requires a plural verb.

25. (4) *We* is a subject pronoun. Here the pronoun is the object of the preposition *from,* so an object pronoun is needed.

26. (4) Two things are being compared, so the *er* form of the adjective is needed, not the *est* form.

27. (1) With *neither . . . nor,* make the verb agree with the part of the subject closest to it. Here it should agree with *Craig.*

28. (3) The canceling of the credit card occurred in the past before another past action, so it should be described in the past perfect tense.

29. (5)

30. (1) *Scarcely no* is a double negative and is never correct.

31. (1) *Hairdressers'* is a plural, possessive noun. Here, the word should be plural but not possessive. Therefore, no apostrophe is used.

32. (3) Always use *well,* not *good,* when referring to health.

33. (2) In this sentence, the subject pronoun *I* is used incorrectly. An object pronoun, *me,* is needed to follow the preposition *to.*

34. (5)

35. (1) The announcement is a completed action that occurred in the past before another action completed in the past. Therefore, it should be described using the past perfect tense.

36. (2) When you see *than,* mentally complete the phrase. Here the understood phrase is *than she does. She* is the subject of the verb *does.*

37. (2) The underlined words are repetitive. Choice (2) gets rid of the repetition without losing any meaning.

38. (4) *Since the rain had been so heavy* is not a complete thought. Choice (4) changes it into an introductory dependent clause.

39. (1) In the original sentence, the phrase *singing on a crowded bus* is not parallel with the other items in the series.

40. (3) The verb *going* in the original sentence does not have a subject. Choice (3) adds a subject.

41. (1) *The cost of* and *the price of* say the same thing. Choice (1) gets rid of the repetition without changing the meaning.

42. (3) Since the modifying phrase *in full uniform* modifies *soldier,* it should be placed as close as possible to *soldier.*

43. (2) *Instead* suggests a contradiction of ideas. *In fact* suggests the development of the same idea. The conjunctive adverb should be preceded by a semicolon and followed by a comma.

44. (4) The conjunction *because* suggests that the flight was canceled because they had planned to fly that day, which is not correct. *Although* correctly expresses a contrast between the two parts of the sentence. The first part of the sentence is an introductory dependent clause, which is followed by a comma.

45. (3) You cannot tell to whom *he* refers in the original sentence. It is also unclear whether or not someone actually spoke about being sorry. Choice (3) makes it clear that *he* refers to the owner and that the apology was stated in the letter.

46. (1) Christy is in her department, so she earned more than anyone *else.*

47. (5)

48. (2) The series in the original sentence is not parallel. Choice (2) gets rid of the preposition *with* so the items will all have the same structure.

49. (1) The original sentence is wordy. Choice (1) keeps the meaning and makes it more direct.

50. (5)

51. (3) Cause-and-effect order tells how one event is related to another.

52. (1) Time order tells about events in the order they happen. If someone is to know how to change a faucet, he or she needs to know what to do first, next, and so on.

53. (2) Use comparison-and-contrast order to show how two things are alike and different.

54. (1) The two main purposes of prewriting are to find ideas and to organize them.

55. (2) During drafting, you put your ideas on paper. During later stages of the writing process, the grammar, spelling, word choices, and other parts of the writing can be improved.

Post-Test Evaluation Chart

On the following chart, circle the number of any item you got wrong. Next to each item, you will see the pages you can review for items that gave you trouble. Pay special attention to skills on which you missed half or more of the questions.

Skill Area	Item Number	Review Pages
Nouns	5, 31	24–31
Pronouns	22, 25, 33, 36	32–47
Verbs	18, 20, 28, 35	50–72
Subject/Verb Agreement	21, 24, 27	73–86
Modifiers	19, 26, 30, 32	89–114
Sentence Combining	23, 38, 43, 44	119–130
Sentence Problems	39, 40, 42, 45, 48	131–146
Style and Diction	37, 41, 46, 49	147–154
Capitalization	11, 13, 16	162–171
Punctuation	9, 10, 12, 14, 15	172–185
Writing and Organization	51, 52, 53, 54, 55	189–224
Spelling	1, 2, 3, 4, 7, 8	225–239
No Error	6, 17, 29, 34, 47, 50	

Answer Key

CHAPTER 1

EXERCISE 1
Page 14

1. Sarah <u>attacked the chores with enthusiasm</u>.
2. <u>Indira's kitchen table</u> <u>was piled high with fresh baked bread</u>.
3. <u>High winds</u> <u>broke several windows in downtown buildings</u>.
4. <u>Jevon</u> <u>raced to the telephone in the living room</u>.
5. <u>Mr. Zimmer's house</u> <u>will always be our least favorite</u>.
6. <u>The woman</u> <u>answered the police officer carefully</u>.
7. <u>The doctor</u> <u>arrived at the office at 8:30 A.M.</u>
8. <u>Soon Young</u> <u>prepared a huge meal for her parents</u>.
9. <u>The forest fire</u> <u>had destroyed several thousand acres of trees</u>.
10. <u>Marek's grandmother</u> <u>will turn eighty-five this year</u>.

EXERCISE 2
Page 16

1. The team's <u>manager</u> <u>should win</u> an award.
2. <u>Everyone</u> <u>has ordered</u> something different to eat.
3. <u>Andrej</u> <u>fumbled</u> in his pockets for his car keys.
4. <u>Mr. and Mrs. Hastings</u> <u>complained</u> about the defective lamp.
5. The run-down old <u>bus</u> <u>pulled</u> slowly out of the station.
6. The previous <u>receptionist</u> <u>had been</u> more efficient.
7. <u>Pak Ku</u> <u>runs</u> during his lunch hour every Friday.
8. <u>Christy and Jan</u> <u>became</u> good friends last year.
9. My brother's <u>apartment</u> <u>was burglarized</u> recently.
10. The brilliant <u>writer</u> of this movie <u>has created</u> a suspenseful plot.

EXERCISE 3
Page 18

1. **S** *You* is the subject, and *need three stamps on that envelope* is the predicate. It expresses a complete thought.
2. **S** In this complete thought, the subject is *Sam and his nephew* and the predicate is *fished all morning.*
3. **F** *That thick magazine on the sofa* is a subject, and *fell* is a verb, but this group of words is a fragment. Because the word *when* introduces the sentence, a complete thought is not expressed.
4. **S** This complete thought is made up of the subject *this room* and the predicate *is a mess!*
5. **S** The subject *my client in Dallas* and the predicate *will send you the brochure* make up a complete thought.
6. **F** This group of words lacks a subject to tell you what *rattled and chugged all the way down the street.*
7. **F** This group of words could be a subject. There is no predicate to complete the thought to tell you something about the neighbor and friend.
8. **S** The subject *the workers* and the predicate *walked carefully through the construction area* express a complete thought.
9. **F** *You and your co-workers* is a subject and *are dependable* is a predicate. However, this group of words does not express a complete thought and therefore is a fragment.
10. **S** This group of words expresses a complete thought. *Florentia* is the subject and *received dozens of cards during her illness* is the predicate.

PRE-GED PRACTICE
PARTS OF A SIMPLE SENTENCE
Page 19

1. **(1)** The original is a fragment because it lacks a predicate. What about people with homes on the Mississippi floodplain? Choice (1) adds the verb *fled* to tell what people with homes on the floodplain did.
2. **(4)** The original is a fragment because it lacks a subject. What migrated south from Canada? Choice (4) adds the subject *wolves* to tell what migrated.
3. **(2)** The original is a fragment because it does not express a complete thought. What was a result of the air pollution being so bad? Choice (2) provides a subject, *laws,* and a predicate, *were enacted.*
4. **(3)** The original is a fragment because it lacks a predicate. What about the car's electric window? Choice (3) adds the verb *became jammed.*
5. **(5)** The original is a complete sentence.
6. **(5)** The original is a complete sentence.

EXERCISE 4
Page 22

1. Brian slowly got to his feet _._
2. Be careful with that lawn mower _!_
3. Smoke is coming from the roof _!_
4. Where did you find the book _?_
5. Stop jumping on the bed _!_
6. The train stops here every fifteen minutes _._
7. Have you seen my radio _?_
8. Ms. Luna left here at least twenty minutes ago _._
9. What a nightmare _!_
10. Can you see her yet _?_

PRE-GED PRACTICE
TYPES OF SENTENCES
Page 23

1. **(2)** This is a statement of surprise or urgency.
2. **(2)** This is a question.
3. **(5)**
4. **(2)** This is a statement. No excitement or surprise is shown.
5. **(4)** This is an exclamation of surprise. Use an exclamation point.

EXERCISE 5
Page 24

1. <u>Hilda</u> says she will return <u>home</u> soon.
2. <u>Construction</u> of the <u>Alaska Highway</u> began in <u>1942</u>.
3. <u>Superman's</u> first home was <u>Cleveland, Ohio</u>.
4. Two high school <u>students</u> created the <u>superhero</u>.
5. Last <u>year</u>, <u>Louis Padilla</u> moved into an <u>apartment</u> in <u>Washington, D.C.</u>
6. <u>Padilla</u> visits the <u>Smithsonian Institution</u> at least twice a <u>month</u>.
7. The <u>Smithsonian</u> is <u>one</u> of the largest <u>museums</u> in the <u>world</u>.
8. <u>Toni</u> is learning to paint <u>landscapes</u>.
9. <u>William</u> wants to capture the <u>beauty</u> of the <u>outdoors</u> in his <u>photos</u>.
10. <u>Shawna</u> captured the <u>colors</u> of the morning <u>sky</u> in her <u>painting</u>.

EXERCISE 6
Page 26

1. The two <u>friends</u> traveled to <u>Chicago</u> and visited the <u>Sears Tower</u>.
2. The <u>salesperson</u> showed <u>Melanie</u> two navy blue <u>jackets</u>.
3. While riding on the <u>train</u>, an <u>attorney</u> read the <u>St. Louis Post-Dispatch</u>.
4. The <u>nurse</u> took <u>James's</u> <u>blood pressure</u> and recorded the <u>numbers</u> on the <u>form</u>.
5. My <u>friend</u> <u>Yolanda</u> wants to learn more about <u>Hinduism</u>.
6. Many <u>people</u> go out of <u>town</u> over <u>Memorial Day</u> <u>weekend</u>.
7. A <u>chef</u> from <u>France</u> prepared a fabulous <u>meal</u> for the special <u>event</u>.
8. Let's go into the <u>museum</u> when <u>Mark</u> and <u>Noriko</u> arrive.
9. There are <u>geysers</u> and <u>hot springs</u> in <u>Yellowstone National Park</u>.
10. Can <u>Jeremy</u> stop at the <u>Quikstop Food Store</u> and pick up some <u>milk</u>?

EXERCISE 7
Page 28

1. **(3)** scratches
2. **(5)** correct
3. **(3)** sheep
4. **(4)** lives
5. **(2)** spies
6. **(5)** correct
7. **(2)** trout
8. **(4)** skies
9. **(3)** dishes
10. **(1)** handkerchiefs

EXERCISE 8
Page 30

1. **country's**   This is a possessive noun. The problem belongs to the country.
2. **women's**   *Women* is a plural noun that does not end in *s.* To make this plural show possession, add an apostrophe and an *s.*
3. **C**
4. **Millers**   The verb *have* shows possession, so no apostrophe is needed on the noun *Millers.*
5. **C**
6. **books**   This noun is plural, not possessive. No apostrophe is needed.
7. **C**
8. **boss's**   This noun is possessive. A singular noun ending in an *s* is made possessive in the same way as other singular nouns, by adding an apostrophe and an *s.*
9. **years'**   The noun is plural and possessive. Add an *s* to form the plural and an apostrophe to show possession.
10. **citizens'**   This noun is plural and possessive. Add an *s* to form the plural and an apostrophe to show possession.

PRE-GED PRACTICE
NOUNS
Page 31

1. **(4)** There is only one team. Form the possessive by adding an apostrophe and an *s.*
2. **(1)** Nouns ending in *ch* are made plural by adding *es.*
3. **(2)** *Mysteries* is plural but it is not showing possession. Drop the apostrophe.

4. **(1)** Words ending in *x* are made plural by adding an *es.*
5. **(2)** The sun possesses the rays. Form the possessive by adding an apostrophe and an *s.*

EXERCISE 9
Page 34

1. **they**   Since *they* and the *guests* refer to the same people, you should use a subject pronoun.
2. **He and I**   A subject pronoun is needed because *he* is part of the compound subject *he and I.*
3. **Julian and she**   The subject pronoun is used because *Julian and she* is giving more information about the subject, *my two friends.*
4. **they**   *They* is the subject of the verb *sell.*
5. **you and he**   The subject pronoun *he* is correct because it is part of the compound subject of the verb *should plan.*
6. **we**   *We* is the subject of the verb *learned.*
7. **I**   The verb of being, *is,* is the clue that a subject pronoun is correct.
8. **the Porters and we**   A subject pronoun must be used here because *we* is a part of the subject of the verb *have lived.*
9. **he**   The verb of being, *is,* is the clue that a subject pronoun is correct.
10. **I**   *I* is the correct pronoun here because *you* and *I* are part of the subject of the verb *love.*
11. **We**   *We* is the subject of the verb *invited.*
12. **I**   A subject pronoun is needed because *I* is part of the compound subject *Tina and I.*
13. **He**   *He* is the subject of the verb *asks.*
14. **she**   A subject pronoun is needed because *she* is part of the compound subject *William and she.*
15. **You and he**   The subject pronoun *you and he* is used because it is part of the compound subject of the verb *did.*

EXERCISE 10
Page 36

1. her   *Her* is the correct possessive pronoun to show the "ownership" of knowledge.

2. yours   No noun follows the possessive pronoun, so *yours* is correct. *Yours* never has an apostrophe.

3. hers   No apostrophe is used with possessive pronouns.

4. your   *Your* always goes with a noun. Possessive pronouns never have apostrophes.

5. its   No apostrophe is used with a possessive pronoun. Remember that *it's* stands for "it is" or "it has."

6. ours   No noun follows the possessive pronoun, so *ours* is correct. No apostrophe is used with a possessive pronoun.

7. their   *Their* is the correct possessive form because it is followed by a noun, *break time*. *They* is a subject pronoun and cannot be used to show possession.

8. mine   No noun follows the possessive pronoun, so *mine* is correct. *Mine* never has an *s* at the end.

EXERCISE 11
Page 38

1. us   The pronoun is the object of the preposition *between*.

2. her   *Her* is the object of *followed*. Therefore an object pronoun is needed.

3. him and me   When two or more pronouns are used and one of them is *me*, *me* always comes last.

4. her   The pronoun *her* tells more about *customers*, which is the object of the verb *asked*. An object pronoun is needed.

5. them   The object pronoun *them* is correct because it answers the question, "For whom is there enough food?"

6. you and me   These pronouns are objects of the preposition *between*.

EXERCISE 12
Page 39

1. ourselves   The correct form of the pronoun is *ourselves*. There is no singular form.

2. she   The subject pronoun is used because *she* is part of the compound subject. Remember that *herself* is not a subject pronoun.

3. I   Use a subject pronoun for the subject of the sentence.

4. themselves   The correct plural reflexive is *themselves*. *Theirselves* and *themself* are never correct.

5. me   An object pronoun is correct because *me* answers the question, "To whom did the bus driver give transfers?" Remember that *myself* and other reflexive pronouns can never substitute for subject or object pronouns.

6. themselves   This is the correct plural reflexive pronoun.

7. herself   This is the correct singular reflexive pronoun.

8. I   Use a subject pronoun for the subject of a sentence.

EXERCISE 13
Page 42

1. he   Remember that with pronouns after *than* or *as*, you should mentally complete the sentence. Amy is just as qualified as he (is).

2. him   The correct pronoun is the object pronoun *him* because it answers the question, "Whom did we voters want?"

3. me   The object pronoun *me* should be used instead of the reflexive *myself*. *Me* is the object of the preposition *between*.

4. us   Since *parents* is the object of *give*, the object pronoun *us* is correct.

5. she   The subject pronoun *she* is correct here. I work harder than *she* (works).

6. my   Since a noun follows the possessive pronoun, *my* is the correct pronoun.

7. whomever The object pronoun *whomever* is correct. It is the object of the verb *brings*.

8. Whoever Since you can substitute the subject pronoun *he, Whoever* is the correct pronoun.

9. Ted and I When a noun and the pronoun *I* are connected by *and* or *or*, the pronoun *I* should go last; *Ted and I* continued laughing.

10. Correct

11. I The correct pronoun is the subject pronoun *I* instead of the object pronoun *me*.

12. she The subject pronoun *she* is correct and not the reflexive pronoun *herself*.

EXERCISE 14
Page 49

1. <u>Someone</u> who forgets to pay (*his or her, their*) electric bill may end up without lights.
2. The <u>woman</u> (*which, <u>who</u>*) plays the guitar used to play the drums.
3. When <u>Sergeant York</u> tells you to do something, he expects (*him, <u>you</u>*) to do it.
4. The <u>players</u> must have (*his, <u>their</u>*) luggage on the bus by noon.
5. Although I've had (*<u>it</u>, them*) for years, this <u>pair of scissors</u> is still sharp.
6. If <u>people</u> want to succeed in life, (*you, <u>they</u>*) must make plans now.
7. The <u>group</u> was sure (*<u>its</u>, their*) performance would win first prize.
8. The <u>couple</u> giving this party have plenty of food for (*his, <u>their</u>*) guests.
9. Frank put his <u>sunglasses</u> back in (*its, <u>their</u>*) case.
10. <u>Everything</u> must be put in (*<u>its</u>, their*) place before the guests arrive.
11. <u>Everyone</u> should sign (*<u>his or her</u>, their*) name to register for the workshop.
12. <u>Politics</u> has (*<u>its</u>, their*) own set of rules.
13. The <u>pair of pants</u> is missing (*<u>its</u>, their*) belt.
14. The <u>tailor</u> (*which, <u>who</u>*) altered the suit did an excellent job.
15. <u>Neither Velma nor I</u> can work any harder no matter how hard (*I, <u>we</u>*) try.

PRONOUN REVIEW
Page 50

1. **that** <u>They</u> have a cat <u>who</u> is always following <u>them</u>.
2. **We** <u>Us</u> lazy people cannot understand why <u>he</u> works whenever the boss asks <u>him</u>.
3. **Correct** <u>She</u> and <u>I</u> told <u>him</u> that everyone should be well organized.
4. **Correct** <u>He</u> told <u>us</u> that having three jobs made <u>his</u> life hectic.
5. **Correct** Just between <u>you</u> and <u>me</u>, Sam, <u>whoever</u> gets this job deserves it.
6. **he** If <u>you</u> were <u>him</u>, would <u>you</u> want this job?
7. **Correct** When the United States elects <u>its</u> president, <u>your</u> vote will count as much as <u>his</u>.
8. **myself** <u>I</u> left <u>me</u> a note so <u>I</u> would remember to write a letter.
9. **whoever** <u>He</u> will give a ticket to <u>whomever</u> wants to attend <u>his</u> comedy act.
10. **us** On <u>their</u> vacation, <u>they</u> sent greetings to <u>we</u> slaves still on the job.
11. **he** That baby boy showed <u>his</u> parents that <u>it</u> was ready to walk by pulling <u>himself</u> up to a standing position.
12. **who** <u>She</u> proved <u>herself</u> the person <u>which</u> is most qualified.
13. **Correct** <u>They</u> claimed the money <u>that</u> was on the table was <u>theirs</u>.
14. **I** Do <u>you</u> remember when <u>you</u> and <u>me</u> visited Washington, D.C.?

PRE-GED PRACTICE
PRONOUNS
Page 51

1. **(4)** *It's* is a contraction meaning "it is." Here the possessive pronoun *its* is needed.
2. **(2)** The subject pronoun is used because *Alicia and she* is giving additional information about the subject, *Our friends*.
3. **(2)** The object pronoun *me* is correct because it follows the preposition *between*.
4. **(1)** When *me* and another pronoun are linked, *me* always goes last.
5. **(2)** Reflexive pronouns should not be used as subject pronouns.

1. **(3)** The original is a fragment. What happened while the ducks rose? Choice (3) creates a complete sentence.
2. **(2)** The original sentence is a fragment because it lacks a subject. *Himself* is the correct reflexive pronoun. *Hisself* is always incorrect.
3. **(2)** The original is a fragment because it does not express a complete thought. What was a result of his cold being so bad? Choice (2) provides a subject, *John,* and a predicate, *stayed home.*
4. **(2)** The original is a fragment. What happened during that night? The correction adds a simple subject, *fire,* and a predicate, *kept them warm.* (In the original sentence, *fire* is an object.)
5. **(4)** *Bookshelf* is made plural by changing the *f* to a *v* and adding *es.*
6. **(4)** *Had jumped over a wall* is a sentence fragment. Adding *They* to the fragment makes it a complete sentence.
7. **(4)** *It's* means "it is." The possessive form is *its.*
8. **(4)** The pronoun follows a preposition, *with,* and therefore should be an object pronoun.
9. **(5)**
10. **(3)** *Who* is correct because it is a subject pronoun that goes with the verb *ate. Whom* is an object pronoun.
11. **(4)** This is an exclamatory sentence and needs an exclamation point.
12. **(4)** Part of this sentence is understood. Read it as "he shoots better than she shoots." *She* is correct because it is a subject pronoun; *her* is an object pronoun.
13. **(1)** *Us* is an object pronoun. Here the pronoun is the subject, so use *we.*
14. **(2)** *Somebody* is always a singular pronoun. *Their* is plural. Somebody can be either male or female so use *his or her.*
15. **(4)** The pronoun refers to people who are being spoken about. The pronoun should be in the third person. *You* is in the second person and refers to a person spoken to.

CHAPTER 2

EXERCISE 1
Page 56

1. Sidney <u>will come</u> to the table when you <u>call</u> him.
2. <u>Did</u> you <u>know</u> that my aunt <u>is</u> still <u>living</u> in Canada?
3. When Veronica <u>saw</u> the picture, she <u>was</u> very <u>surprised</u>.
4. I <u>will be coming</u> to work early tomorrow.
5. When <u>can</u> you <u>come</u> and <u>see</u> my new baby?
6. During our vacation, we <u>camped</u>, <u>cooked</u>, and <u>hiked</u>.
7. By the time we <u>finish</u> this job, our boss <u>will have found</u> two new ones for us.
8. <u>Can</u> you <u>describe</u> the man who just <u>left</u> the store?
9. Although her manager rarely <u>talked</u> to her, Akiko <u>liked</u> her job.
10. Cindy <u>has</u> never <u>missed</u> an Elvis Presley movie that <u>has been shown</u> on television.
11. I <u>will</u> always <u>be grateful</u> that I <u>got</u> a good education.
12. Since she <u>came</u> back from her trip, Raisa <u>has felt</u> much more relaxed.
13. After <u>cleaning</u>, <u>shopping</u>, and <u>fixing</u> lunch, Ida <u>took</u> a nap.
14. What <u>will</u> it <u>be like</u> when we <u>arrive</u> in Florida, I <u>wonder</u>?

EXERCISE 2
Page 60

1. **called** — The word *yesterday* is the clue that the past tense is necessary.
2. **waits** — Use the present form here. It shows an action that is performed regularly. *Every afternoon* is the clue. Remember to add an *s* to the base form for a singular noun, *Stan.*
3. **moved** — The past tense of *move* is correct. The phrase *two years ago* tells you that the action occurred in the past.
4. **enjoy** — The present form is used for something that is always true.

5. will work *Next week* tells you that this verb should be in the future tense.

6. happened *Last night* is the clue that the past tense is correct.

7. demand *Today* shows that this sentence
or is making a statement that is
are true now. Therefore, use the
demanding present tense.

8. will end *Next Tuesday* tells you this sentence is in the future tense.

9. owns The word *now* tells you that the verb should be in the present tense. The subject *Simon* requires an *s* at the end of the base form of the verb.

10. talked *Yesterday* tells you that this happened in the past.

11. will *Tomorrow* tells you that the
discuss verb is in the future tense.

12. parked *Last Sunday* tells you that the verb is in the past tense.

13. answered *Last night* tells you that the verb is in the past tense.

14. will smile *Next Tuesday* tells you that the verb is in the future tense.

EXERCISE 3
Page 65

1. Brian __threw__ out the runner trying to steal second.
2. The rain __freezes__ as soon as it hits the pavement.
3. Please __give__ this package to the delivery person.
4. I didn't know what she __meant__ when she said she was skating home.
5. Jill's babies __clung__ tightly to her when she left home.
6. Dilip is the most helpful real estate agent I have ever __dealt__ with.
7. Anna __spun__ another tale of horror for her young listeners as they squirmed in their seats.
8. If you value your life, don't __set__ that can on the table.
9. Ms. Tso __swore__ to the judge that she was telling the truth.
10. Javier leaped excitedly as he __pulled__ the huge fish ashore.
11. The bread dough had __risen__ after a few hours.
12. I __dreamed, dreamt__ I won the lottery.
13. He __burst__ the balloon with a pin.
14. Mr. Hanley was __bitten__ by a dog.

EXERCISE 4
Page 68

1. will begin *In two more weeks* tells you that this will happen in the future.

2. tastes The present tense is used for action that is always true.

3. had taken The past perfect form is correct because this action took place before another action.

4. rushed The simple past is correct since the action was completed yesterday. The past perfect would not be correct, because there is no other past action in the sentence.

5. will have The future perfect shows that the
swum action will be completed before another future action. By the time they finish the race, the action of swimming twenty miles will be completed.

6. had asked The past perfect is correct because Charles had asked the questions before another action in the past *(noticed)*.

7. will *Tomorrow* is a clue that this will
prepare take place in the future.

8. have said The present perfect is used to show an action that has taken place in the past and is still true in the present.

9. has Use the present perfect tense
memorized because the action took place in the past and has continued into the present.

10. had tried First Curtis tried to reach the landlady; then he reached her. The past perfect shows the action that took place first.

11. will have The future perfect tense shows
earned what will happen by a certain time in the future.

12. has ridden The present perfect tense shows that an event was done in the past and is still being done.

13. invented The action was completed in the past.

14. will have The future perfect tells you that
finished by a certain time in the future the action will be completed.

15. stole Use the past tense because the action was completed in the past. The past perfect cannot be used here because the two actions occurred at the same time.

EXERCISE 5
Page 70

1. complete
2. were
3. be drunk
4. were
5. pay

EXERCISE 6
Page 71

1. My grandparents deserted the old house.
2. Large shrubs hide the doorway.
3. A fallen tree has jammed the cellar door shut.
4. The wrecking crew will tear down the old house.

EXERCISE 7
Page 72

1. rode, rides
2. measured, had grown
3. had bought, discovered
4. do, are
5. began, was
6. will finish or will have finished, begins
7. was sweating, returned
8. opens or opened, had been hidden
9. hope, gave
10. shook, talked
11. planted, sees
12. realized, will take
13. dropped, will be ready

PRE-GED PRACTICE
VERBS AND VERB TENSES
Page 74

1. (3) John was at the track before Javier crossed the finish line. Therefore, the verb *arrives* should be in the past perfect tense to show that this action occurred before the action of Javier's crossing the finish line.
2. (3) When a verb ends with a *ch,* an *es* instead of an *s* is added to form the simple present tense. *Reachs* should be *reaches.*
3. (2) *Swear* is an irregular verb. The correct spelling of the past participle is *sworn,* not *swore.*

4. (3) Yolanda wrote the address at the same time she stood at the station. Therefore the verbs should be in the same tense. The simple past tense *wrote* agrees with the simple past tense *stood.*
5. (1) This statement takes the subjunctive form of the verb *connect* because it expresses urgency. The subjunctive form does not add an *s* to the base form.
6. (1) The verb *exchange* should be in the past tense, so the correct form is *exchanged.*
7. (3) *After Ted gets his tax return* is in the future tense, so the verb *bought* should be changed to *will buy.*
8. (4) The verb *thank* should be in the past tense, so the correct form is *thanked.*

EXERCISE 8
Page 76

1. Those <u>fish</u> (*has,* <u>*have*</u>) been jumping since we got here.
2. Our <u>problem</u> (<u>*is,*</u> *are*) getting the tent set up.
3. <u>We</u> in the jury (<u>*believe,*</u> *believes*) he is innocent.
4. My <u>muscles</u> (<u>*ache,*</u> *aches*) from all the exercise.
5. The security <u>guards</u> at the store (<u>*want,*</u> *wants*) a raise.
6. <u>I</u> (<u>*come,*</u> *comes*) to all my son's baseball games.
7. The <u>order</u> (*include,* <u>*includes*</u>) paper clips, folders, and tape.
8. My favorite <u>movie</u> (<u>*is,*</u> *are*) The African Queen.
9. Michiko's three huge <u>dogs</u> (<u>*pull,*</u> *pulls*) her helplessly along.
10. The <u>price</u> of those strawberries (*seem,* <u>*seems*</u>) awfully high.

EXERCISE 9
Page 78

1. were — *Mr. Fletcher and Ms. Ortega takes were* because it is a compound subject joined by *and.*
2. appears — This compound subject is joined by *not only . . . but also.* The verb should agree with the subject closest to it.
3. is — The simple subject is *lunch,* so use the singular verb form. Remember that the verb does not always agree with words following the linking verb.

4. plans   The form of the verb ending in *s* is correct because the verb must agree with the part of the subject closest to it, *Jeffrey.*

5. have   With compound subjects joined by *either . . . or,* the verb must agree with the subject closest to it, *they.*

6. gives   Both parts of the compound subject, *my roommate and best friend,* refer to the same person. Use the singular verb form.

7. are   The subject takes a plural verb because the parts are linked by *and.*

8. complain   The plural verb form is correct because the parts of the compound subject are linked by *and.*

9. figures   Since the compound subject is connected with *either . . . or,* the verb agrees with the part closest to it.

10. want   Since the compound subject is connected with *not only . . . but also,* the verb agrees with the noun closest to it, *actors.*

EXERCISE 10
Page 81

1. stand   The simple subject is *pumps,* so use the plural verb *stand.* If you have trouble finding the simple subject, put the sentence in normal subject-verb order: *Two old water pumps stand at the end of the dusty road.*

2. are   Since *there* is neither a noun nor a pronoun, it cannot be the subject. The subject is *clues,* so the correct verb is *are.*

3. waits   Don't be confused by the interrupting phrase. *Antonio* is the subject of the sentence.

4. stretches   The word order of this sentence is inverted. Change it to *A yellow ribbon stretches across the front windows* and you will see that the subject is *ribbon.*

5. walk   Ignore the interrupting phrase, *including my collie.* The subject is *dogs.*

6. are   In this inverted sentence, *boots* is the subject and takes a plural verb.

7. grow   Ignore the interrupting prepositional phrase, *in the west. Clouds* is the subject and takes a plural verb.

8. do   *Plants* is the subject of the verb and agrees with the verb *do.*

EXERCISE 11
Page 83

1. argue   The pronoun *who* refers to *people,* not *Molly.* Since *people* is plural, the plural verb *argue* is correct.

2. are   The pronoun *that* refers to *orders* and is in agreement with the verb *are.*

3. need   The pronoun *that* refers to the plural noun *lamps.*

4. seems   The pronoun *which* refers to the simple subject *solution,* which takes a singular verb.

5. require   The pronoun *that* refers to *books,* a plural noun, which takes the plural verb *require.*

6. appears   *Appears* agrees with the singular noun *plan.*

7. love   The pronoun *who* refers to the plural noun *children.*

8. are   The pronoun *that* refers to the plural noun *computers.*

9. drive   The pronoun *that* refers to the plural noun *inventions.*

10. like   The pronoun *who* refers to the plural noun *brothers.*

11. appears   The pronoun *which* refers to the singular noun *answer.*

12. plans   The pronoun *who* refers to the singular subject *Mr. Lee,* which takes a singular verb.

13. arrive   The pronoun *who* refers to the plural subject *nephews.*

EXERCISE 12
Page 87

1. **makes** *News* is one of the nouns that is always singular. Use it with a singular verb.

2. **rides** *Everyone* is a pronoun that is always singular. Always use a singular verb.

3. **is** *Most* is a pronoun that refers to the singular noun *meat.* Use the verb form that goes with *he, she, it.*

4. **gives** The simple subject of the verb is *pair,* a singular noun.

5. **looks** *Everything* is a pronoun that is always singular. Choose the singular verb.

6. **laughs** *Crowd* is a collective noun. Here it is used to refer to the whole group acting as a unit. Use a singular verb.

7. **are** When *none* is used to refer to a plural noun, as in *voters* in this sentence, use the plural verb.

8. **serve** *Few* stands for a plural noun, *restaurants.* Use the plural verb.

9. **was** *Each* is always singular. Use a singular verb.

10. **are** *Half* can be plural or singular. Here it refers to the plural noun *people.* Use a plural verb.

11. **appeals** *Neither* is always singular, so a singular verb is correct.

12. **belong** *Scissors* is plural and takes a plural verb.

PRE-GED PRACTICE
SUBJECT-VERB AGREEMENT
Page 88

1. **(3)** *Neither* is a pronoun that is always singular. It takes the singular verb *wants.*

2. **(1)** Ignore the interrupter. The verb *jump* should be changed to its singular form to agree with *Rosa.*

3. **(4)** With *neither . . . nor* the verb agrees with the subject closest to it. Here the closest subject is the singular noun *Andrew.*

4. **(5)** All the verbs are in agreement with their subjects.

5. **(1)** *Tickets* is the subject of the sentence, not *here.* The verb must agree with this plural noun.

6. **(1)** The choir is acting as a group, so the singular verb *performs* is required.

7. **(1)** Ignore the interrupter. The singular verb *runs* agrees with the singular noun *Jed.*

8. **(3)** The committee is acting as a group, so the singular verb *decides* is required.

9. **(5)** All the verbs are in agreement with their subjects.

10. **(4)** The verb *is raising* agrees with the verb *is speeding.* Both verbs are in the present tense.

PRE-GED PRACTICE
VERBS
Page 90

1. **(5)** *Is exhausted* agrees with *guard. Who* is a pronoun that refers to *guard,* so it agrees with the singular verb *walks.*

2. **(3)** The subject of *are welcome* is the pronoun *everyone. Everyone* is a singular pronoun so the verb should be *is.*

3. **(3)** Use the past perfect tense to show that the action of the sale ending happened before Lucinda got to the store.

4. **(4)** Ignore the clause *whom I do not know* and check the agreement between *somebody* and *send. Somebody* is a singular pronoun and takes a singular verb.

5. **(2)** The word *while* tells you that both events happened at the same time. Therefore the verbs should show the same tense.

6. **(2)** *Athletics* is a singular noun, even though it ends with an *s.*

7. **(2)** This sentence is in the subjunctive mood because it creates a sense of urgency. Therefore the verb *sign* should not end with an *s.*

8. **(2)** Ignore the interrupting phrase *along with her two little brothers.* The verb agrees with the simple subject *Sonia,* which is singular.

9. **(4)** The correct past participle of *hide* is *hidden.*

10. **(1)** When words like *not only . . . but also* split up a compound noun, the verb agrees with the noun closest to it. Here the plural noun *cousins* is closest to the verb, so the verb should be plural.

11. **(2)** Two events occur at different times. *Martha and Kim had never seen such a large roller coaster* occurs before the amusement park opened. Therefore the amusement park opening occurs in the simple past tense to show that it occurred in the past but more recently than the other event.

12. **(5)** *Jury* is a collective noun. Here it is plural and takes a plural verb, *do look,* because each member looks unhappy. All the action occurs in the present, so the use of present tense verbs is correct.

13. **(3)** *Eyeglasses* is a plural noun, so it takes the plural verb form *slip.*

14. (1) This sentence expresses a statement contrary to fact, so the verb should be in the subjunctive form. *Were* is always used in the subjunctive mood, not *was.*

15. (1) The first sentence is inverted. Its subject is *carpenters,* which is plural.

CHAPTER 3

EXERCISE 1
Page 94

1. arrived   *Late* tells you when the mail arrived.
    adverb   *Arrived* is a verb, so *late* must be an adverb.

2. dinner   *Late* tells you what kind of dinner.
    adjective   *Dinner* is a noun, so *late* must be an adjective.

3. children   *Four* tells you how many children.
    adjective   *Children* is a noun, so *four* must be an adjective.

4. moved   *Quickly* tells you how Andrew moved.
    adverb   *Moved* is a verb, so *quickly* must be an adverb.

5. amazing   *Absolutely* tells you to what extent the discovery is amazing.
    adverb   *Amazing* is an adjective, so *absolutely* must be an adverb.

6. chair   *This* tells you which chair.
    adjective   *Chair* is a noun, so *this* must be an adjective.

7. played   *Quietly* tells you how the music was played.
    adverb   *Played* is a verb, so *quietly* must be an adverb.

8. lives   *Here* tells you where Juan lives.
    adverb   *Lives* is a verb, so *here* must be an adverb.

9. noise   *Awful* tells you what kind of noise.
    adjective   *Noise* is a noun, so *awful* must be an adjective.

10. car   *New* tells you what kind of car.
    adjective   *Car* is a noun, so *new* must be an adjective.

EXERCISE 2
Page 96

1. rapidly   The modifier tells how the runners moved. *Moved* is a verb, so use the adverb *rapidly.*

2. easily   The modifier tells how the calculator should work. *Work* is a verb, so use the adverb form.

3. C

4. C

5. extreme   *Extremely* is an adverb. Here it is used incorrectly to modify a noun, *heat.*

6. C

7. carefully   The modifier tells how the contract is being read, so the adverb form is needed.

8. badly   The modifier tells to what extent Molly hurt her foot, so an adverb is needed.

9. straight   *Straight* does not change form when used as an adverb.

10. practical   *Practically* is an adverb. It is being used incorrectly to modify a noun, *solution.*

11. C

12. crookedly   The modifier tells how the old road winds, so the adverb form is needed.

EXERCISE 3
Page 99

1. dark   *Became* is a linking verb. *Dark* describes the noun *sky,* so the modifier should be an adjective.

2. sad   *Sad* modifies *you,* a pronoun. Use the adjective.

3. quickly   The modifier describes the verb *crosses,* telling how Gopal crosses the street. An adverb is correct.

4. carefully   *Carefully* tells how the doctor felt Ann's arm. It modifies the verb *felt.* An adverb is correct.

5. sure   *Seems* is used as a linking verb. The adjective *sure* is used to modify *Kyle.*

6. happy   The modifier *happy* modifies the pronoun *I,* so use the adjective.

7. brightly   *Brightly* tells how the sun shone. It modifies the verb, so use an adverb.

8. evilly   *Evilly* tells how the robber looked at the woman. *Evilly* modifies the verb *looked,* so use an adverb.

9. C

10. loud   *Loud* modifies the noun *volume,* so use an adjective.

11. slowly   *Slowly* tells how the weeds covered the backyard, so use an adverb.

12. C

ANSWER KEY

EXERCISE 4
Page 103

1. least Use *least* because more than two things are being compared. The phrase *we have ever had* is the clue that more than two things are being compared.

2. cheapest The comparison is between more than two things—rice, beans, and macaroni and all other items bought. Since *cheap* is a one-syllable adjective, use *est* instead of adding *most.*

3. faster Two people are being compared. Use *er* instead of *more* because *fast* is a short word.

4. best *Good* is an irregular adjective. Use *best* because more than two people are being compared. *Among all those people* tells you many are being compared.

5. neater Two people are being compared, so the *er* ending is used for the adverb.

6. fewer Duties at two jobs are being compared, so the *er* ending is used for this adjective.

7. more serious Two people are being compared. *Serious* is a longer word, so add *more* to the adjective.

8. most exciting *Of all the movies* is your clue that more than two things are being compared. Add *most* to the adjective because it is a long word.

9. more Two activities are being compared. *Much* is an irregular adverb. *More* is used to compare two things.

10. happier Two time periods are being compared—before and now. Change the *y* to *i* and add *er* to make the correct form of happy.

11. best Use *best* because two or more markets are being compared.

12. farther Use *farther* because two distances are being compared.

13. worse Use *worse* because Anita's allergies are being compared for two seasons.

EXERCISE 5
Page 106

1. those *Them* is a pronoun, so it can't be used to modify a noun. *Those* is an adjective.

2. had scarcely *Scarcely* is a negative. *Hadn't scarcely* is a double negative.

3. bitter *Taste* is used as a linking verb in this sentence. *Coffee* is the subject, and it cannot perform the action of tasting. Use an adjective here.

4. well The modifier refers to health, so use *well,* not *good.*

carefully *Carefully* describes how the person nursed Jon. Since it modifies the verb *nursed,* use the adverb.

5. an *An* comes before *easier,* which begins with a vowel sound.

would hardly *Hardly* is a negative word, so *wouldn't hardly* is a double negative.

6. an *An* comes before *ideal,* which begins with a vowel sound.

7. any *Don't* is a negative. Use *any* to avoid the double negative *don't no.*

8. these *Carrots* is a plural noun, and *this* only modifies singular nouns.

that *Cup* is a singular noun. *Those* can only modify plural nouns.

9. anything *Isn't* is a negative, so using *nothing* would create a double negative.

better Two things are being compared here, how I feel when I'm sick and how I feel when I'm not sick.

10. a *A* comes before *variety,* which begins with a consonant.

11. anywhere *Couldn't find* is a negative, so using *nowhere* would create a double negative.

12. this *Basket* is a singular noun, and *this* modifies a singular noun.

13. can hardly *Hardly* is a negative word, so *can't* would create a double negative.

14. an *An* comes before *unusual,* which begins with a vowel.

more angular *More angular* is used because two houses are being compared.

PRE-GED PRACTICE
ADJECTIVES AND ADVERBS
Page 108

1. **(2)** *Careful* is an adjective that is being used to modify the verb *drove.* The adverb is *carefully.*

2. **(2)** Use *well* to refer to health after a linking verb.

3. **(1)** *Didn't hardly* is a double negative.

4. **(4)** The manager is trying to hire the best people of all those available. The comparison, therefore, is between more than two.

5. (1) *Wise* is a short adjective. When comparing two things, add *er.* Never use both *more* and *er.*

6. (2) When comparing two things, add *er,* not *est.*

EXERCISE 6
Page 110

1. bus	Louis saw the bus <u>at the corner</u>.
2. Shen	<u>Opening the door</u>, Shen looked outside.
3. smell	The smell <u>of barbecued chicken</u> made Shawna hungry.
4. runner	The exhausted runner, <u>seeing the finish line</u>, speeded up.
5. was sorry	Julie was sorry <u>to lose the watch</u>.
6. books	Jacobo left his books <u>at the library</u>.
7. Ms. Atole	<u>Already soaked to the skin</u>, Ms. Atole opened her umbrella.
8. soon	The basketball game ended soon <u>after sunset</u>.
9. left	The police car left the crime scene <u>in a hurry</u>.
10. manager	<u>Hoping to get more customers</u>, the store manager lowered prices.
11. Mr. Henshaw	<u>Locking the door</u>, Mr. Henshaw left his apartment.
12. Mrs. Cosmos	Mrs. Cosmos crossed <u>over the Canadian border</u>.
13. Lenore	<u>Sitting between her parents</u>, Lenore felt quite happy.

EXERCISE 7
Page 112

1. Yuri Gagarin, the first human in space, was from the Soviet Union.

2. Ham, a chimpanzee, tested the U.S. spacecraft.

3. Alan Shepard, the first American in space, wrote a book about the early space program.

4. Shepard went into space in Redstone 3, a tiny spacecraft.

5. Shepard, an astronaut and test pilot, went to the moon many years later.

PRE-GED PRACTICE
PHRASES AS MODIFIERS
Page 113

1. (2) A comma should be used to separate an introductory phrase from the rest of the sentence.

2. (4) Except for introductory phrases and renaming phrases, phrases are not usually separated from the sentence by commas.

3. (3) *An expensive Japanese model* is a renaming phrase that describes *camera.* It should be set off with commas.

4. (5)

5. (1) An introductory phrase should be set off by commas.

6. (1) An introductory phrase should be set off by a comma.

PRE-GED PRACTICE
MODIFIERS
Page 114

1. (4) *The produce manager* is a renaming phrase. It should be set off with commas.

2. (1) *Can't hardly* is a double negative.

3. (1) *Them* is always a pronoun. It can never be used to point out a noun.

4. (3) *An* is used before all words that begin with a vowel sound. *A* is used before words that begin with consonant sounds.

5. (3) *That* means "there," so saying *that there* is like saying *there there.*

6. (1) *Looks* is sometimes a linking verb, sometimes an action verb. Here it is used as an action verb. *Nervously* modifies *looks,* telling how the letter carrier looks at the dog. *Nervous* is an adjective.

7. (5)

8. (3) *I have ever read* is the clue that this book is being compared to all other books. *Funnier* compares only two things.

9. (1) *Well,* not *good,* is used to describe health.

10. (2) The word *more* should not be used with an adjective to which the ending *er* has been added.

11. (4) *Easy* is an adjective. In this sentence it is used to modify the verb *sets,* so an adverb, *easily,* is needed.

12. (3) *Isn't scarcely* is a double negative.

13. (4) *Loud* modifies *screamed,* so the adverb, *loudly,* is needed.

14. (4) *Those* means "there," so *there* is not needed in this sentence.

15. (5)

CHAPTER 4

EXERCISE 1
Page 122

1. Ann starts a new job soon, but she hasn't told her present boss.
2. There are no good movies in town; however, a great rock band is playing.
3. My house is a mess; I never seem to have time to clean it.
4. The plane's wings were covered with ice; as a result, the departure was delayed.
5. The waitress took their orders; then she brought us coffee.
6. I could never keep the washer fixed, so I bought a new one.
7. Snow is forecast for tonight; therefore, we should change our travel plans.
8. Max is a good dog; nevertheless, I don't want him eating off the table.
9. The storm knocked out electric power; lights are off all over town.
10. Janet has a sore arm, yet she's going bowling.
11. The game was really exciting because Hugo made the winning touchdown.
12. We had a good time at the party, but it ended too soon.
13. I went swimming at the beach yesterday; the water was just the right temperature.
14. Alexandra got the flu yesterday, so she will stay home for a few days.

EXERCISE 2
Page 127

Answers will vary. Sample answers are given.
1. <u>After</u> backing into the garage, Sarah loaded the truck.
2. Melissa wants to go to the zoo <u>unless</u> the weather turns cold.
3. <u>Although</u> the bats still live in Carlsbad Caverns, there are fewer of them today.
4. Gilbert cast his fly <u>where</u> he had seen the large trout jump.
5. <u>As soon as</u> I tell Santwana I saw a spider, she will want to leave.
6. Few salmon live in the Snake River <u>because</u> huge dams were built.
7. <u>Even though</u> that dog has a loud bark, it's really very friendly.
8. <u>Since</u> you said the dog was friendly, I tried to pet him.

9. <u>In spite of the fact that</u> you were bitten, I still say the dog is gentle.
10. The doctor says the wound will heal <u>if</u> I keep it bandaged.

PRE-GED PRACTICE
COMBINING IDEAS IN SENTENCES
Page 128

1. (3) *As soon as* shows a time relationship between the two clauses.
2. (1) *When* is the best choice. It says these two events—reading a magazine and eating lunch—happen at the same time. *As soon as* also relates the ideas by time, but it doesn't make sense.
3. (4) *Unless* shows a condition: one thing will happen if something else happens.
4. (5) *But* shows a contrast between the two ideas.
5. (2) *While* shows a time relationship between the ideas.
6. (3) *Whether* doesn't make sense. *Because* introduces the reason why he won't pay his bills on time.

EXERCISE 3
Page 131

Revised sentences may vary. Sample sentences are given.
1. before going on vacation
   Your bill should be paid before you go on vacation.
2. Hanging on the wall
   Javier stared at the beautiful painting hanging on the wall.
3. After cooking breakfast
   After breakfast was cooked, the fan had to be turned on to remove the smoke.
4. C
5. beginning on Bradford Road
   The parade, beginning on Bradford Road, included clowns, elephants, and bands.
6. When only six years old
   When I was only six years old, my grandfather gave me his big pocket watch.
7. Being very proud
   Being very proud, Emily showed her new ring to everyone.
8. Driving down the highway
   Driving down the highway, Pam saw beautiful scenery.

EXERCISE 4
Page 133

1. I spent the weekend working in the yard, painting a door, and fixing a cracked window.
2. Regina said she would fix supper, set the table, and clean up afterwards.
3. That candidate has energy, concern, and honesty.
4. When Taro got home, he found mud on the carpet, scratch marks on the furniture, and broken glass on the floor.
5. Jo likes people who are kind, thoughtful, funny, and rich.
6. The fortune teller told Ana that she would get a great job, that she would lose money, and that she should move to another city.
7. The workshop explained how to speak clearly, how to appear skilled, and how to ask for a raise.

EXERCISE 5
Page 137

1. **would get**   Because *was convinced* is in the past tense, *will get* is not correct.
2. **C**
3. **had locked**   *Realized* is in the past tense. Use the past perfect tense to show that Leroy locked himself out before that.
4. **could**   *Asked* is in the past tense. *Can* cannot be used with the past tense, so *could* is the correct helping verb.
5. **C**
6. **will**   *Says* is in the present tense, and you know that Sonia has not yet washed her hair. Use the future tense *will* in place of *would*.
7. **would**   *Said* is in the past tense. *Would* is correct with the past tense.
8. **would not have panicked**   The conditional clause is in the past perfect, so you use *would have* with the past participle, *panicked*.
9. **C**
10. **will**   *Will* is used with the future tense, since the interview is happening tomorrow.

EXERCISE 6
Page 140

Some sentences can be corrected in other ways. Samples are given.

1. C
2. Cathy told her son to clean his closet and his room since they were a mess.
3. The walls were bright green and the carpeting pale gray, a combination which we thought was really ugly.
4. People are actually living without heat and hot water, and this situation must be taken care of.
5. The police department says that crime is increasing in our city.
6. Rosa told her daughter that Rosa would be able to drive in two weeks.
7. Thaddeus helped Steve move into Steve's new house.
8. Beth talked with the girls as they walked down the street.
9. The police officer said I have to buy a parking sticker for my windshield or I will have to pay a fine.
10. The person fixing my car said that the tire should be taken care of immediately.
11. Angel gave Noreen the coat that Noreen had left at Angel's house.

PRE-GED PRACTICE
SENTENCE PROBLEMS
Page 142

1. **(2)** The snow occurred during the night, before the sun came out. The simple past shows that the sun came out after the snow fell.
2. **(3)** This is a conditional statement. The first verb, *had gone,* is the past perfect. It must be paired with a verb such as *would have* along with a past participle.
3. **(3)** In the original sentence, the pronoun *she* could refer to either Isabel or her daughter.
4. **(4)** The story is not about a house on the train. *On the train* is a misplaced modifier.
5. **(5)**
6. **(4)** Changing the second use of the pronoun *he* to *Barry* makes the sentence much clearer.

ANSWER KEY

EXERCISE 7
Page 146

There are other ways to revise each sentence. Sample revisions are given below.

1. The temperature should get to eighty degrees.
2. I often forget people's names.
3. The first step is to list the necessary ingredients.
4. I don't write letters because I never have enough time.
5. He said the new salespersons were ready to go into the field for further training.

EXERCISE 8
Page 149

1. Lee told us that Greg *should have* received the package by now.
2. *As* I've said before, most people never know how well off they are.
3. Sarah divided the remaining cake *among* the three of us.
4. Roland will certainly be *at* the game Saturday to see his brother play.
5. When she got up *off* the ground the last time, Yoko gave up skating.
6. Tina's got a sharper memory than any *other* person I know.
7. That movie was so realistic, I *couldn't help screaming.*
8. Sid said he knew someone who would *try to* get us some tickets.
9. Do you think you could borrow a snow shovel *from* the neighbor?
10. C
11. Garlan *could have* gotten home sooner if his train hadn't been late.

PRE-GED PRACTICE
SENTENCE STRUCTURE
Page 152

1. **(4)** *Would of* is incorrect diction. *Would have* is correct. Choice (2) is also incorrect because *different from* is correct. No punctuation is needed.
2. **(2)** The original sentence has incorrect verb sequence. All the action occurs in the past. *Has discovered* is the present perfect tense, showing that an action is continuing.
3. **(3)** The original sentence lacks parallel structure.

4. **(1)** The original sentence is a run-on sentence. Choice (1) turns one of the clauses into a dependent clause. Since it is an introductory clause, it must be followed by a comma.
5. **(3)** *Even though* is a conjunction showing contrast. Here the writer is telling why the Caribbean is considered tropical.
6. **(2)** The original sentence leaves it unclear whether the dog belongs to John or to his brother.
7. **(1)** The original sentence has two repetitive ideas: *the future time before us* and *world leaders around the globe.*
8. **(1)** *If* says that if the first idea is true, then the second will be true too, which doesn't make sense. *Unless* shows that if you do one thing, then the other won't happen, which does make sense.
9. **(2)** The original sentence says Cheryl's serve is faster than a tennis player.
10. **(4)** The original sentence contains a misplaced modifier. It says the auto dealership was on sale.
11. **(2)** *Like* is incorrectly used with a subject-verb combination: *Mr. Murry said.*
12. **(5)** The original is correct.
13. **(3)** The sentence contains an *if* clause with *were,* so the correct form for the main clause is *would* plus the base form *be.* Choice (4) is incorrect because it does not use a comma after the dependent clause.
14. **(4)** The original sentence has nonparallel structure. The first two items are nouns, the third was the *ing* form of a verb.
15. **(2)** The modifying phrase should be as close as possible to the word it modifies.
16. **(3)** *At last* and *finally* are repetitive. Also, the sentence is wordy because it is in the passive voice.
17. **(1)** The transition word *Because* explains why Ted and Sonia left the country.
18. **(3)** Use *between,* not *among,* when referring to two people or things.
19. **(3)** The original sentence contains two nonparallel elements.
20. **(2)** This sentence has two problems. First, *both . . . and also* is repetitive and incorrect. Second, the phrases joined by the conjunction are not parallel. *Dramatic* is an adjective and *it inspired* is a subject-verb combination.

CHAPTER 5

EXERCISE 1
Page 160

1. east	Do not capitalize *north, south, east, west* or other directions when used to tell a general direction.
2. President	Here *President* is used as a title for a specific person.
3. English	*English* is an adjective formed from the proper noun *England,* which names a particular place.
4. high-fat	The term *high-fat* is a general term for a kind of diet.
5. Southeast	*Southeast High School* is the specific name of a particular high school.
6. program	The sentence does not give the specific name of the program. The word *program* is only a general noun.
7. Langston Hughes	*Langston Hughes* is the name of a specific person.
8. North Carolina	*North Carolina* is the name of a specific place.

PRE-GED PRACTICE
WHEN TO CAPITALIZE
Page 161

1. **(2)** Names of specific places are capitalized. *Los Angeles* is the specific name for a city.
2. **(2)** *Rivers* is a general name. It would only be capitalized if it were part of the name of a specific river, such as the *Kennebec River.*
3. **(5)**
4. **(5)**
5. **(2)** This could be any baseball game, so *baseball* should not be capitalized.

EXERCISE 2
Page 164

1. weekly	Since *weekly* states a general time, not a specific one, it is not capitalized.
2. unless	This complete quotation is divided by words telling who the speaker is. *Unless* introduces a clause. It is not a complete sentence by itself and should not be capitalized.
3. ACLU	Capitalize abbreviations that stand for specific organizations.
4. Sr.	Capitalize abbreviations.
5. Biology 340	*Biology 340* is the name of a specific course. It should be capitalized.
6. Children's Aid Society	The names of specific organizations should be capitalized.

PRE-GED PRACTICE
OTHER CAPITALIZATION RULES
Page 165

1. **(4)** *Physical fitness* is a topic, not the specific title of a book.
2. **(5)**
3. **(4)** The names of government organizations are always capitalized.
4. **(2)** *Northwest* is used as a direction rather than as the name of a specific place or region.
5. **(2)** The title *senator* is not used in place of a specific name in this sentence. Therefore, the title should not be capitalized.

EXERCISE 3
Page 168

1. Mrs _._ Rachet completed the annual report _._
2. Look out for that bus _!_
3. Her address is 321 Lake St _._
4. Did he pick the winning lottery number _?_
5. "Did he already spend all the money _?_" Georgia asked _._
6. As the ladder slipped, Lynn screamed, "Help _!_"
7. "Who was that masked man _?_" the salesperson asked _._
8. My uncle named his new business the Rivets Co _._
9. "Quick _!_" shouted the police officer over his car radio _._
10. As she looked all over the house, Maxine moaned, "Where are my keys _?_"
11. Wow_!_ That's the best news I've ever heard _!_
12. "What's your favorite movie _?_" Derrick asked _._

ANSWER KEY

PRE-GED PRACTICE
USING END PUNCTUATION
Page 169

1. **(3)** The quotation is a question, so it should end with a question mark inside the quotation marks.
2. **(4)** The quotation is an exclamation; the exclamation point goes inside the quotation marks. No other end punctuation is needed.
3. **(2)** This sentence is a simple statement, not a question. It only states that Mercedes had a question. It should end with a period.
4. **(5)**
5. **(3)** The entire sentence is a question, but the quotation by itself is not. Therefore, the question mark should go outside the quotation marks.

EXERCISE 4
Page 175

1. When Akiko came by the office ⌞,⌟ she fixed the copy machine. Set off dependent clauses with a comma when they begin a sentence.
2. The little boy asked ⌞,⌟ "How can I get home from here?" Use commas to separate quotations from the rest of the sentence.
3. On January 3, the Bombers will play at Johnson Field, Omaha ⌞,⌟ Nebraska. Separate city from state with a comma.
4. It was ⌞,⌟ in fact ⌞,⌟ the best cheesecake she had ever had. Interrupters such as *in fact* should be set off from the rest of the sentence with commas.
5. Jim picked up the trash can ⌞,⌟ and a rat came flying out. Use a comma before the conjunction linking clauses in a compound sentence.
6. Why don't you wear your yellow sweater ⌞,⌟ Tomás? Use commas to set off the name of a person addressed in a sentence.
7. This exercise program is easy for me; moreover ⌞,⌟ I have lost ten pounds. When compound sentences are joined by a conjunctive adverb, place a comma after the adverb.

8. Yolanda ⌞,⌟ the woman who got me this job ⌞,⌟ has now quit. Set off renaming phrases with commas.
9. Mr. Chung hurriedly left his house after getting the telephone call. When a nonrestrictive dependent clause comes at the end of a sentence, do not use a comma to set it off.
10. "Gina will pick you up in an hour ⌞,⌟ " the woman replied. Use a comma to separate a quotation from the rest of the sentence.

EXERCISE 5
Page 178

1. Teresa really wanted to go to Mexico ⌞;⌟ nevertheless ⌞,⌟ she agreed to spend her vacation at the lake.
2. At the supermarket, we ran into our old neighbors ⌞,⌟ the Okaras ⌞,⌟ who lived next door ⌞;⌟ Jill and Sean ⌞,⌟ the ones who gave noisy parties ⌞;⌟ and Marianne ⌞,⌟ our babysitter.
3. Keisha cried, " He forgot my birthday ⌞;⌟ / ⌞,⌟ then he went to a hockey game ⌞.⌟ "
4. Paulo wished he could remember everything ⌞;⌟ however ⌞,⌟ he was already forgetting the details.
5. He gave these reasons for moving ⌞:⌟ a bigger yard ⌞,⌟ more bedrooms ⌞,⌟ lower taxes ⌞,⌟ and a better school district.
6. It is now 7 ⌞:⌟ 00 and Stan just got here ⌞;⌟ nevertheless ⌞,⌟ we're still going to the game.
7. Jan yelled to her brother, " Who's going to feed the dog? "
8. Dear Madam ⌞:⌟
   I bought a SlimMachine because I wanted to lose weight ⌞.⌟ It broke the first day I used it ⌞.⌟ Please refund my money ⌞.⌟
   Sincerely ⌞,⌟
   John Arocha
9. We're looking for a new car ⌞;⌟ the one we have is worn out.
10. I want a job downtown ⌞,⌟ not one out in the suburbs.

Page 180

1. **(3)** Only the quotation is a question, so the question mark should be inside the quotation marks. Only one end punctuation mark is needed.
2. **(3)** *It's* is a contraction meaning "it is." In this sentence, the possessive *its* is needed.
3. **(5)**
4. **(1)** Use a colon when a complete thought is used to introduce a list.
5. **(1)** Use a semicolon to join independent clauses in a compound sentence when a conjunction is not used.
6. **(3)** *In fact* is used as an interrupting phrase. It should be set off with commas.
7. **(3)** The two parts of this quotation make one complete sentence. *Will* should not be capitalized because it continues the sentence.
8. **(5)**
9. **(2)** *Uncle* is not used here to replace a name, so it should not be capitalized.
10. **(3)** Use an apostrophe to show that the *o* in *not* is the missing letter in this contraction.
11. **(4)** *French* is a word taken from the specific name of a country.
12. **(4)** Here the quotation itself is a question. The question mark belongs inside the quotation marks.
13. **(1)** Seasons should not be capitalized.
14. **(5)**
15. **(4)** *Doctors* refers to a general group of people. It is not used as a title for specific people.
16. **(1)** A comma should not be used to separate the month from the date.
17. **(2)** A dependent clause that comes at the end of a sentence is not set off with a comma.
18. **(3)** One complete thought in this sentence is *I suppose that all your work was worthwhile.* No comma is needed.
19. **(1)** A complete thought introduces a list in this sentence. A colon is needed.
20. **(2)** *Funds* is used as a plural here. No apostrophe is needed.
21. **(4)** The quotation is an exclamation. The exclamation point should go inside the quotation marks.
22. **(1)** *Junior college* is not the name of a specific place.
23. **(3)** *They're* is a contraction meaning "they are." Here *their* is needed to show possession of the breakfast.
24. **(4)** The writer is not asking a question but is telling about the mother asking a question.
25. **(1)** *As a result* is a conjunctive adverb connecting two main clauses. It should have a semicolon before it.

CHAPTER 6

EXERCISE 1
Page 188

1. The answer is given.
2. 5
   2
   1
   4
   3
3. 2
   5
   4
   1
   3
4. 3
   5
   1
   2
   4

EXERCISE 2
Page 191

1. **(2)** The fact that electric cars are not practical is not a cause of air pollution.
2. **(4)** The fact that every big city in America now has more homeless people on the streets is not a cause of homelessness.

ANSWER KEY

EXERCISE 3
Page 192

Here are some possible causes for violent crime:
- violence on TV may make people more violent
- broken homes cause stress on children and adults, which often results in violence
- drug abuse
- abused children often become violent adults

Here are some possible effects of violent crime:
- people feel unsafe
- people feel more vulnerable
- need for more jails
- need for stricter laws against violence to deter criminals

Here are some possible causes for lack of basic educational skills:
- failure of schools to educate all students
- language problems experienced by immigrants
- lack of family support for education
- learning problems are often unrecognized or go untreated

Here are some possible effects of the lack of basic educational skills:
- fewer jobs available to unskilled workers
- less pay for unskilled workers
- poorer quality of life
- often caught in a poverty or welfare cycle

EXERCISE 4
Page 195

Answers will vary. Possible answers will be similar to the following:
Care: Cats have to be fed and cared for daily.
Behavior: Cats are very independent; may or may not like people or other cats; and are sometimes lazy.

PRE-GED PRACTICE
PATTERNS OF ORGANIZATION
Page 200

1. **(1)** When describing an event, you will probably want to use time order. It helps the reader know what happened first, next, and so on.

2. **(4)** Comparison and contrast clearly shows how one choice is similar to, better than, or not as good as another choice.
3. **(3)** Cause-and-effect organization helps you show how doing one thing (forgetting to put oil in the engine) caused something else to happen (the engine to become damaged).
4. **(3)** There is probably no special order the examples should be put in. Simple listing gives examples.
5. **(5)** The paragraph tells the story in time order. It begins with the arrival of the first settlers. It ends with the final destruction of wolves in the nineteenth century.
6. **(5)**
7. **(5)** Wolves' disappearing altogether happened after people decided to poison and shoot them.
8. **(4)** Except for one sentence that is out of order, the paragraph first tells the advantages and disadvantages of buying a home. Then it tells the advantages and disadvantages of renting a home.
9. **(3)** The paragraph is organized in a whole-to-whole pattern. Sentence 6 refers to renting, so it should be moved to the discussion of apartments.
10. **(3)** This sentence tells you that if one thing happens (a repair is needed) something else will result (you will have to pay for it).

CHAPTER 7

PRE-GED PRACTICE
PROCESS OF WRITING
Page 215

1. **(1)** Brainstorming is the second step in the prewriting process.
2. **(4)** Editing is the step in which you look for errors in grammar, punctuation, spelling, and capitalization.
3. **(2)** The introduction gives the writer's topic, or main idea.
4. **(4)** You should decide upon your main idea and organize your details during prewriting. Errors can be corrected during editing.

5. (1) One of the main purposes of the introduction is to tell what the main idea is.

6. (2) The conclusion does not give new information. It reminds the reader of the main idea of the writing.

7. (5) Any way in which you share writing with others is a means of publishing it.

8. (3) The main idea is that the cabin was important to everyone in the family.

9. (1) The writer tells about the cabin from the time Grandfather built it until the present.

10. (2) *Then* makes a time connection between paragraphs 2 and 3. It shows that events in paragraph 3 happen after those in 2.

11. (3) The sentence makes more sense if it follows the discussion of what Grandfather called the cabin and what he used it for.

12. (3) *When the logs were cut down* is a dependent clause. When a dependent clause comes at the beginning of a sentence, it should be followed by a comma.

13. (2) This paragraph is about cutting the logs. Telling about the weather is not needed.

14. (1) *Porch* is a more precise word choice than *front part.*

15. (4) Dad received the cabin at the time that Grandfather died. Both actions are in the simple past, so *got* is correct.

CHAPTER 8

EXERCISE 1
Page 220

	Prefix	Root Word	Suffix
1. untruthful	un	truth	ful
2. disappearance	dis	appear	ance
3. quickly		quick	ly
4. prearrangement	pre	arrange	ment
5. misconnection	mis	connect	tion
6. illogical	il	logic	al
7. singer		sing	er
8. replacement	re	place	ment
9. nonexistence	non	exist	ence
10. courageous		courage	ous

1. disapprove The prefix in this word is *dis* and the root word is *approve.* When adding a prefix to a root word, do not change the spelling of either word part.

2. inferring The final consonant, *r,* should be doubled since the stress of the root word *infer* is on the last syllable, its final consonant is preceded by a single vowel, and the suffix *ing* begins with a vowel.

3. valuable The root word is *value,* and the suffix is *able.* Drop the final silent *e* of the root word when adding a suffix beginning with a vowel.

4. encouragement The root word is *encourage,* and the suffix is *ment.* Do not drop the final silent *e* of the root word unless the suffix begins with a vowel.

5. bookkeeper The compound word *bookkeeper* is made up of *book* and *keeper.* Do not change the spelling of either word.

6. C

7. opening The stress of the root word *open* is on the first, not the last, syllable. The final consonant should not be doubled.

8. C

9. definable Drop the silent *e* from the root word *define* before adding the suffix *able.*

10. limited The stress of the root word *limit* is on the first syllable. Do not double the final consonant before adding *ed.*

Page 224

1. **(5)**
2. **(3)** The root word *embarrass* already ends in a double consonant. Do not change the spelling of the root word here.
3. **(3)** When a root word ends in a silent *e*, keep the *e* before adding a suffix beginning with a consonant.
4. **(2)** When a root word ends in a *y* that is preceded by a consonant, keep the *y* if the suffix begins with *i*.
5. **(1)** When a root word ends in a silent *e*, the *e* should be dropped before adding a suffix beginning with a vowel.

EXERCISE 3
Page 226

1. **succeed** *Succeed* is one of the three words that end in *ceed*.
2. **deceit** After the letter *c*, the *e* usually precedes the *i*.
3. **brief** Place the *i* before the *e* when no *c* comes before.
4. **weird** *Weird* is one of the exceptions to the general rule.
5. **precede** *Precede* is not one of the four words spelled with either a *ceed* or a *sede* ending.
6. **neither** *Neither* is an exception to the rule and must simply be remembered.
7. **yield** *Yield* follows the rule of *i* before *e*.

PRE-GED PRACTICE
SPELLING
Page 229

1. **(1)** Drop the final *e* before adding a suffix beginning with a vowel.
2. **(3)** The spelling of neither the prefix *dis* nor the root word *appoint* changes.
3. **(2)** The root word *fail* has two vowels; do not double the final consonant before adding the suffix *ing*.

4. **(4)** This word is an exception to the "*i* before *e*" rule.
5. **(1)** There are three words ending in *ceed*. They are *proceed*, *exceed*, and *succeed*.
6. **(4)** The prefix of this word is *ir*, and *relevant* is the root word. Do not change the spelling of either word part.
7. **(5)**
8. **(3)** *Courageous* is an exception to the rule that calls for dropping the *e* before a suffix beginning with a vowel.
9. **(1)** The plural of the singular noun *half* is formed by changing the *f* to a *v* and adding *es*.
10. **(3)** No spelling rule applies to *cemetery*. You must simply memorize it.
11. **(1)** *Realize* is another word whose spelling must be memorized.
12. **(4)** Remember the rule "*i* before *e* except after *c*."
13. **(2)** The final *y* of the root word *theory* is preceded by a consonant. Change the *y* to an *i* before adding the *es* to form the plural.
14. **(5)**
15. **(1)** The root word *admit* has the stress on the final syllable, it ends with a single consonant, and the suffix to be added begins with a vowel. Therefore, double the final consonant, *t*.
16. **(5)**
17. **(2)** No rule applies here. You'll have to memorize the spelling.
18. **(3)** This word fits the conditions for doubling the final consonant. The stress is on the final syllable, it ends with a single consonant that is preceded by a single vowel, and the suffix begins with a vowel.
19. **(5)**
20. **(1)** The root word *claim* does not fit the rules for doubling the final consonant when adding a suffix beginning with a vowel.

Glossary

A

action verb: a kind of verb that tells what the subject does

active voice: the way a verb is used to show that the subject does the action

adjective: a word that modifies, or describes, a noun or pronoun

adverb: a word that modifies, or describes, a verb, an adjective, or another adverb

B

base form: the most basic form of the verb; the form you begin with when you form all verb tenses

body: the main part of a piece of writing, which gives the details and facts about the main idea

brainstorming: a way of gathering ideas to write about, in which the writer lists every idea that comes to mind

C

cause-and-effect order: a way of organizing information that tells how one event made another event happen

clause: a group of words that contains a subject and a verb

collective noun: a noun that names a group of people or things

command: a type of sentence that gives an order or makes a request

common noun: a type of noun that names a whole group or general type of person, place, thing, or idea

comparison-and-contrast order: a way of organizing information to show how one thing or idea is similar to or different from another thing or idea

complex sentence: a sentence that contains one independent, or main, clause and one or more dependent clauses

compound sentence: a sentence that contains two or more connected independent clauses or simple sentences

compound subject: a subject of a sentence that is made up of more than one word; the words are connected with words like *and* or *or*

compound word: a single word that is made by combining two or more words

conclusion: the last part of a piece of writing, which summarizes or draws the writing to an end

conjunction: a type of word that links parts of a sentence by showing how the parts are related

conjunctive adverb: an adverb or adverb phrase that works like a conjunction

contraction: a word that is made up of two words with some letters left out; an apostrophe is used in place of the missing letters

D

dangling modifier: a modifying phrase or clause that does not modify any word in the sentence

dependent clause: a group of words that contains a subject and a predicate but does not express a complete thought

diction: how words are chosen and used

drafting: the second step in the writing process, in which ideas are written as sentences and put down on paper in an organized way

E

editing: the step in the writing process in which mistakes in grammar, punctuation, capitalization, and spelling are corrected

exclamation: a type of sentence that expresses surprise or excitement; it always ends with an exclamation point

exclamation point: a kind of punctuation that is used to end a sentence that shows strong emotion or excitement

F

fragment: an incomplete sentence

future perfect tense: a verb tense that shows an action that will be completed by a specific time in the future

H

helping verb: a verb that is used with other verb forms to form different tenses

I

idiom: a group of words that have been used together so often and for so long that they have developed a special meaning; an idiom cannot be understood just by knowing the meaning of the individual words

independent clause: a part of a sentence that contains a subject and a predicate and expresses a complete thought

infinitive: a verb form that begins with the word *to*

introduction: the first part of a piece of writing, which tells what the topic and main idea are

introductory clause: a dependent clause that is used to begin a sentence

introductory phrase: a modifying phrase that is used to begin a sentence

inverted sentence: a sentence in which the usual subject-verb order is reversed, so the verb comes before the subject

irregular verb: a verb that does not form its past and past participle forms in a regular, or predictable, way

L

linking verb: a kind of verb that tells what the subject is or that links the subject with a word or words that describe it

M

misplaced modifier: word or phrase whose meaning is unclear because it is out of place

modifier: a word or group of words that describes other words in a sentence; adjectives and adverbs are modifiers

N

noun: a word that names a person, place, thing, or idea

O

object pronoun: a type of pronoun that is the object of a verb or a preposition

P

passive voice: the way a verb is used to show that an action is done to the subject

past perfect tense: a verb form that tells that an action was completed in the past before another event or before a certain time in the past

perfect tenses: verb forms that tell that an action has been completed before a certain time or that will be continuing until a certain time

period: a kind of punctuation used to end a sentence that gives information or that states a feeling or wish

plural noun: a noun that names more than one person, place, thing, or idea

point-by-point pattern: a way of organizing comparison-and-contrast writing by telling about one point, or feature, of one item and then comparing and contrasting the same feature of a second item; after that, another feature is compared for the two items, and so on

possessive noun: a type of noun that shows that one thing is owned, or possessed, by another person or thing

possessive pronoun: a type of pronoun that replaces a noun that shows ownership

predicate: the part of a sentence that tells what the subject is or does

prefix: a word part that is added to the beginning of a root word

preposition: a word that connects a noun with another part of the sentence

prepositional phrase: a word group that begins with a preposition and ends with a noun or pronoun

present perfect tense: a verb form that tells that an action was started in the past and is continuing in the present or that it has just been completed

prewriting: the first step in the writing process, during which ideas are found, developed, and organized

pronoun: a word that replaces and refers to a noun

proper noun: a type of noun that names a specific person, place, thing, or idea; always capitalized

publishing: the final step in the writing process, in which the piece of writing is shared with others

Q

question: a type of sentence that asks for or about something

question mark: a type of punctuation that is used to end a question

R

reflexive pronoun: a type of pronoun that shows action is done by the subject to himself or herself

regular verb: a verb that forms its past and past participle forms in a regular, or predictable, way

renaming phrase: a modifying phrase that gives more information about a noun; it is made up of a noun and other words that modify that noun

revision: the step in the writing process in which the rough draft is changed and improved

root word: the main part of a word before anything else is added to it

rough draft: the first draft of a piece of writing, in which ideas are put into sentences and paragraphs for the first time

run-on sentence: a compound sentence that is incorrectly joined so the ideas run together

S

sentence: a group of words that contains a subject and a predicate and that expresses a complete thought

simple future tense: a verb tense that shows an action that will occur in the future

simple listing: a way of organizing writing by simply giving details to show the characteristics or to give examples of a main idea

simple past tense: a verb form that shows actions that occurred at a specific time in the past

simple present tense: a verb form that tells what is happening or is true at the present time, that shows actions that are performed regularly, or that tells what is always true

simple sentence: the most basic, or simple, form of the complete sentence; it has one subject and one predicate and expresses a complete thought

simple subject: the most basic part of the subject of a sentence; it is what or whom the sentence is about but does not include any descriptive words that are part of the subject

singular noun: a noun that names only one person, place, thing, or idea

statement: a type of sentence that gives information or tells something

style: how words and sentences are used to express meaning

subject: whom or what a sentence is about

S

subject pronoun: a type of pronoun that takes the place of a noun that is used as the subject of a sentence

subjunctive mood: a verb form that expresses a command, wish, or condition that is contrary to fact

suffix: a word part that is added to the end of the root word

T

tense: the time shown by a verb

time order: a way of organizing writing according to the order in which events happen

transition words: words that give the reader clues about the order of events or how the events are connected

V

verb: the most important part of the predicate, which tells what the subject is or does

verb phrase: a group of words that begins with a verb and that acts as a modifier

W

whole-to-whole organization: a way of organizing comparison-and-contrast writing by first telling all about one item and then telling how the other item is alike and different from the first one

Index